# "Any Old Iron"

# "Any Old Iron"

*Graham Martin Johnson*

# "Any Old Iron"

Spiderwize
Remus House
Coltsfoot Drive
Woodston
Peterborough
PE2 9BF
UK

www.spiderwize.com

'Book Title - Tony Goode'

ISBN 978-1-908128-25-6

## MUM....... My Sixth Sense

Only a heart as dear as yours, would give so unselfishly

The ENDLESS things you've done,

With ALL THE TIMES you were there

Help me know deep inside, just how much you really care

Even though I might not say, I appreciate all you do,

RICHLY BLESSED is how I feel, having a mum just like you.

This Book MUM... I Dedicate to You... Graham Xx

# Table of Contents

# Foreword

On meeting Graham unexpectedly he was to tell me of his writings and asked would I consider putting a few words or even a foreword should his manuscript go for publication. In this brief meet I told him that foremost I was a Football Supporter and that seemed to touch an approving nerve with him as he picked up on this straight away. He went on to tell me he had the same views and told me he mentions this within his introduction. He told me he hit on factors of his family life, childhood and life experiences that in many instances, was/would still have a West Ham United or football association.

I must say this book is all as he said, with his personal life and times as a West Ham United Supporter and most importantly Football Fan spanning a period of five decades, it also gives rise to his personal views of/and the changing face within the game.

This book is most informative and detailed and amongst many matches of re-living during my two spells as a Hammer at Upton Park, I took a personal pleasure in his recollections of the 1985/86 season and the Boys of '86 20th year anniversary. For me the Introduction of this book with its description says it all, and I have no doubt this is a read that will be enjoyed.

**Tony Cottee (West Ham United and England)**

# Preface

W hen you are playing you do not realise how passionate supporters are. Graham's words bring home the passion that is in a true West Ham supporter and it's nice to be able to read thoughts, experiences and stories from the terraces. As players we do not always realise what goes through the minds of supporters. It is a well-known fact that West Ham supporters are amongst the most passionate, loyal, knowledgeable and understanding fans.

**Alan Devonshire and Tony Gale**

# Testimonial

The words written in this book are how many of us West Ham Fans would love to be able to put in writing. Not only is it a very interesting and enjoyable read, it also invokes so many of my own personal memories. Like Graham I have many fond memories and stories of my time following the 'Irons', and this book is a must for any true West Ham Fan.

**Len Herbert-Secretary of the Boys of '86**

# Introduction

## The Memories/The Times

**T**HESE ARE THE INDIVIDUAL GAMES and days as well as 'happenings' that readily came to mind when flicking through my West Ham programmes and then entering them onto home and away listings for my own reference. There are of course memories that just can't be written or described; it is a case of 'you had to be there' or 'not there' as in some instances. I think and thought of so many people who I hope are happy, healthy and well, but also have no idea if in fact are still alive and kicking.

Having heard anecdotes and stories that I told on travels, two lads said to me at separate times and without duel consultation that the stories I told may be of interest and/or amusement to others, and that I should consider seriously about putting 'pen to paper'. Trust me, at the time of telling of an incident or happening it was only because it may have been relevant to a conversation or subject brought up or mentioned at the time, and all I was doing was adding 'my bit' as a matter of throwaway conversation. I can truly say I never at any point thought that an interest to the point of 'you should write about'…had ever crossed my mind, but now having the suggestion put to me by two 'not silly people', without their prior together consultation or knowledge, the consideration was in my thoughts, then more in my thoughts and then even more in my thoughts, and so…

The starting happened; the writings were to put me through memory emotions of all kinds, the smiling and the laughter, the tears and the joy, the frustrations and elations, the excitement and disappointment, the travelling and the weather, be it the hot, cold, wet if not the freezing, the deep thinking and wanting to see people again, even the open singing of terrace songs and of course 'Bubbles' and the chant of United, United—all returned, sometimes in the morning early hours when writing enthusiasm had taken over. All this was to happen when at home alone in my small second bedroom and I'm not embarrassed to say so. It seemed that when I was writing I was transported back in time; it all felt so real again and I felt the emotions as if a recurrence and déjà vu. These feelings had started when I started and were to prevent any thought of not wanting to finish. The Memories/The Times came back and possibly, if not probably, would not have returned to the forefront of my memory or mind if the starting hadn't started. The reminisce was one proper reminisce and I thank Dave Radisic (Dave the Post) and Tony Goode (Tony G), the two lads who suggested this project along with Wolves lifetime fan Steve McCormack who on more than one instance insisted that I should 'Do It'. Together, these lads in their very own but different ways willingly gave advice, suggestions and support. Then of course there was my mum, who in her own considerate, warm, thoughtful, helpful, not interfering but quietly encouraging way was a rock as ever Xx.

These writings are totally honest, they are my opinions that will be agreed and disagreed by whoever and for whatever reason, and so be it. They are written openly and from the heart, and if not outwardly but again sometimes between the lines, my thoughts on modern day 'top flight' football may not be that difficult to pick up on. Everything I have written is how it is or how it was, is spelt out in layman's terms and has no deliberate exaggeration or play down. The writings do not contain one swear word unless you class the word 'inconvenience' as such, and is most definitely in no way associated with personal involvement with physical violence as that just wouldn't be me. It is nothing more than a normal man's life and football fan experience, supporting a club and team with passion but never forgetting that football itself is the priority. Take away football and you take away the team to be passionate about because in four words, the team wouldn't exist. (Is that five?)

After Dave and Tony's suggestion of writing about my stories I couldn't help but be sent down my very own memory lane, be it in the main still attached in one way, shape or form to West Ham United or football in general. I felt also that I should include mum and dad's pre-me 'basics' as well as brother Terry and sister Elaine's 'basics' also. These writings I can only hope are informative, be of interest and give enjoyment to those of more tender years than myself as, I hope also, those of similar and more senior years to me will possibly, if not probably, relate as well to the comings, goings, life and times of my memory lane, and not only for the West Ham United or football association

# Coincidences Happen

It is true to say and a fact of life—the more people you know or come into contact with, the bigger the chance and possibility of a coincidence! A repeated coincidence however that I have that has nothing to do with people and will be subjected within, is that on the Saturday I was born West Ham United were to play Fulham, the first match I was to see West Ham play live, they were to play Fulham! My first FA Cup Final, West Ham were to play Fulham.

During the reading of this book, some 'down the line' page references are made for information only. I'd like to bring to attention that full explanation, in its written order, is made during and along book progress. However, it gives you, the reader, the option and choice to attend these pages prior to returning and "staying the course" should you so wish, but realising at same time, all will be revealed!

## The Beginning - (Refer to Coincidences Happen, Page XXIII)

### East End Maternity Home/E14 to SE16/FULHAM
### 01/02/1958/Division Two Champions

I N SEPTEMBER 1958, seven months after my entrance into the world, my immediate family of George (dad), Joan (mum), Terry (brother), and Elaine (sister), moved from number four Akbar House, Cahir Street, Isle of Dogs E14 to number four Cranemead, Silwood Estate, Bermondsey SE16. A new estate just built that year with residents moving in for the first time. The two-bedroomed flat that was the family home in Akbar House had severe damp problems; one bedroom was so seriously affected that all five members of the family were to share and sleep in the one bedroom not affected.

I had been born on Saturday 1st the previous February mid-morning in The East End Maternity Home, Commercial Road, Stepney E1, my birthplace being not more than a ten-fifteen minute walk or so from the north side entrance/exit of the Rotherhithe tunnel, on the left-hand side if walking in the direction of Watney market, Aldgate and the City of London. The building fifty years on is now named Steel's Lane Health Centre and has been named such for some time. To be found on the level of the first floor wall of the outer building, between two rectangular maternity ward windows vertically placed, is a round roman numerical back-to-back two-faced clock, approximately three and a half feet in diameter. The clock is confined in a rectangular black casing and is again vertically positioned but outwards and not flush to the wall, thus preventing northward facing and limited viewing. The back-to-back outward facing clocks therefore are positioned in the directions of east and west and can be seen by oncoming vehicles and pedestrians alike from both directions. Mum on occasions would come out for a ride with me when I'm working in my van as a courier driver. On one such occasion we were passing my place of birth when mum pointed out and informed me that it was there, separated by the clock behind one of the two ward windows: was where we were to spend our early days after my birth.

1

Which one of the two wards – although I did ask her, mum was not in a position to commit to.

One thing though that I can commit to is that on the day of my birth, West Ham United were to play Fulham Football Club at Fulham's home ground Craven Cottage; it was to be a second division football league match that at the time saw West Ham pushing for promotion. In the match programme that I was to obtain in my teen years, a 2-2 draw is written. Hammers went on to clinch promotion as champions that season, scoring 101 goals and with a points tally of 57. Blackburn was to finish runners up with Charlton Athletic finishing third. Third being an "also ran" place in those days as three up three down had not been introduced and play-offs weren't even a figment of the imagination.

## Silwood Estate 1958-1969

**O**F COURSE not knowing anything personally about my first seven months Akbar House, Isle of Dogs start in life, my Silwood Estate recollections are simple. Cranemead where I and my family were to live until the month of September 1969 was a block of maisonettes and accompanied by three identical buildings, all known as Moland Mead. Cranemead was one word but Moland Mead was two—I don't know why so perhaps someone else knows the answer to that one! The three Moland Mead blocks were divided by two situated directly behind Cranemead making a row of three; the third Moland Mead block ran lengthways to the side of the three buildings; thus, if looking down from above, they formed the shape of an E. These "Mead" buildings consisted of nine ground-floor three-bedroomed self-contained properties with nine placed directly above. Cranemead being the lead block, faced two large high-rise nine-storey buildings known as Oldfield Grove. Between Cranemead and Oldfield Grove was a fair sized perimeter fenced-in green that for two or so months every year that I could remember, and before November 5th firework night, kids from the estate would spend much of their time collecting wood and whatever they could put their hands on including discarded furniture to make and create one proper, proper bonfire. So much was always gathered and success if not guaranteed was always achieved. Where they got the 'totem pole' as we called the build around centre pole each year I would never know, but it was of some height, I can tell you, twenty-five foot plus looking back many years later would be my imagined prediction. I've no doubt in later, reflecting years such an acquisition, although not proven, could only have been with the knowledge and knowhow of parents, but for sure that would have been their only role play as most definitely the rest was down to us kids.

Such great fun, getting stuck in and dirty, having one or two little fires on the side, pushing a stick through a spud and cooking it was so normal. Even with all this going on the green was of a size that could still be used for kicking or playing football, general mucking about and by the roaming dogs. Sometimes though, we would want to play our "own game" of kick about which meant that we didn't want to be interrupted by "joiner inners"; to do this we would go to Southwark park, just a ten-minute walk away, or under the railway arches into Bolina road from Silwood Street to "The New Park", a new development and commonly used term as nobody seemed to know its true name. Senegal Fields it was, as we were to discover in later years, but The New Park sufficed and every kid knew where it meant.

Senegal Fields was demolished in the 1990's and made way for the development of The New Den, home and new ground name of Millwall Football Club. This after moving from their previous dwelling of The Den and Cold Blow Lane, just a stone's throw away or so. Silwood kids, as probably on all similar types of estates, could be so imaginative and spontaneous but no doubt even more so at weekends and in school holidays when spare time can be a bore or at a premium. It was nothing to go out of the near vicinity of the estate to play in outer areas of surround, or to go to Surrey Docks tube station and buy a three bob (15 pence) red bus rover and jump on buses that took us wherever we randomly chose or ended up. At times we may just decide on getting a 70 or 188 bus to Greenwich Park and go boating or to the Maritime museum or stay in the park and do whatever. Take a 47 bus and we'd end up in Kent's Farnborough and go egging, an enjoyment that was not just confined to Farnborough woods or its farm(s), but parks such as Southwark Park would be raided also—an enjoyment I now wish had not taken place BIG TIME. Such a hobby or activity I would not be able to bring myself to do now as an adult. It is with regret and youthful cruelty, with limited or no understanding of consequence, that I did this, and a number of boys, too, had collections. Other pleasures or ways of killing time would be to have fun over the canal and have a campsite hidden close by; other places for a campsite would be near the train arches and railway lines, and then it was a matter of trying to keep it a secret, knowing that lads not included would take great pleasure in doing a demolition job. Other pastimes and friendship bonding would be to go to the pictures, either Saturday mornings or for more serious viewing in the afternoon, whether it be to Deptford Broadway or the Regal and Astoria down the Old Kent Road, or the two cinemas opposite each other at the Elephant and Castle. These were all favourite pastimes on a Saturday, in school holidays or after school and I give these as examples. It was all such normal practice.

## FULHAM (Home) League Division One 03/02/1968/This was not MILLWALL/This for me is Different/Alf Garnett/Till Death us Do Part

IT WAS THURSDAY 1st February 1968 and my tenth birthday. All family members other than those that had by now passed on, still lived in the East End Limehouse and Poplar London E14 areas, except Nan and Granddad Martin who had now crossed the water since departure from The Hearts of Oak home and public house, St Leonards Road Poplar in 1958 (told of in **Immediate Family Mum Page 201**) and who now lived in Kidbrooke SE3.

Terry my brother and ten years my senior came into our bedroom where I had been sleeping for some time. He woke me to tell me he had asked dad if it was OK to take me to West Ham on Saturday for my birthday treat and that dad had said he could. I still recall the happiness and excitement of the next thirty-six hours and the fact that I was going to be going to West Ham. MY TEAM! The team ALL MY family, certainly from dad's side, had supported dating I know back to World War One days and probably Thames Iron Works also. The family that at any function attended belted out "Bubbles" with Uncle Fred if there was a piano providing the music. It is without doubt family influence that was to make me the avid Hammer I was to become. It's my tenth birthday and I've been told I was going to be going to West Ham. How was I meant to deal with this? This was NOT Millwall who it was quite normal to go and watch at times with other kids from the estate. I'm ten. I'm going to West Ham. We're playing Fulham and this for me IS DIFFERENT.

My first proper impact recollection looking back now after all those years wasn't the tube rides from Surrey Docks to Whitechapel then Whitechapel to Upton Park, or the excitement of walking within the crowd to the ground—it was the claret sign WEST HAM UNITED written on the West Stand wall facing Green Street! This now had made it real—I really was at West Ham, and this is the ground and IT IS GOING TO HAPPEN. I recall also Alf Garnett of 'Till Death Us Do Part' television fame, walking around the pitch in true TV program West Ham claret and blue colours and style before kick-off, waving to the crowd, and that the North Bank were chanting his Alfie, Alfie – Alfie Alfie Garnett name. Alf played a proper East End "Family man", a Hammer through and through, devout to Queen and Country and professed to have high moral standards. When television in those times finished, say approximately midnight and resumed on the following morning, the national anthem was always played out; others in the Garnett household would often have retired and gone to bed, but Alf, on his own or if still with company, would always stand to attention and honour the national anthem. Alf liked his pint and in the odd episode would be seen staggering home to a rather out of tune chorus of 'I'm Forever Blowing Bubbles'.

So much of Alf Garnett I could relate to in my own father, not necessarily in appearance but certainly in particular mannerisms, and "Bubbles", in a pub or club, was a dad forte. The Garnett home and family cast consisted of Tony Booth (father of Cherie Blair, Prime Minister Tony Blair's wife), who played Mike (a Liverpool supporter often referred to by Alf as "you scouse git"), husband to Alf's daughter Rita (Una Stubbs). Dandy Nichols played Alf's longsuffering wife Elsie, often referred to by Alf as "Silly Moo". Johnny Speight wrote this sitcom and I would sometimes think that due to many similarities of behavioural pattern, certainly in home life between Alf and my father, that he must have known dad and then based a played-down version of him? The part of Alf Garnett was played by Warren Mitchell who in reality was a Tottenham Hotspur supporter.

I'm not aware of any filming that day, although filming at West Ham on another or other occasions I'm sure did take place. Warren Mitchell, when 'Till Death Us Do Part' and spin-off series 'In Sickness and in Health' no longer continued to be televised, diverted and performed his one-man theatre show 'The Thoughts of Chairman Alf' in London's West End; he afterwards toured locally in the home counties and possibly further afield. Although not having seen the show, the/my imagination does not need stretching!

## The First and Last/Certificate 0335

S TANDING AT THE VERY FRONT for the first time in the North Bank, pressed against the wall separating terrace to pitch, five or six yards to the right of the goal facing the South Bank, was where I was to watch Alan "Sniffer" Clarke open the score for Fulham before West Ham were to run out convincing winners by seven goals to two. Trevor Brooking two, Geoff Hurst two and one a piece for Brian Dear, Bobby Moore and Martin Peters were to be the scorers for The Hammers. To see all three 1966 World Cup winners Hurst, Moore and Peters score along with Brian Dear, who I understand holds the fastest five goals scored in an English domestic professional football match (20 minutes either side of each half) against West Bromwich Albion in a 6-1 home win season 1964/65 and Trevor Brooking, who was to become what can only be described as a future West Ham great, proved to be one right good happy home debut for me.

Alan 'Sniffer' Clarke at the end of the season was to move from Fulham to Leicester City for £150,000, spending one season before further moving on to Leeds United for £165,000. Clarke continued regularly to score goals gaining nineteen caps as an international for England. Later in my older, I've-grown-bigger years, I stood higher up in the terracing, but still about the same distance to the right of the goal facing the South Bank. I was to stand there for the vast majority of matches that I attended until closure for redevelopment to all seating in 1994. The last terraced match was to be played against Southampton on May 7th and those in attendance who stood that day should they apply received a signed Terence Brown (Chairman) and Billy Bonds (Manager) numbered certificate. On this certificate a brief history of the North Bank is given and having applied my certificate was numbered 0335. (Pictured Page 92)

## IPSWICH TOWN (Home) League Division One
## 21/03/1969/Tony Gray/First defeat or was it?

I WASN'T TO SEE West Ham lose in a live match until Ipswich Town in March 1969. It was my tenth match, OR WAS IT? All matches I attended I put a small asterisk in the top left-hand corner of the match programme as a proof or cross reference of my attendance. I had always thought my first defeat was the eleventh but the asterisk on the top of my programme listing says otherwise. Tony Gray, a friend and primary school mate, came with Terry and me that Friday night; Tony had said to me he was going to be a West Ham fan like me so I asked Terry if he could come to the match also. Tony didn't appear disappointed that we had lost, but it was my first time and I didn't take it too well. I was to leave my Rotherhithe primary school that summer and soon after in September, two weeks into my new senior school, South East London Creek Road Deptford SE8 my family were to move to Eltham SE9.

After leaving primary school I was never to see Tony again but I can't help thinking he went to Scott Ligget School which had a swimming pool and in its first year of opening. All these years after I do hope Tony is happy, healthy and well, but as I write I wonder if he is "still" a Hammer? On only one more occasion was I to go to a home match that season and it was to be the final home match against Arsenal on a Monday night. Prior to this however and just two days before and on the 19<sup>th</sup> April, I was to go to my first ever away match and it was away to Arsenal's arch rivals Tottenham— and so unexpected!

## TOTTENHAM HOTSPUR (Away) League Division One
## 19/04/1969/Greavsie-'Our' Bobby Arm in Arm Jig/Eddie
## Wise/Peter Grotier

L EON NICHOLSON, A MATE OF MINE who lived in the high rise flats of Somerfield House, identical to those of Oldfield Grove (Lambourne House was one such other) asked, "Fancy coming Tottenham?"

I knew they were playing West Ham and that would have been the reason for him to ask me. I don't remember too much about the day or match but I do remember Jimmy Greaves and "Our" Bobby Moore ("Our" so known to me as an expression during/from early days of my life and told of in **Immediate Family Dad Page 204**) doing an arm in arm jig (they were good friends off the pitch) close to where I was standing (shelf side) near the halfway line, and that Greavsie scored early in the second half against West Ham's debutant goalkeeper Peter Grotier with Tottenham winning the match 1-0. I do however recall that we journeyed on the tube and overground trains probably from Surrey Docks to Whitechapel, changing for Liverpool Street and once again for White Hart Lane.

Still only being eleven, kids could be allowed and given so much more freedom back then, as explained with examples previously. I'd often go out in the morning and stay out until whenever before going home, perhaps if it had started raining, got cold or if getting dark or hungry. Leon was however, three years or so older than me. Some thirty-eight years or so after my first away match debut in 1969, by chance only when looking through home programme back issues, I came across a Christmas card drawing by Eddie Wise of Bristol; it was in the postponed Nottingham Forest match programme of Boxing Day 1970. The drawing is an amusing mock of Bobby and Jimmy's arm in arm dance/jig around that I recall having taken place on my first away match debut. In Mr Wise's amusing picture, Jimmy is seen sporting a West Ham shirt and not a Spurs shirt that he would have been wearing on the day. Debutant goalkeeper Peter Grotier was to play 54 matches for West Ham, a figure made of fifty first division matches and four cup tie appearances in the League Cup. Peter was never to play in any FA Cup matches for West Ham in his period with The Hammers. My first what I would think at the time as being a "real" away match, meaning outside London and some distance to a fifteen-year-old, was to be at Derby County's Baseball Ground on the 21$^{st}$ May 1973. The match was to end in a 1-1 draw with The Hammers goal being scored by Bertie Lutton. It was also to be Peter Grotier's last appearance as a first team goalkeeper in a West Ham shirt before moving on to Lincoln City in 1974.

## Jimmy Greaves/Ronnie Boyce and "What Happened Next?"

**B**OBBY MOORE AND JIMMY GREAVES were to join up as team
mates in March 1970. Martin Peters was to transfer to Tottenham
Hotspur with Jimmy Greaves reversing in the opposite direction to West
Ham in an exchange player plus cash transaction. The reported deal was that
Peters had been valued at £200,000 with Greavsie entering into his twilight
years valued at £80,000.

Having had the enviable record of scoring on all his previous debuts for
Chelsea, A.C. Milan, Spurs, England at full international and under 21 levels,
Jimmy Greaves' West Ham debut was to be away at Maine Road to
Manchester City. Greavsie was to continue his most impressive record of
debut scoring by converting two goals in an impressive away win of 5-1.
Some turnaround also, as the corresponding home fixture earlier in the
season had seen The Hammers lose 0-4. Geoff Hurst was to score two that
day also, but what sticks out in my mind and so distinctively, is that while
watching Match of the Day that same Saturday evening, was seeing Joe
Corrigan, City's goalkeeper boot the ball up the park, turn to return towards
his goal only to see the ball entering at speed into his empty net. Ronnie
"Ticker" Boyce had whacked the ball on full volley from just inside City's
halfway line. I was watching Match of the Day that night with dad. We
hadn't heard how "Ticker" had scored his goal and we were in fits, seeing
Joe Corrigan turn to look up field in surprise, shock and bewilderment added
to our amusement. That highlight has been shown and repeated at varying
times on television over the years. I was indoors one evening sometime way
back and my amusement was roused once again; my memory had been
triggered as I watched Joe Corrigan bounce the ball before unleashing it up
the park. The film was then halted and it was used as a subject question What
Happened Next? on television's long... LONG running series 'A Question of
Sport'.

## The 1970 World Cup Car Rally/Bobby Moore-Jimmy Greaves and "That" Bracelet

T HE SUMMER MONTHS of 1970 and the England national side are in Mexico preparing for the defence of the Jules Rimet World Cup trophy, won so gloriously four years earlier on what was that most famous of famous Wembley days, July 30th 1966, a date so shared also with brother Terry's birthday. Preparation for World Cup defence had begun some weeks before the competition was to commence, a precautionary decision taken as Mexico was much higher than England (as in altitude) and it was deemed the change in air quality, humidity and therefore breathing ability would be of such significance, player acclimatisation was of essence and necessity.

During this preparation Bobby Moore was to be accused of a bracelet theft and was subsequently held on house detention in Bogota, Columbia. It so happened that Jimmy Greaves had teamed up with British Rally Driver Tony Fall and was to be taking part in what was known as The London to Mexico car rally—an event that was to be the idea of Wylton Dickson, an Australian advertising guru to mark the fact the World Cup of 1966 had taken place in London and that the upcoming 1970 World Cup was to be held in Mexico. Dickson, so it has been said, had a way about him that didn't encourage people in the right places to warm to his suggestion. There was one, however, that did like Dickson's idea and that was Paddy Hopkirk, a renowned British rally driver of the time and together, they were to get the backing of *The Daily Mirror* tabloid newspaper and the Royal Automobile Association, who supplied office facilities to initiate and develop the idea. Their no doubt very committed and determined ambitions were to pay off and the London to Mexico car rally was commissioned. *The Daily Mirror* sponsoring the race with The Royal Automobile Club and Motor Sports Association being the institutions organising the event.

Ninety-six cars were to take part in the event and the cars were not restrictive; a selection of entries was to include a BMW 2002ti, Datsun 1600SSS, Ford Lotus Cortina, Ford Escort 1850GT, Hillman Hunter, Mercedes Benz 280SE, Rolls-Royce Silver Shadow and a Rolls-Royce Silver Cloud, a Peugeot 404 and a Porsche 911. Due to the demanding nature of the course, modification work on entries was prepared and sanctioned.

The event was to attract many car rally drivers of the day but also attracted well known people of status and celebrity fame. Vehicles were to consist of two or three driver teams that included women entrants. Wylton Dickson's suggestion of holding the rally prior to the World Cup was due to his inner feeling that it would enhance interest in the England football team profile and yet at the same time, also open a shop window for the British Motor Industry. The race was to start from Wembley Stadium on 19th April 1970 and was seen off by England manager Sir Alf Ramsey and team captain Bobby Moore. Over and above 16,000 miles were to be driven and in excess of twenty countries were to be trekked. Shipping of cars was to be between Lisbon (Portugal) and Buenos Aires (Argentina) and then Buenaventura (Columbia) and Cristobal (Panama)  The race was to finish in late May and when cars did arrive in Mexico City they were escorted into the Aztec Stadium, the venue for the 1970 World Cup Final itself.

## Insufficient Evidence/Four Days House Arrest/Unexpected but Welcome Guest

**B**OBBY MOORE'S alleged stealing of the publicised £600 bracelet had happened when visiting a jeweller with team mate Bobby Charlton. Bobby Charlton was looking to buy a gift for his wife Norma when the lady shop assistant "saw" Bobby Moore slip a bracelet into his pocket before leaving without paying. Bobby Moore was arrested on suspicion of theft but later released through insufficient evidence. The England team were due to play Ecuador in Quito in a Pre-World Cup friendly; after winning 2-0 and returning by plane Bobby was again detained and put under four days house arrest. It was at this time in the latter days of the month of May, that Jimmy Greaves arrived in Mexico at the end of the 16000 mile plus London to Mexico World Cup Car Rally with companion driver Tony Fall.

Greavsie had concerns for his friend and now West Ham colleague and was quoted as saying that "Mooro wouldn't take a liberty let alone a bracelet". Greavsie of course kept himself aware of any developments; he followed the situation via media and information given very closely and was to visit where Bobby was being held at an ambassador's residence as an 'unexpected but welcomed guest'.


## A Sporting Dinner with Jimmy Greaves/Inquisitive Curiosity/The Knowledge and Ammunition I Needed


IN MARCH 2008, thirty-eight years after this most well publicised incident, I was to be invited by a good friend, Chris Deady, to go to his work's social "governor's treat". Chris informed me one colleague had dropped out and a ticket was up for grabs. The ticket was for "A Sporting Dinner with Jimmy Greaves". I had heard before about Jimmy doing entertainment evenings, where he would tell football stories of fact and humour along with the amalgamation of a question time and perhaps a quiz. I had always wanted out of inquisitive curiosity, other than the well-publicised goings on around the happenings surrounding the bracelet saga, to know the true story behind Jimmy Greaves' subsequent 'bunking in' of where Bobby was being held. Jimmy was the one who had the knowledge and ammunition I needed and this was an opportunity to get my inquisitive curiosity for this knowledge quenched.

After dithering but more importantly making sure I wasn't treading on anybody's toes I accepted Chris' invitation. All that needed to be done now was to try and get a quiet private moment with Jimmy and I knew that would or wouldn't be easy. Jimmy's entertainment evening was to take place at The Beaverwood Club in Chislehurst, which held at my estimate around 140/180 seated guests, occupied by varying company parties and individually selected people groups alike. On my suited and booted arrival Chris introduced me to his workmates. I was instantly made welcome but I still couldn't help feeling slightly embarrassed, if not intrusive for a short while before relaxing and settling in. All drinks amongst Chris' work contingent were to be paid for by management, although having been offered a beer on arrival, I chose to stick to myself drinkwise and explained the cost of the ticket as well as the gesture of invite I felt was credit enough.

I would say not much more than fifteen minutes had passed before I saw Greavsie standing around in company but with nothing of significance going on, feeling this was a good time and taking my chance, I seized the opportunity. On introducing myself, we talked briefly and I mentioned his arm-in-arm jig around with Bobby Moore all those years previously and he recalled the happening with an almost unnoticeable, very slight approving three of four nods of his head with a gentle solemn smiling face, saying, "Yeh...yeh." We talked for a few more moments, but knowing this one-on-one exchange was to be very shortlived, I brought up the subject of the 1970 Mexico Car Rally and him "bunking" in the ambassador's residence to be with Bobby Moore during the "stolen bracelet affair". Greavsie became a little reluctant to talk but shall I say, "lightened up". My memory tells me he told me he got in by scaling a wall of the premises before dropping into the perimeter grounds. He then came across an unlocked door and on entering it found he was in the kitchen amongst cooks and staff. "Nobody seemed to take a blind bit of notice," he told me, and when he opened a door leading from the kitchen he continued to explain that he found himself looking into a very large room with Bobby Moore sitting in the middle, wearing his track suit and reading a newspaper. He went on to tell me they had a very brief, surprised to see you hello sort of communication before being spotted by officials. Greavsie then went on to tell me he was gently but firmly led towards a door, but Bobby of course, on seeing this, got to his feet and explained who Jimmy Greaves the 'intruder' was. After this intervention-cum-explanation, Greavsie was escorted to the front entrance and told if he knocked on the door he would be allowed in. This is my recollection of the happenings at that time after my brief chat with Jimmy Greaves; I can only personally assume his being taken to the front door and being allowed in was to give the appearance that security had not been breached and that Greavsie was 'in fact' on the premises as a visiting guest. With Bobby and Jimmy now sorted and at ease, why not enjoy a chat and a few bottled beers together and that, my friends, is exactly what they did... NICE. Bobby Moore, talking after his ordeal and of this meeting with Jimmy Greaves, was to be quoted as saying, "It was just the relaxation I needed."

Sometime after my short but informative 'pass time' with Greavsie, I attended a talk show starring said man and Sir Geoff Hurst with compere Terry Baker. On this night before an attendance approaching a thousand or so and in an almost identically worded manner to mine, Jimmy was again asked about Bobby Moore and 'that bracelet', but this time, and without any form of hesitation or reluctance, Jimmy recited almost to a word his story given me prior but added that he had climbed a tree before scaling a wall etc etc.

Diplomatic pressure and subsequent intervention by the then Prime Minister Harold Wilson along with obvious weakness in evidence saw the case dropped entirely. On his release Bobby said, "I would not wish my ordeal on anybody."

MICKY CANTWELL PRESENTS

A SPORTING DINNER WITH

# JIMMY GREAVES

YOUR CHANCE TO MEET A REAL SPORTING LEGEND

WEDNESDAY 19TH MARCH 2008 · BEAVERWOOD LODGE

COMEDY & LAUGHTER FROM THE HILARIOUS

**RUSS WILLIAMS**

SPONSORED BY

www.contractflooringservices.co.uk

*And Signed by the Man Himself... Thank You to Jimmy Greaves*

## Tony Fall-Jimmy Greaves Finish a Credible 6th/WEST GERMANY get Revenge

**A**FTER in excess of five weeks and on information given, Jimmy Greaves and driver partner Tony Fall finished a credible 6th in the final placing of the London to Mexico Car Rally, their vehicle having been a Ford Escort 1850GT. H. Mikkola and G. Palm were the race winners, also driving a Ford Escort 1850GT. Race favourites Paddy Hopkirk with driver colleagues A. Nash and N. Johnston in a Triumph 2.5PI were to finish 4th. Ms Rosemary Smith was lead member of a three-woman team and was first to cross the finish line in 10th position. They had completed the course in an Austin Maxi and were the coveted winners of the ladies' award. Of the ninety-six cars that commenced the race twenty-three were to finish, HRH Prince Michael of Kent being one participant who failed to complete the course.

England's were to exit their football defence of The World Cup in the quarter finals to West Germany, ironically the team they beat in the previous tournament's final at Wembley in 1966 four years prior. Having led by two goals to no reply by scorers, Tottenham captain Alan Mullery and now Tottenham player from West Ham Martin Peters, England eventually succumbed to a three goals to two defeat after extra time. Back Home the official World Cup single record release by the England squad players was to enjoy much success and spent at least three weeks as a chart topper between May and early June.

## The Royal British Legion Band/Paddy/Truly 'My Heroes'

**W**HAT I REMEMBER clearly in the early years of my Boleyn Ground attendance in the late sixties and into the seventies was The Royal British Legion Band. The band was to be the 'before the match and half time entertainment' that consisted of a bandleader, a number of brass instruments and a cymbal player who, I recall, would step into the ring with much enthusiasm when it was coming close to the appropriate time for him to give them a smash. Just twenty yards or so on pitch entrance was where they would form a circle in front of the West Stand; from here they would play many a varying tune but as kick-off time approached, it was customary for them to play the amalgamated jazzed-up versions of "Bubbles". I remember also Paddy; who he was I can't remember, or what his role was other than coming out seconds before Bobby Moore (and later Billy "Buccaneering Bonzo" Bonds) to gee-up the crowd I do not know, not now anyway. With the crowd becoming expectant and me on tiptoes leaning forward, I could see the ball that Bobby had hit with his inner or outer wrist flying into the air; from where I was, I always saw the ball before Bobby and the players. As time got close and my excitement grew, my eyes were always glued, set on that tunnel. 'Come on, Hurry Up!' was always my chain of thought. As an early years teenager, these players truly were 'My Heroes'.

## Culture Shock/Dave and Keith Miller/Woolwich Ferry/Chips out of a Newspaper

**M**OVING TO ELTHAM was to be a culture shock to me. It was the country in comparison to the Silwood estate and Bermondsey. It was so nice and certainly I appreciated the fields, parks and woodland but SO quiet. Almost every Saturday morning for a good few months after the family move, I'd walk to Eltham Park railway station and travel to New Cross before getting the underground metropolitan line tube train to Surrey Docks. Although I started to meet new lads in Eltham, the adaptation took me some time to get used to. After school one evening and taking my football with me, I went to Eltham Park South in the hope I might meet up with lads who I would get a kick about or a game of football with. It worked; I met this group of six or so who I became mates with. Two of these, Dave and Keith Miller, were brothers and were also Hammers fans. They went to home matches and after this initial first time meet up, asked if I wanted to go with them "This Saturday" (4/10/69) to West Ham for the game versus Burnley? I said I would have to ask dad first. Dave was a couple of years older than Keith and in later discussion, we discovered that Keith was 11! Not only was he the same age as me in years but we were also to establish we had both been born on the same day and year as each other, though I was to be two or so hours his senior. Dave and Keith explained to me that they went via the Woolwich ferry and I asked expectantly what the cost would be, but they told me that you didn't have to pay. After mentioning about my new-found West Ham friends and gingerly asking dad if I could go to football that Saturday, dad replied with a "Yes" and that was that. A one o'clock knock on my door meet up would mean missing "On the ball", commentator Brian Moore's television preview of that day's Saturday football and mid-week round up of league and cup matches. We were to get a 161 bus from Eltham Well Hall Pleasance to Woolwich, take the ferry to North Woolwich and then the 101 bus to East Ham town hall, a fifteen minute walk or so along the Barking road completed the journey! Going to West Ham with the brothers became a regular event; on the odd times it happened and a 101 wasn't waiting but a 69 was, (North Woolwich being a terminus), we would swing to a 69 and walk from Plaistow tube station, a similar distance to the ground as if from the town hall. I remember that occasionally after a match we would walk to the Woolwich ferry as this would save pocket money. We also decided sometimes not to use the ferry but chose to take the foot tunnel instead; if ever a choice was taken, walking to North Woolwich was always from Upton Park, we never walked to Eltham from Woolwich

One night match, on getting to Woolwich, we jumped on the 161 bus in Powis street and where we got off at Eltham Well Hall Pleasance was a fish and chip shop just by Dunvegan road, the road also where Dave and Keith lived. We bought six of chips (six 'a' chips); nothing unusual in that, I know, but it was what Dave said: "Do you know what? There's something about eating chips out of a newspaper!" I had always thought that but had never said it. 'Sixpance' and not 'six pence', often referred to as a tanner, was the pronunciation, and in today's decimalised currency, would be two and a half pence and what's more, it wasn't unusual for chip shops to use newspaper for carry-out food.

**Boys Brigade Intro/Car Cleaning Entrepreneurs/Brighton Vintage Car Rally/Push Bikes/Sitting in the West Stand**

S OON AFTER MEETING Dave and Keith, I met a new friend who was to become I can only describe as a true...true friend. Michael Voce is just under two years younger than me and comes from a family originating from Liverpool. It is no surprise then that Liverpool FC is the family team but I would often sense that they had a soft spot for Tranmere Rovers. Adrian his brother is eighteen months or so older than Michael and we also became great pals in our teenage and early twenties years before he followed oldest brother Chris and went to live in Australia. Michael's Mum and dad, three brothers Chris, Adrian ('Age') and Stephen along with their three sisters Anne, Carole and Julia completed the family.

Somewhere along the line during this jumbled, finding my way in my new surroundings period, I had become a member of The Boys Brigade, an organisation I had not previously heard of. I had become part of an organisation that was to give me in time the most fulfilling and in comparison, happiest and contented for varying reasons period of my life and by an unusual circumstance.

It was a Wednesday evening and the time between 9.30pm and 10.00pm. Dad walked in with two flustered if not somewhat not at ease young lads wearing uniforms; they appeared to be of a similar age to me which at the time would have been twelve. The boys had been witnesses to a car accident that had happened in Westmount road, adjoining Elibank road where we as a family now lived. Dad had brought the boys home to relax and calm them over a hot drink. Dad asked the boys the reason why they were out so late, and the reply was they had been to Boys Brigade in the Methodist church opposite and were waiting for the 160 bus. The following Wednesday the boys Gary and Dave were to knock on our door unexpectedly and asked if I wanted to go with them to Boys Brigade. Surprised, feeling obliged and a little embarrassed, I said "Yes". I recall mum polishing my shoes whilst I went upstairs to find a pair of school trousers in an attempt to smarten up. In nine words of that once again coming together and previous week to the day introduction, I can honestly say, hand on heart, "It was to change my life… and possible direction."

In later months I introduced Michael and he, like me, was to spend a number of years in the 22nd West Kent Boys Brigade Company, culminating in us both becoming officers.

Michael and I were, I guess, no different from most boys of our age and years, and over the coming three or four year period, amongst improvising for fun and enjoyment, we would go egging up in the woods of which Eltham had an abundance of, play lots of football whether it be in the street or up the park and travel around riding our push-bikes. In perhaps a little more adult way we would take the train to Charing Cross and go to Cheapo Cheapo's in Rupert Street W1, a shop that bought, sold and swapped records with the general public and when we were up that way we would also take in Football's Hall of Fame, a museum for lovers of football that was a ten-minute walk or so away in Newman Street. We also had our own little "car-cleaning business" where we would clean motors at weekends. As little entrepreneurs we would extend our car-cleaning 'habit' and together would go out and clean cars after school in the light night summer months just for that little extra pocket money. We kept our own "business" book and had our regulars; many benefits came from having "on-going customers" and one of these was being taken to travel with and watch The London to Brighton Vintage Car Rally in Doug and Tina's jaguar. I remember times when we would pedal to Woolwich and take the ferry journey to North Woolwich and then continue on to West Ham on our push-bikes in the school holidays; we would go into the Hammers shop where I would look at the merchandise. Sometimes I would buy a badge or photograph of a player to take home. I also remember walking into the ground and sitting high up in the empty West Stand on more than one occasion, just looking round and watching the sweeping up process of the terracing after a Saturday or midweek match.

## Geoff Hurst/Bobby Moore 'Clear Offs'/I'm Safe, No World Cup Hat-Trick for me (Thank You Martin Peters)

**T**HERE WAS HOWEVER, one occasion that sticks out most prominently, and that was as I was walking down the West Stand exit stairs I could see Geoff Hurst talking to this big black man. Being nervous but so inquisitively interested, I planted myself close enough to hear what in effect they were saying: "Is that the car they gave you?" to which Geoff replied, "Yes." I then, looking over to the car, saw it was a Ford Escort Mexico. Thinking back on memory, I do believe all members of the 1970 World Cup Squad were given these vehicles as gifts. Geoff at the end of this brief conversation walked over to his car and, on getting in and closing the car door, was surrounded by a group of kids I was very near to, and it was possible to hear Geoff assertively saying words to the effect, "Why don't you lot just clear off!" Did Geoff include me? I was close.

On another of my school holiday Upton Park trips, I was walking out the main gates in Green Street when I looked across the road and saw Bobby Moore. My luck was right in, or was it? Bobby had a sportswear shop opposite and he was chatting away to who I thought was probably a shop assistant; correct I was, but this did not help my cause. I went into the shop excited, and not thinking, I immediately started to look for a pen and paper so I could ask for and hopefully obtain Bobby's autograph. What I mean by this not helping my cause was the fact IT WAS the, yes THE shop assistant! The shop was empty; it was a small shop and on non-match days only required the one. Our Bobby walked in and told me to "Clear Off". Bobby had got one most definite wrong idea and impression! I was shocked—'Our'

Bob and I'd been told to "clear off"! It took a while but I've now smiled about that for years!

Thinking back, perhaps it was fortunate that I did not come across Martin Peters on my school holiday visits; with the way it was going and my previous "luck" with two of our World Cup hero trio, I could have ended up with a World Cup "Clear off" hat trick of my own. Now that would have cracked me up…I'm enjoying this!

## Clyde Best/Epic STOKE CITY/Gordon Banks Saves Penalty

T HE BLACK MAN I referred to talking to Geoff was a young Clyde Best, who later partnered Geoff up front many times and played in those epic League Cup semi-final matches against Stoke City in 1971/72. I did not go to any of the four matches that made this semi-final so memorable for me but, oh, how I would have liked to write about these matches with first-hand experience. I remember watching them on the television highlights so clearly. My dream of Wembley and it was to be so, SO close. Winning at The Victoria Ground in the first leg 2-1, Clyde Best and Geoff (penalty) converting our goals. John Ritchie scored late in the 2$^{nd}$ half to force extra time in the return leg at the Boleyn. Gordon Banks brought down Harry Redknapp in the penalty area very late into the second half of extra time. Geoff took an almost identical penalty as previously at The Victoria Ground but this time it is saved (Gordon had got a hand to Geoff's penalty in the first match). The first replay ended 0-0 at Hillsborough; however, it was the 2$^{nd}$ replay at Old Trafford Manchester that was to have all the excitement and drama.

## Bobby Ferguson Injuries/Bobby Moore Saves Penalty/Brookings Finest Strike?

**H**AMMERS' SCOTLAND GOALKEEPER Bobby Ferguson goes down if my memory serves me correctly at Stoke player Terry Conroy's feet, gets a head concussion and has to go off. Clyde Best is the on-pitch reserve goalkeeper but nerves get the better, so who goes in goal? None other than Bobby Moore. Bobby not only goes in goal but he then saves a Mike Bernard penalty, only for Bernard to follow up and convert the rebound. Bobby Ferguson later returned to the match but said afterwards, that he had no recollection of the game. Hammers lost 2-3 that night with Billy Bonds scoring; a shot from not too far outside the penalty area beating Gordon Banks helped with a deflection off Stoke centre half Dennis Smith. Trevor Brooking was to score this night also with Gordon Banks commenting on Trevor's goal, saying it was one of the finest struck shots that had ever beaten him. Trevor in later years said his possible favourite strike was away to Hungary (where the ball gets stuck high in the goal between cross bar and post) in the World Cup qualifying match in June 1981. I tend to reflect also to the goal that won Sunday afternoons televised highlights, the Big Match Goal of the Season (1975/76) at the Baseball ground against Derby County, a goal so fuelled in my mind having eye witnessed and with the high energy celebration that took over me. Clyde Best was also in the match against Leeds but this time subbed in goal after goalkeeper Bobby Ferguson went for a high ball and came down landing on his neck—I can still see it! I thought he was dead, it was so horrific. The ground went silent, AND IT DID. Bobby Ferguson recovered fully but that occurrence is visually mind-set fixed.

## Peter Batt Concedes/Colin Hart/Did They Know Each Other?

**P**ETER BATT, *Sun* newspaper sports columnist and writer, wrote in his report of the Stoke West Ham League Cup semi-final match at Old Trafford that he had always refrained from committing himself to what was the best match he had ever seen. In his sport page paper report the following morning he finally conceded, in an opinion of mine and mine alone, his concession was influenced not only through the head-on determination, passion, commitment and skill shown that night in conditions that should have made a football match a mockery, but also because of the unusual, perhaps never seen before circumstantial incidents that made up this fantastic football spectacle. Colin Hart boxing columnist of *The Sun* newspaper sat a couple of seats to the right of me in the West Stand cum 'The Dr Martens Stand' in later years and I'm wondering now whether he knows or knew Peter Batt? A question that until doing these writings and after many chats between us, I had never thought to ask.

## Ferguson-Parkes/World Record Goalkeeper Signings/Mervyn Day/Clyde Best MBE Award

**H**AGGIS, OR FERGIE, as he would often be referred to by fans, had been signed in 1967 by West Ham from Scottish football club Kilmarnock for £65,000, then a world record fee for a goalkeeper. In the early to mid-1970's Bobby Ferguson was stretched to keep a permanent place in the side, firstly with Peter Grotier and then with the emergence in his first and second seasons (1973-75) of twice runner-up hammer player of the year of young Mervyn Day, awards compounded with the winning and to date the only goalkeeper to do so, of the PFA Young Player of the year award 1974/75. Bobby Ferguson now found himself more times than not playing reserve team football. In February 1979 West Ham were to buy goalkeeper Phil Parkes for £565,000 from Queens Park Rangers for what was another world record fee for a goalkeeper. In November 1979 Fergie ended his first team West Ham playing career in a 1-2 defeat league division two match at Chelsea. Clyde Best played his last matches for West Ham in January 1976; he was to play for and at a later stage coach his national side Bermuda. In 2006 he was honoured with the MBE award for services to football and the community in Bermuda.

## South East London School Deptford SE8 1969/74

**M** R FOTHERBY (Fov) was our form teacher and was one of the school French teachers. There were two at our school. My school was South East London School, Creek Road, Deptford SE8 from 1969-1974, the other French teacher being Miss Shaw. There was a group of us lads at school who were well into progressive music; it would be an understatement to say it was never far away from our ears or conversation; dominated by music of The Deep Purple/Led Zeppelin/PinkFloyd/BlackSabbath/Who/Free/Focus/Yes/Uriah Heep and so on kind. I would go to "Rock" concerts on a regular basis; although I had this music interest with a section of school mates, I had the same interest with another group from Boys Brigade and others in Eltham. Depending on the band popularity and/or venue size, obtaining tickets would sometimes mean getting up at the crack of dawn and then meeting up for the first bus and/or first train journeys. It made for stronger friendship bonding; it was perhaps even a little adventurous and importantly, it was all part and parcel of getting as close to the front of the venue queue as we could, making it less possible for a sell-out and therefore disappointment. In latter years, with credit cards, debit cards and ticket agencies, the purchasing of tickets over the telephone made the accessibility of tickets so much more simplified. Would I do the queuing now or would I even want to? With the coming of my older years it was one progress I appreciated, although from a youngster's point of view and with my previous experiences, somewhat a little less adventurous. With my school mates and me living some distance away in Eltham, we lacked the facilities or a base to play and listen to our in common liking of progressive music as a group together. Miss Shaw became aware of this and Miss Shaw after cottoning on to our 'plight', and who shared living quarters with other, I assume. student/teacher types in Blackheath, said to us that we could go to their/her place if we wanted to. This offer was so appreciated and taken up. The fictitious drums, keyboards, imaginary hand-held microphones and air guitars came out and no doubt Miss Shaw, along with her student/teacher types in an adjoining room, had many amusing comments to make attached with one right good giggle listening at us lot doing what they privately/probably did also?... (I was in no way a hippie type but for sure the hair was long…ish.) Miss Shaw was a tiny, pretty little thing. She told me she was 24. At that time, I probably never gave it a thought how old that was but now I think how young that is!

## HEREFORD UNITED (Home) FA Cup 4th Round Replay 14/02/1972

**G**OING TO WATCH WEST HAM and missing school: only once did it happen—during the electricity wage claim strikes of February 1972. Hereford United it was, conquerors of Newcastle in the FA Cup 3<sup>rd</sup> round; now they were to play at the Boleyn as this 4<sup>th</sup> round match had been originally drawn 0-0 at theirs. Hereford, what's this all about? They're non-league (they were then); don't remind Newcastle but please do remind West Ham! Lower division league sides loved West Ham, not only at this time or as well as the previous six or so years that I knew and suffered (school mates can be so cruel), but also the many matches over the years that were to follow. It's the morning of the game, I walk in with my claret and blue scarf tucked in my trouser belt loops so either end of the scarf hangs down each leg to the knee. "Alright Fov, got dentist this afternoon." With that sorted, Upton Park here I come, but not before enrolling three or even possibly four recruits! After being prevented by police from walking through the Blackwall Tunnel south side, the 108 bus was caught from Tunnel Avenue. The first bus stop is only about a third of a mile after exiting the tunnel and placed immediately after passing under the over the top East India Dock road, walking up the stairs onto the East India Dock road where The Sir John Franklin pub sits to the right of the bus stop, and on the corner of that part of "once" St Leonards road was where we were to get our number 15 bus connection. The Blackwall Tunnel is not open to pedestrians, but taking chances and playing pranks is what kids do. Rightly or wrongly, IT IS WHAT KIDS DO. We're fourteen. Should we know better? Of course we should. Were we 'Herberts'? (Mischievous). On this day I guess we were?

Oh well, we get to the ground and no chance. With thousands outside, getting in was going to be a problem. Shouldn't this lot be at work? Shouldn't those kids be at school? We headed to the high-rise flats behind the North Bank looking over and into the ground. Many others had that same idea and were already on the roof. We were to attempt this also, but "grown up kids" with their kids who had tried moments before told us that you couldn't see anything. Although the flats were built higher than the North Bank roof, the roof itself made looking down onto the pitch impossible. It became apparent that seeing the match this way wasn't really going to be an option! Hereford had brought their town down or so it seemed. They appeared to have more supporters locked out than West Ham, possibly due to arriving that much later but closer to kick off. I very much doubt though, that anybody had envisaged such a large crowd turnout. No, surely not, not on a weekday, workday, school day! Terry my brother got in though—he had taken time off from work and his ploy was a blinder; he told me he went to one of the gates and just told the steward that he "was from the press" and the steward let him in without question, or even asking to see his pass. Good job too. Why? BECAUSE HE NEVER HAD ONE!

Geoff Hurst scored all three in a 3-1 win. "I've been to the dentist"—and was back in school next day as normal. Three or four others though had some explaining to do.


## Brian Moore—The Big Match/Brian Yeo Testimonial
## GILLINGHAM (Away) 09/04/1973/Kia-Ora Orange Drinks


I HAD BECOME A GOOD FRIEND of John Sweet, some two, three or so years older than me from playing park football in Eltham. Brian Moore, presenter of Sunday afternoon's televised football highlights 'The Big Match' and a director of Gillingham Football Club, announced that West Ham were to be the opposition in what was to be Brian Yeo's testimonial 'tomorrow night'. After the Sunday tele football there was a group of us lads who went to Eltham Park South for a kick about. John and I talked about West Ham being at Gillingham and decided to go to the game. I used to lie in bed on a Sunday morning reading all the back page sports and although not having seen Brian Yeo play, I was aware he was regularly mentioned in the goal scoring credits. I had never been to a football match at The Priestfield Stadium before, but had delivered Kia-Ora plastic container drinks made at/in the Kia-Ora factory on Silwood Street in my school holidays along with cinemas in the Kent county area. My brother in law Richard (Dick to family members) worked for Kia-Ora as did my father some time before him. I would often go on this particular 'once a week in the country' trip with Dick and give a hand.

## Hey Jude/Music Clubs/Wings/Scruffy Dog/Horses at the Garden/3-0 Win at CRYSTAL PALACE 30/10/1971/Ade Coker Scores on Debut

**I** **T WAS AROUND THE TIME** of the Brian Yeo Gillingham testimonial match that I was also to meet Lorraine. John Sweet asked if I along with two other lads would attend a meeting with him before parishioners of St Luke's Church on Westmount road and ask if it would be possible to use the small upstairs hall, which I estimate from memory to be about twenty feet by ten feet in size for a Rock 'n' Roll club on a Sunday night. A short while after this meeting, with Boys Brigade friends and 'senior' members Gary Fisher and Michael Voce, we asked Dave Hodgekiss (Hodge) Company Captain if it would be possible to use the fellowship room of the Methodist Church for a progressive music night on a Tuesday. This room was smaller than the hall at St Luke's but still big enough should we get them out of the BB games room, to use pool cues as imaginary guitars.

Both clubs were given go ahead trial periods that were to prove successful. Lorraine was introduced by Alison to the Rock 'n' Roll club in the first or second week of opening. Alison was Simon and Jonathon Dobson's sister. Simon never came along but Jonathon, like John Sweet, was also a massive rock 'n' roll music lover. Lorraine got on with everyone; she was of a very outgoing nature but this did not prevent her desire to do well in her studies at school. Lorraine adored horses, loved her music and was a big fan of The Beatles. On her birthday a card was given signed by four or five of us lads but it was me who got the kiss. I was 15, Lorraine was now 14 as of years, but 22 months was the separation. We squared up many times after that initiation and one Sunday morning she arrived at the gate of our small Elibank road front garden. Mum called to me to say, "Graham, look out the front window." Lorraine was with Alison: they were both on horseback, and it was not a common sight normally associated in Elibank road or anywhere else locally for that matter.

One club night Lorraine asked if I knew the words to 'Hey Jude' and smiled with a sense of shy embarrassment. Being a Beatles fan myself and having sung the song many times before, I said "yes". After she left, even knowing the words inside out, I had to sing them in my head. I looked for something in the lyrics that may be detrimental but it was all plus signs. As if to rubber stamp the occasion, Lorraine came round to our house in Elibank the following evening and passed me the record on an Apple labelled single. The coming months were such happy times; I would meet Lorraine from school or she would come to mine and play music. We would take our dogs Scruffy and Sally for walks in the parks and woods or go swimming at Eltham Park lido with other friends for a cool down. My brother-in-law Dick, aware that Lorraine was a big Beatles fan, made enquiries and was successful in getting us both complimentary tickets when working with Kia-Ora for Paul McCartney and Wings at Hammersmith Odeon, now known as The Apollo.

Scruffy was our family dog. Dad had brought Scruff home one Saturday afternoon in October 1971. Dad phoned mum and told her he was bringing a dog home. Mum described the dog and she was correct in her description; earlier in the day she had seen a confused, panic stricken dog running around aimlessly in the area, and it was assumed the poor thing was no longer wanted and had possibly been put out of a window of a pull-away car? After taking the dog to the police station and supplying home details to police should the dog be claimed, this poor, overly long haired, dirty and matted, running around, confused and desperate dog was brought home with dad using his tie for a collar and lead. I was in the bath having played football for the Boys Brigade when dad walked in calling this dog "Pooch". This was how scruffy was to be known in the early days before deciding on a name. Scruffy was a fitting and descriptive name for his appearance when he was found, and perhaps a little soppy also, due to his loving nature that this multi-mongrel dog openly displayed. This day was also the day Ade Coker had scored in the opening minutes of his debut at Crystal Palace in a 3-0 away win for West Ham. Lorraine's dog Sally was a cross between a Labrador and Boxer and, like Scruffy, beautifully behaved with the most wonderful temperament, although it would be agreed Scruffy was the more inquisitive if not mischievous of the two.

Now working my way up the ranks within the Boys Brigade, playing three football matches over the weekend for my school and Boys Brigade on a Saturday, then Endeavours Football club on the Sunday, the two music clubs as well as all and sundry in the way of activities that an organisation such as the Boys Brigade enabled, it was such a fun time for sure; but on the negative side I was as you may have gathered, somewhat slapdash as a pupil at school and now, as I reflect, I'm not sure whether I have or should I have regrets or not. It was for me, being young, youthful and socially happy, at times being serious and yet free. 'Hey Jude' with all the songs lyrics fulfilled, was to be proved quite poignant and my memories of that time period and through first love emotions will last my life time.

## Failed Journey/SOUTHAMPTON

**H**OVERING AROUND this same period I had been camping with Boys Brigade mates at Five Arches (Foots Cray Meadows) North Cray, a small area in Kent sandwiched by the bigger and better known places of Bexley and Sidcup and had arranged with Terry Randall who was not a BB boy, that if I came home early we would go to the Southampton match. Dad was not in any way impressed that I had come home early and would often say to me if I stayed away and didn't go 'they would win', and this was another such time this sentence was drummed in. Crunch time was coming and he asked me how I was intending to get to Southampton. I replied with the money I had in my pocket and his and mum's pocket money I was due. Well, I did say dad was not impressed and so it proved, for there was no pocket money for me—not on this day anyway.

Terry had a large family and one of his three sisters, Tracey via Crown Woods School and before I met her, was already a good friend of Lorraine's. It was Tracey and not Terry that would accompany me sometimes to Hammers matches and now, looking back on it, this possibly was the only time I was to get together with Terry with the sole intention of going to a West Ham match. The family had three Staffordshire bull terrier bitch dogs, Letty, Katie and Gabby of which her puppy litter delivery I was to witness and attend. I told Terry of the situation and my predicament and that I still wanted to go. Terry had no qualms so off we went. Our idea was to get a 108 bus from Eltham through the Blackwall Tunnel and then thumb a lift from a West Ham travelling to the match car. I had seventy pence and together we agreed that with what money he had, we would have enough to get us both in and a programme, assuming whoever we thumbed a lift from would bring us back to London and the Blackwall Tunnel and so therefore and finally, the 108 bus back to Eltham. Together we walked to each and the next bus stop along the Rochester Way, approaching The Dover Patrol pub at Kidbrooke and then with the donkey field to our left and claret and blue openly on display, a not known to us family and friends Arsenal minibus unexpectedly pulled over. Two harmless Hammers fans looking probably as if they were on a mission must have come across as 'alright' because the Arsenal fans were heading, I believe, north to a match and a lift through the Blackwall Tunnel with two seats vacant was offered and accepted. This getting a lift lark to Southampton had got off to a blinder, especially as at this stage we weren't even thumbing; what's more, not only did we get taken through the tunnel but got dropped off at Aldgate, which at the time going on conversation within the Arsenal group was to be more beneficial to us.

These Arsenal supporters chatting amongst themselves had been putting their heads together to come up with what best to advise for our quest to reach Southampton. Collectively they came up with the suggestion we should follow signs for the A3 as that was what they felt would be our best option. "Walk across Tower Bridge towards The Elephant and Castle," was where they told us we would pick up signs for the A3 and, true to their word, A3 signs appeared. We walked and walked, we followed the A3 signs through Kennington, Stockwell and Clapham, but it was only at Wandsworth we saw our one and only West Ham car. A lack of cars was talked about between the pair of us but as for why never crossed our minds. This 'one' car was stopped at traffic lights but fifty yards or so ahead, we both 'legged it' in the hope of catching up and a possible lift, but of course the lights changed, and what was to prove our one and only opportunity was missed. It was now one o'clock and giving in became a reality as the match was a 3pm kick off. Our fruitless 'walk in the dark' had come to an end and other than the compensation and benefit of exercise, which trust me was not thought of or even mentioned, we ended up at Earlsfield train station. It was from here we set off for home, and this also is what I used my seventy pence for. We didn't know the car journey way to Southampton and neither, despite their chat among themselves and good intentions, did the Arsenal fans. This was to explain in later years why we hadn't seen any West Ham 'away' travelling vehicles apart from the one and it's possible he had got his bearings wrong also? The A3 is in fact the most direct road for Portsmouth although, in saying that, it may have been this driver lived south of the river and intended to cut across country from the A3 at Guildford onto the A31 towards Winchester before heading south towards Southampton, of which my information now tells me would likely have been the A33 and not the M3 which was not due for completion until many years later, as was the M25. With Terry and me of course acting on good intended guidance but now having the experience, I feel it would be true to say if we had stayed north of the river and not walked across Tower Bridge but towards Blackfriars and Parliament, continued along the river embankment onto Earls Court and even if necessary as far as Hammersmith who knows, our required hitched lift may have been hitched? It's always easy to look back and hindsight is 'a wonderful thing', but this route was far more likely to have been used by many West Ham travelling fans driving from east to west London north of the river with intentions of a more direct route for them to Southampton. My road study of the routes back then tells me that taking the A4 at Hammersmith would have been the best option, leading onto the A316, A30 and then the A33 into Southampton?

## The Dream-The Dream/The DREADED Monday Morning

**T**HREE YEARS after the very so close against Stoke and Wembley dream of a League Cup final in 1972, came the FA Cup run of 1975. I recall in my early years and then early teens when sitting in front of the tele from around 10.30am to kick-off time, how much I would get glued and sucked into the build-up. The scenes, the interviews with the players, the re-runs of 'the road to Wembley' matches or showing of the fans from their hometowns and the street 'dressings' in the build-up week, or perhaps arriving at Wembley on the day, the colour, the atmosphere, everything the FA Cup final IS. The dream and, Oh, how I wanted it! I had no distractions. West Ham weren't playing, and the league programme had shut down for FA

Cup Final Day. I remember mum coming in the living room one cup final day and behind me, where I sat, I sensed her looking at me, knowing my thoughts, pondering and then with a delayed hesitancy saying, "Don't worry son, they'll get there one day..." After a couple of seconds thought but no more and no less, a solemn angled look down at my outstretched feet and without looking round, I replied with words to the shoulder shrug off effect: "Will they?"—not believing they ever would. I felt/knew that mum wanted it for me even more than I wanted it for myself and that would have been typical. But do you know what? West Ham and football really did mean everything to me in my youthful, younger years. I'll never forget (it may go distant and to an extent fade) the dreaded Monday morning at school if "we" had lost.

### IPSWICH TOWN FA Cup Semi-Final Replay (Stamford Bridge) 09/04/1975

I**T WAS POURING BUCKETS**. West Ham supporters were in the open to all the elements opposite end to the semi-covered end known as The Shed where, on this night, the Ipswich Town hordes were housed. After a 0-0 draw at Aston Villa's Villa Park on the previous Saturday, battle was to recommence. Ipswich...West Ham was the song of the night as it was at the match four days prior at Villa Park, made famous from chart record releases by bagpipes and vocalists alike to the tune of Amazing Grace. One lot would start and then the competition of who could be the loudest began. Another two goals are scored matching his two in the 6th round victory over Arsenal at Highbury from Alan 'The Whippet' Taylor or 'Sparrow' as he would also be known. All supporters know what it is like: seconds feel like minutes and minutes feel like hours. It doesn't always mean the same thing in your own team's match either; it could quite easily be the importance of a result that affects your team in a match being played elsewhere. In this case I was in a total state of being "all over the place" with Ipswich losing 2-1 and pushing for an equaliser. The whistle blows, it's 'Wembley here we come!' and I can now pulsate into the human form of visual delirium. After a win of such proportion self-control doesn't really matter; singing, jumping and running up and down the terracing to me was quite normal behaviour, as I could see amongst the embracing hugs and cheering of the majority, it was also for the odd other. On leaving the ground I remember being in the Kings Road, arms aloft in the cold damp air as the rain had stopped, singing to my heart's content and then, without warning, my Hammers bobble hat being pulled down over my face.

### Pat/Football Specials/King William 1V Pub Celebration

**I**NSTANTANEOUSLY TURNING, I saw it was Pat, who I had met on my away travels on 'run down' trains that had seen 'better days' known as football specials. These trains that would often appear as if they were soon to be taken out of service took football supporters to matches up and down the country at discounted rates. Pat normally went to away matches with his girlfriend Sue; however, Sue on this occasion was not with him but by coincidence was from Ipswich.

With this brief moment of embrace we continued on our separate ways and I walked along the streets away from the Kings road with fellow pals Steve James, John Sweet and I'm sure brother Terry. It was a sure fact that the further away from the ground we walked the thinner the departing fans got, we ran into a group of Ipswich supporters who made the point they had been the better side over the two games. I agreed, it was in my opinion that referee Clive Thomas blew his whistle on occasions when advantage could have been played and that at times this had broken down Ipswich's rhythm. I felt it helped West Ham. We finished up our celebrations of the night in The King William IV pub on the Grosvenor road, between Chelsea and Vauxhall bridges on the embankment north side.

### Disc Jockey/Claret and Blue Rugby Shirt/Contact Eroded

**P**AT CAME FROM BERMONDSEY and I remember going into the Victoria pub with girlfriend Lisa where, unknown to me, he was a disc jockey. This must have been late 1979, early 1980, and after the surprise of this meet up he remarked on what I was wearing and where I was, Pat duly pointed out the fact I was in an area with pubs frequented by Millwall supporters and wearing a claret and blue rugby shirt would not be received with approval. In the previous two or three years or so prior to this meeting and through no real reason, we had lost contact; natural changes in direction happened with "at the time" in common acquaintances and it would be true to say Pat and I never socialised away from football; mobile telephones were not in existence and we had never exchanged landline numbers, be it work or home, so for that reason we lacked the means for staying in touch. In conversation in the pub that night Pat was to tell me he still travelled with West Ham fans on trains or by other means and I told him that "these" days I went by car. As time went by my contact with Pat completely eroded; whenever I returned to the Victoria on the very rare times I did, Pat was never in attendance.

*Lisa with me wearing my West Ham rugby shirt*
*Pat duly pointed out the fact I was in an area frequented by*
*Millwall Supporters. This picture however although taken in a pub,*
*was not The Victoria*

## Seamus/The Monty Club/2012 Olympic Implications/Pat Reunion/The Victoria Pub/Manze Pie and Mash

*A Fabulous Social and Family Sports Club. Snooker/Pool/Darts/Quiz Nights/Trips to the Theatre/Car Rally's/Hastings/Chessington World of Adventures/Disco's/Live Bands/St Georges Nights/St Patricks Nights. It just went on and on with any competitions or arrangement for examples given above being sorted 'in house'. So many people would pull together for its continued continuation with children having the safest of environments playing in the hall or on the outside grounds.*
*The Monty Club was all about Volunteers. Kevin Dooley is seen here with me pouring a pint and doing a stint behind the bar leading up to Christmas.... Year?*

**M**ANY YEARS LATER though, through a chance conversation with occasional beer pal Seamus at the Monty club, Christ Church Eltham High Street, we got to talking over a pint about his Stratford London E15 work premises and about it being required for the forthcoming 2012 Olympics; he was explaining to me his plus and minus concerns as well as the implications this was having on him or will have on him and his partner Pete, then stressing more fervently on his staff. During the course of an evening's session, many topics are conversed over and natural changes in subject just occurr. One such change in subject this evening was to make a lasting impression; for some reason we went on to talk about pubs we used to drink in down the Old Kent road many years ago and way before we had met. Seamus dropped in the conversation that he now, if ever down that way, would drink in The Victoria. I mentioned about Pat all those years ago and he told me it was a Pat who was now the tenant, and that also he was a West Ham supporter.

I decided before the Brighton FA Cup 3rd round home tie of 6th January 2007 to have pie and mash in Manze, Tower Bridge Road SE1, before venturing to The Victoria not too many minutes' walk away. Curiosity told me I had to find out if it was the same Pat who had been my West Ham travel mate and DJ in said pub twenty-seven years plus previously. My curiosity thirst was quenched—I walked into the pub and recognised him straight away! Before I could re-introduce myself his jaw hit the deck. He made an instant recovery and after giving him my order, a light and bitter with a warm light ale on the house was poured my way. Memory lane was to become the natural focal of conversation and the "Do you remember?" backward and forward banter cum reminisce was a natural course and direction in the conversation that followed.

Patricia was now Pat's partner and she was standing with him on my walking through the door entrance; understanding this most unexpected reunion, Trish stood watching and listening before saying, "I'll leave you two to it, I've got shopping to do." I've been back to see Pat from time to time since, but generally it's been with mum and not before a Hammers match of which a simple journey over Tower Bridge, through the Limehouse Link towards Canning Town and Greengate parking can take less than twenty five minutes. Mum. like me, also has a big liking and always looks forward to the enjoyment of our trip back to Bermondsey for Manze pie and mash where, afterwards, she is quite happy to sit with her thoughts whilst Pat and I discuss common ground.

## Ballot Card-Vouchers/FULHAM and Wembley 03/05/1975

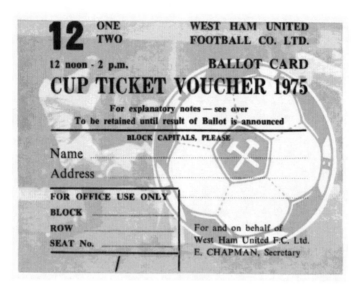

**12** ONE TWO    WEST HAM UNITED FOOTBALL CO. LTD.

12 noon - 2 p.m.    BALLOT CARD

## CUP TICKET VOUCHER 1975

For explanatory notes — see over
To be retained until result of Ballot is announced

BLOCK CAPITALS, PLEASE

Name ...........................................................

Address ........................................................

FOR OFFICE USE ONLY
BLOCK ................................
ROW ................................
SEAT No. ................................

For and on behalf of
West Ham United F.C. Ltd.
E. CHAPMAN, Secretary

### RETAIN THIS CARD CAREFULLY
#### EXPLANATORY NOTES

The holder of this card will automatically enter the Club's Ballot for tickets as notified.

The significant feature of this Ballot Card is the CODE NUMBER in the top left-hand corner.

The result of the Ballot will be announced as follows (Example Only): "CODE NUMBER 9; Colour: WHITE."

THIS CARD MUST BE RETAINED. The result of the Ballot will be published in the Press and Official Programme.

Holders of winning Ballot Cards MUST insert their full name and address on the front of this card in BLOCK LETTERS and MUST present it at the Club Offices on a date to be notified between the times shown on the front of this card. They will be entitled to purchase ONE TICKET. This will prevent unnecessary waiting-time.

NO POSTAL APPLICATIONS FROM WINNING HOLDERS CAN BE ACCEPTED UNDER ANY CIRCUMSTANCES.

**B**EFORE that fantastic Stamford Bridge night and win over Ipswich Town some three or four weeks before and with the possibility of a cup final approaching, ballot card cup ticket vouchers 4.5x3.5 inches in size were issued at a not announced pre-selected home match. The match then chosen without supporter knowledge was to be the first division league match against Burnley in March, although there may have been another? These ballot vouchers were to have a number stamped on them and issued to paying fans at terracing entrance turnstiles around the ground. Should a cup final ensue, it was deemed by the club this was the fairest way to allocate terrace fans a ticket as seated season ticket holders would automatically be guaranteed a place. A similar system I understand was also used for the cup final against Preston in 1964.

Hundreds of ballot vouchers bearing the same number were issued and a series of numbers were to be picked "out of a hat" (say from 1-30); should you then have a ballot voucher with a successful corresponding number, you were guaranteed a cup final ticket if claimed at the time given on the ballot voucher but on a date to be notified. Results of this ballot with any further information such as the date of ticket purchase would have been published in the press and any official programme(s) prior to sale; this process was then repeated until all tickets had been sold. What actual numbers were used I can't say, but I can say it is my belief letters of the alphabet were considered as a possible way of balloting but was not accepted as after further consideration and understanding, it was deemed letters would be "easier" for alteration and therefore abuse by either 'keen' fans or for plain profiteering. For all my happiness and joy of being in the FA Cup Final and having more than one numbered ballot voucher (a friend or two had donated theirs to me), not one of my ballot card numbers proved to be in my favour.

Having no memory and being only 6 at the time of 1964 Preston, I was now to go through the thrill and the build up to my first ever FA Cup final— milking the thought of West Ham at Wembley, walking around in a dream on cloud nine and even answering the home telephone "West Ham for the cup" before saying the telephone number. For some I must have been one right pain, absolutely no doubt about it, but even without a ticket I could not help but continue the feeling of immense excitement. I was and had been I guess in the sense of the word 'desperate' for a ticket, but the euphoric feeling of Wembley somehow made me thick skinned to the fact no ticket was in my hand. It did not matter who I came in contact with or how brief an introduction to an acquaintance was, it would be true to say in the next few weeks approaching May 3rd, I made it quite known to all and sundry my determination to obtain a ticket. Perhaps that was the reason for my not having a ticket denial; the belief that a ticket was going to show, and this effort combined with confident belief, was going to pay off. It worked! From a week before the match having no ticket to the lead up to twenty-four hours before the match, I had four. Five of us now were to be going by car but two already had tickets. Three tickets went to deserving "homes" but having obtained these four tickets via various quarters our place of standing was to be in different sections of Wembley Stadium. The other ticket, obtained only the night before, I failed to offload.

Standing and walking around outside Wembley amongst the thousands I just couldn't find one deserving supporter. Not one West Ham or Fulham fan did I come across looking for a ticket. I ended up selling the spare to a tout for £2.50; to this day it is something I didn't want to do, but hopefully a West Ham or Fulham devotee would now have a ticket opportunity? For a fan all I would have wanted in return would have been the face value price of £1.50, but where were they?

Not a great final but then not many, it seems, are. Shame really, because I have always been one for entertaining, fair, flair and fluent football. It is something also that is a desire within me that I want other supporters to see when West Ham play, and in this match Hammers were playing on the world stage. Fulham on balance of play and though not a spectacle in my opinion, just edged it, but two goals again from Alan 'The Whippet/Sparrow' Taylor and a 2-0 win, sent a number of celebratory fans at the final whistle on to the pitch. Not an ounce of trouble witnessed by myself or told of or read about. It was The Friendly London FA Cup Final. On leaving the ground we had banter with Freddie Starr, the extravert stage show and television stand-up comic comedian in his Rolls Royce as we pushed out into the traffic before him, us in our little whatever it was blearing out "Bubbles" on the cassette player. HAPPY… JUBILANT… ECSTACTIC… Such minor words really and not entirely descriptive.

## The Cockney Pride, Piccadilly Circus/Trafalgar Square/Mate... Mate, Your Shoes...Your Shoes

**I** **JUMPED** out of the car with Steve James in Piccadilly and headed straight to the Cockney Pride pub situated between Regents Street and Haymarket on Piccadilly Circus. I had met Steve some seven or so years earlier; we were both members of a Cub Scout group based on Ilderton Road opposite Ilderton Road primary school, Bermondsey SE16. Our re-meeting happened when he joined the Boys Brigade sometime after me, having moved to Eltham also with mum Pauline, dad Jim and twin sisters Julia and Heather.

Having a beer at The Cockney Pride on a Saturday night was not uncommon around this time and we had arranged to meet non-Hammers friends 'Age' Voce, Keith Unitt and Gary Fisher from Eltham there. As the evening wore on the pub became jam-packed with West Hammers. I stood on top of the tables and chairs joining in on all the songs and anything happy. When it was time to leave we headed to Charing Cross to get the train home, only to be hit with the sight of dozens of West Hammers at or in the monument pools of Trafalgar Square! The fountains were not in motion and not to miss out, I took my shoes off, but before I could wade in I was prevented from doing so by a copper. With a little bit of argy bargy I was in. 'Age' followed and amongst other splashing movements we wrestled each other in the water. Tired, worn out, saturated and boozed, we went off to catch the last train home only to hear from behind, "Mate... Mate, Your Shoes... Your Shoes!" I stopped and looked around. It was the copper catching us up with one of my shoes in each hand; he had kept his eyes on us and saw I had forgotten them! Having been so carried away and preoccupied by the magical moment, I had not even realised they were not on my feet. Top Cop and Good Man... Cheers!

## Alan Taylor Fairy Tale/Victory Parade/It May Go Distant and to an Extent Fade. BUT NEVER FORGOTTEN

S O an ALL English team won the 1975 FA Cup and to date are still the last team to do so. The time before this occasion was Manchester City in 1969, but before then it was again West Ham United and that was versus Preston North End 1964. The only difference from the two English produced sides for West Ham was that the 1964 winning team had featured ALL English players throughout the campaign whereas in the 1975 competition Clyde Best (Bermuda), had played in the fourth round tie and then replay win away at Swindon Town. For Manchester City re previous knockout rounds I have not the knowledge. I was an Ever Present attendant of the home, away and neutral ground matches in the reaching of the 1974/75 FA Cup and for the record Alan Taylor had scored the last six West Ham goals in the competition. The two against Arsenal in the 6th round, two in the semi-final replay against Ipswich and of course this day too in the final. Alan had made his debut six months earlier after being bought on the cheap from Rochdale for a reported fee of £40,000. The fairy-tale I recall was well documented. AND WHY NOT!

It was an excited early get-up in the morning for The Victory Parade. As with the night before, I was with Steve James and waiting outside the Bow Bells pub in Bow Road E3 at about 10.30am. This was where the coach was to pass en route to East Ham Town Hall. Silly us, when the coach passed we chased it over the Bow flyover into Stratford High Street but couldn't keep up! Some guy who saw our valiant but futile attempt from the petrol garage opposite the Green Man pub on the junction of Carpenters road took pity on us; he drove us as close to the ground as possible before the crowd got too much and we subsequently ended up by foot power at East Ham Town Hall.

We came across Phil who was a lad I had met on away travels with his younger brother and pals—they were from Hounslow; he asked me to take a picture of him and his group holding a West Ham flag and this I did. It was also the last time we were to cross paths. I used to enjoy talking to Phil; we seemed to share the same views of the beautiful game and how we liked it played. Somewhere in the region of a quarter of a million people attended, stereo systems and speakers balanced on window ledges blearing out Bubbles or West Ham United (B side of FA Cup Final single). A carnival it was and a weekend never to be forgotten. Within the memory, it may go distant and to an extent fade. BUT NEVER FORGOTTEN.

## DERBY COUNTY FA Charity Shield (Wembley)... 09/08/1975

Serial **N°** **1020**

**BRITISH RAILWAYS BOARD**
**SHIPPING AND INTERNATIONAL SERVICES DIVISION**

**EMBARKATION TICKET FOR OVERNIGHT SERVICE**

The holder is not entitled to occupy numbered upholstered seats.
This ticket authorises embarkation on the vessel from

JERSEY depart 21.45
GUERNSEY depart 23.59
to WEYMOUTH QUAY  ~~0~~8 AUG 1975
~~Sunday/Monday, 27th/28th July,~~ 1975

It is valid only in conjunction with a Travel Ticket by the service shown above.
BR 13564/5                                    **Issued without charge.**

**H**AMMERS FANS didn't have to wait too long for a quick return with their team to Wembley. After just three months and six days of the passing of that fantastic first weekend in May, Hammers were now to play for the FA Charity Shield Trophy, but this time it was to be against league division one champions Derby County. The fact is other than losing 0-2 my memory of the match and the day is somewhat elusive. One thing is for sure though, and that is I came home early on a previous night's ferry crossing from the Channel Island of Guernsey with Steve James. We had been camping with our 22nd West Kent Boys Brigade Company and had come home on a previously arranged earlier crossing than with the company, who were due to come home the following day for the sole intention of going to Wembley and seeing the match. The departure from Jersey had left the largest channel Island at 9.45pm and was to pass en route via Guernsey to the port of Weymouth, where we were to catch a connecting train back to

Waterloo and then subsequently a Kent-bound train to Eltham. Mum and dad were still in bed when I walked in; after bacon sandwiches, cups of tea and no doubt a catch up talk about camp and so on, it was time to meet Steve at Eltham Park train station and so off to Wembley.

## The Rolling Stones/'Gimme Shelter'

C ONCERT GOING was a great joy for many of the lads and lassies I knocked about with in the seventies and eighties, and it is with a tinge of regret I wasn't to keep ticket stubs or programmes as record reminders of who I saw and of course dates although another interest would be to compare cost from then to now. The same goes for the numerous West End shows and theatres I've attended and nowadays, the Churchill and Orchard theatres based in Bromley and Dartford respectively due to location and accessibility. The Rolling Stones and the Tour of Europe '76. Together with Adrian ('Age') Voce and Keith Unitt, we applied for tickets for any of the three May gigs to be held at London's Earls Court but no luck was forthcoming. Three more dates were added due to the phenomenal demand of a reported one million applicants but try again by post was something we did not do.

However, try again we did. On the night of the first gig we travelled to Earls Court by train and tube and arrived at around 9pm. It had been advertised that a number of tickets amounting to what I still feel was a hundred for each show had been kept back; tickets from the venue box office for each nightly show were to go on sale from 3pm of the same afternoon. Queuing all night we had cited ourselves up for; mentally prepared we were, but no preparation for weather elements was taken. Luckily the weather was kind to us and so Gimme Shelter were not words that crossed our minds. The Stones were bashing it out inside and here we were outside queuing the night before in the hope of getting in for the following night's gig. Forth, fifth and sixth we were in the queue, as three had already started the formation along the pavement some fifty or so yards from the box office but outside the Earls Court perimeter gates.

## Ticket Tout "Buy or Sell"/Popcorn Making/No Sign Of 'Age'/Choice Words from Clemency

**W**ITH THE CONCERT FINISHING and early 'must get transport home' leavers vacating the premises, ticket touts arrived wanting to buy tickets or if anyone wanted they had tickets to sell. This was so nice to hear and such a pleasing sight as one can imagine. Going into the early hours the queue had increased but by Saturday 10am it had swelled to a considerable amount but 'we knew we were safe'. Having 'roughed it' with other likeminded people and now on friendly terms and with the time approaching 11am, between the three of us we took it in turns to 'hold the fort' whilst the other two went to the Brompton pub just a few minutes' walk back from where we were queuing. With time getting close I returned with Keith but there was no sign of 'Age'. We were told a woman had come out and had asked if anybody would like to help her make popcorn for the evening's show and that 'Age' had 'gone for it'. No way! was our reaction— we were properly baffled as this was not the way we worked, but what could we do? Our feathers were for sure ruffled and no real conversational substance was entered into other than an explanation was most definitely the order of the day from 'Age' when we next saw him.

The perimeter gates opened at the advertised 3pm time and although all night queuing and placed in a no problem of a ticket position, touts arrived again as if waiting to spring with the sole objective of queue jumping. Words were exchanged and pushing and shoving ensued but the choicest of words were coming from Clemency, a girl I hadn't seen in the queue earlier but who I had met at parties before; she was a friend of Lorraine, my first girlfriend. We managed to get our tickets and then some while later we came across 'Age' who had vacated the venue looking for us. He told us he had kept his eye on us when the box office had opened but could not get to that part of the building; he knew also we would have got our tickets and he knew also he hadn't let us down.

## 'Age' Had it Sorted/Girl in the Leopard Two Piece/Girlfriend Popcorn Appetites/Terry 'Goes into One'

'**A**GE' **IN FACT** had arranged with the woman that if he helped her make the popcorn, could his two friends that had been with him all night be part of the team who sold it? 'Age' had sorted this before he had left his 'hold the fort' queuing but was not in a position to tell us. We've got tickets for the Rolling Stones and now having met 'Age' and been explained to, he is now telling us we've got to go with him and NOW! We found ourselves in a similar position that I had found myself in a year earlier at the West Ham/Fulham FA Cup final. Now having spare tickets and due to the urgency, we offloaded our tickets that hopefully went to deserving fans.

Inside the atmosphere was at the point of buzzing, steel bands were playing and girl go-go dancers entertained as people entered the concourse of the exhibition hall cum arena. The go-go girl in the leopard two-piece springs to mind as that day is now thought of and the selling of the popcorn was to prove easy, with disgruntled boyfriends paying for eager girlfriend popcorn appetites and with us making one penny for every box sold. I'm walking around as an 'usherette' when my brother Terry spots me and goes into one. He had taken great pleasure in taking the Michael out of me about him having a ticket and me not. Almost having to pick him up from hysterical laughing, and I do mean convulsion, I gave him the story and he bought a couple of boxes from me before wandering off and me continuing my work.

The concert started, the opening chords of 'Honky Tonk Women' were there for all to hear and from where I was standing on the concourse I could see the popcorn stand. With excitement and without any hesitation or thought, I ran towards the popcorn stand where I met Keith running towards the stand also, but he had come from a different angle; he must have seen me and chose to ditto. Where 'Age' was now we had no idea and we never saw him again that night. Slipping out of the strapping from around our shoulders and neck that held the popcorn tray, and then giving it back with contents to our lady employer, we ran into the Earls Court exhibition hall and arena to witness what we had spent all night and most of the day queuing up for and waiting to see.

## Popcorn Payment/Rude Not To and So We Did

**T**HE FOLLOWING DAY, having discussed it with Keith and not been paid for our popcorn sales, we returned to Earls Court that evening. Banging on an exit door with crowds of people either walking about or mingling, the exit door was opened by two security cum steward type individuals strongly inquisitive as to what we were playing at! Explaining to them our popcorn employment the night before, our attendance for being there was for payment of work done. With this the two security cum steward types escorted us to the popcorn stand. The woman confirmed to them we had worked for her the night before, and on hearing this they wandered off to carry on their duties leaving us to carry out our business. The woman paid me £1.50 but what she gave Keith I do not know, not now anyway. Having now been paid and finding ourselves unattended on the concourse, there could only be one decision: with the Rolling Stones shortly to commence another gig of their Tour of Europe '76 and after such a fantastic night the night before, we felt it would be rude not to pay the band the compliment of staying to watch them again—and so we did.

## Gary Fisher Reminds Me

**I** HAD ALWAYS KNOWN we got in for a Rolling Stones third night and another freebie at that. For the life of me and as time tick-tocked along, when having a beer with great friend Gary Fisher (now living in West Sussex and my knowing him from Boy's Brigade, Football, Holidays and so, So very much more) in the Mug House, London Bridge, many years later, he mentioned about he would never forget when we went to see the Rolling Stones at Earls Court, and me getting us both in with Keith Unitt. I asked if he could recall how and all he said was he remembered me banging on doors and talking to 'bouncers'. Had I used the previous with success payment required from pop corn stand? I have no idea now but for sure, In We Got.

## FC DEN HAAG European Cup Winners Cup (ECWC) 3ʳᵈ Round 03/03/1976

**A**FTER THEIR FINAL Earls Court gig towards the end of May and only two days later, the Rolling Stones were to play in Holland at the stadium of FC Den Haag as a continuation of their Tour of Europe '76. Den Haag had been knocked out of the European Cup Winners Cup (ECWC) by The Hammers on the away goals rule two months earlier in March, the match having ended in a 5-5 aggregate score line. The Hammers had been four goals down at Den Haag when Billy Jennings headed two second half goals that had given breathing space and the lifeline they needed. A 3-1 home win completed the score line and although Jennings played he did not add to his goal tally; the home three goals were scored by Frank Lampard, Billy Bonds and FA Cup Final doubler Alan Taylor.

## 1975/76 Pole Position/FA Cup 3ʳᵈ Round KO/Free Fall/ECWC Concentration?/Thrown out at ARSENAL

**H**AVING HAD THE SUCCESS of winning the previous season's FA Cup and playing in the opening of the season ceremonial Charity Shield match, the season of 1975/76 had started promisingly for West Ham and they found themselves in pole position up in the dizziest of heights of division one after a 1-1 draw at home to Coventry as of 8ᵗʰ November. The season's optimism was to decline in dramatic circumstances after the following league match away defeat to Derby County, and the remainder of the season could only be described as a free fall. A third round home tie 0-2 defeat at the hands of Liverpool was to see the defence of the FA Cup shattered at the first attempt. Having earlier in the season been knocked out of the League Cup in a fourth round replay at home to Spurs again 0-2, it almost seemed Hammers were solely concentrating on their progress within The European Cup Winners Cup competition that had been their reward for the FA Cup triumph the previous season.

Having only lost two matches up until that pole position top spot back in the early part of November, West Ham were to lose seventeen of their remaining twenty-seven fixtures and finished in eighteenth position on thirty-six points. With the ECWC semi-final first leg away to West Germany representatives Eintracht Frankfurt looming at the very end of March, having successful obtained a match ticket and with travel arrangements sorted, I was to attend an away league match at Arsenal some eleven days prior on the 20<sup>th</sup>. It was a match that was to see myself given an early exit from Arsenal North Bank terrace viewing and a game that was to see the Hammers lose 1-6. I can still picture myself being walked around the pitch perimeter by a policeman and passing Hammer player Mick McGiven warming up on the sideline as I made my way and escorted at that, to a pen situated behind a stand that housed so-called hooligans. My concern at the time was that the match was being televised for the following day's Sunday afternoon football highlights program The Big Match and I was wearing a Lep Transport slogan T-shirt, the company I at this time currently worked for, and thinking that this was not the kind of advertising they sought. (Pictured Page 73).

We could hear goals going in and I along with others ejected were kept informed in what direction the goals were being scored. There was no segregation of opposing supporters and although the situation could quite easily have been volatile and aggression was displayed on being led to the pen, once inside calming down was most definitely the order of the day and acrimonious amicability was focused on.

My crime… Mervyn Day had just saved a penalty from 1966 Wolrd Cup Winner Alan Ball and I was a happy, perhaps a little over the top exuberant Hammer, or could it possibly be the bobby was a disappointed 'in disguise' gooner? I along with others was 'released' from the pen some ten minutes from the end of the match and I returned to the North Bank to unite with my pals. They were 'fine' but it was plain to see on my return that in my absence, major disruption and disorder had taken place. The following day I watched the Big Match televised highlights of the game with concern; no sighting of me was observed so no interested company authoritarian or colleague explanation was necessary, unless of course it was told in passing conversation.

## EINTRACHT FRANKFURT ECWC Semi-Final... 1ˢᵗ LEG (Away) 31/03/1976

*Lacey's Coaches, 222 Barking Road, London E6 3BB. Chris Stone (left) with me as an eighteen year old looking forward to an away trip that for us was an away trip with a difference.*

**W**E SET OUT on our travels to Frankfurt on what was an early Tuesday evening. The coach journey was to take us to Dover for the overnight sailing to the port of Zeebrugge, Belgium. With left-hand continental road driving coach continuation, fantastic clear roads, driven at speed and with travel companions Chris Stone, Roy Chenery and Steve Rees, I remember walking along streets of Frankfurt in my claret and blue and a not too small Union Jack Flag that I had borrowed from The Methodist Church I frequented as a Boys Brigade member. Together and as a group we chose to stay more outside of the town/city on arrival where others that had travelled set their sight on I guess, options or livelier activities by going inwards? That may have been the case, but we managed to come across this little café cum bar that had say half a dozen or so German men drinking inside and doing no more than standing about or sitting on bar stools. Together we shared one nice afternoon with communications and understanding being successful. We played pool for steins of beer with losers paying and then afterwards, we went out to an open area opposite and played a German England 4a-side football match using upper clothing as goalposts. I can't remember who played in skins though.

*Walking the Streets of Frankfurt (31/03/1976)*

On walking to the ground and on arrival, we came across what no one in our little group or anyone else who travelled for that matter, could have envisaged. To our complete and total surprise we came across members of the British military stationed in West Germany; on top of this so unexpected visual surprise, we were then staggered by the wide representation of British football clubs in the form of openly worn scarves and colours that were in attendance. I can only assume that given the chance to see a "home" team play it was something many football fans amongst them would not want to miss and I write of a similar situation later re Bobby Moore/Celtic Testimonial under the heading **Bobby Moore (OBE)/What an Inside-Outside Football History/Always Smart and Liked a Lagar Page 179.**

Graham Paddon, 9th minute, twenty-five yards out shoots hard and low… DELIRIUM. Final result was a 1-2 defeat but with the cushion of that all-important away goal if needed. On leaving Frankfurt between 11pm and the midnight hour we arrived back in East London late afternoon or early the following evening. I can't help thinking the travel cost was £20.50 but don't quote me. The home 2nd leg of the ECWC semi-final was to be played on Wednesday 14th April and a home win of 3-1 proportions secured a place in the final that was to be held at The Heysel Stadium in the Belgium capital of Brussels. That return semi-final evening holds special memories for me and although what may appear to be out of place, I will write about that wonderful, wonderful night when all is told in **Atmosphere/Exhilaration/Eintracht    Frankfurt    14/04/1976/All    but Biblical…. Trevor Brooking… Page 174.**

## R.S.C. ANDERLECHT ECWC Final/Heysel Stadium (Brussels) 05/05/1976

**R**.S.C ANDERLECHT was to be The Hammers opponents. West Ham were again just as in the FA Cup Finals of 1964 and 1975 to field another ALL English team, but also in doing so mirrored the ALL English team that took the field and completed the match back in 1965 against TSV Munchen 1860, where on that afternoon and in the same competition at Wembley, became the first ALL English team to win a major European trophy. In 1970 Manchester City as with the Arsenal team of 1994, both started their matches with ALL English ECWC final teams that beat Gornik Zabrze of Poland and Parma of Italy respectively. Arsenal however did not complete having substituted Paul Merson late in the 2nd half for Eddie McGoldrick (Republic of Ireland). It remains to be said then that since starting the major European competitions of The European Cup/Champions League, ECWC and Fairs Cup/Uefa Cup, it is only West Ham United and Manchester City who have won any of these European trophies playing the full match with ONLY Englishmen. It is also my understanding that again, as in 1965, West Ham fielded ALL Englishmen in all knock-out rounds leading up to the final which is something I can't confirm for sure about Manchester City.

Anderlecht were a formidable Belgium team and well known to European football fans over, as in 1965 with West Ham being 'at home', it was now the opposition supporters who were to have the triple bonus and enjoyment of distance to travel, expense and benefit of time. £24 was to include return rail and ferry crossings Victoria/Brussels. Depart London Victoria 0800 hrs 5th May returning London Victoria 0800 hrs 6th May. This was one of the travel arrangements made by Camkin Sports (they did a flight alternative). Although we did the same journey in a similar manner, we did not necessarily travel at the same times or pay the same cost. I seem to recall our group arrived in Brussels in the early hours of the 5th and not via Camkin Sports.

The weather was of full-on sunshine proportions and one of my earliest recollections of the actual day was being in a bar and being interviewed by a Belgian Flemish Radio Reporter. He had seen our happy band on passing and although his intention he told us was to "get a feel of what was going on and talk to supporters later in the day", he went on to tell me he picked on us out of "interest". With the jukebox blasting Bill Hailey's 'Rock Around the Clock' and me with trousers pulled up to the knees balancing a bar stool on my head, what actual sense he got I'm not sure. He did say, however, that a broadcast of the recording would be aired that afternoon around 5pm although your guess is as good as mine. With Hammers fans arriving in their droves, we found self-entertainment and amusement to our liking throughout the day.

## Atomium Monument (Pictured Page 53)/One on One British Bulldog/Fair Ground 'Free Rides'/Heysel Facelift

**W**E VISITED the Atomium monument that was built for Expo '58, The Brussels World Fair; it is 335 feet tall and only a short distance from The Heysel Stadium. The Atomium has nine spheres that are connected by escalators containing exhibit halls and other spaces for the visiting public. A lift is contained in the vertical vertex. We went also to a fairground with John Sweet and me having a one-on-one British bulldog tussle in a sandpit there, before the fairground attendants "allowing" us to enjoy ourselves on one or two of the rides for free. With time getting on and not many being seen until after 3pm but now with Anderlecht fans in full attendance, we entered into The Heysel Stadium only to be disappointed, surprised, dare I say shocked, because for such a prestige occasion, it was obvious for all to see that the venue was in much need of a facelift. I understand also that at the time it had the status of being The Belgium National Stadium. The stadium was open to all elements and the end on which West Ham fans were to stand (and probably the Anderlect supporters too) was of concrete terracing in sore need of repair, where mud had dried to the point of dust and any form of sustained mass crowd movement would bring clouds of this dust rising into the air.

In control? Of course we were! Well, that was my personal view anyway. "Twinge of pain forced me into error"—Lampard (paper cutting saved in programme). Robbie Rensenbrink subsequently scored to equalise Pat Holland (Patsy) opener. Francois Van-der Elst scored early second half with Keith Robson equalising with a low header from a Trevor Brooking cross. Rensenbrink from the penalty spot scored his second and Anderlechts third three quarters or so into the second half and put the Hammers on the back foot. Van-der Elst who later was to join the Hammers for two seasons 1981/82-1982/83 scored a late second goal and Anderlechts fourth that sealed on paper a comfortable 4-2 win for the Belgians.

## Losing Had Never Entered My Head... It Hurt

**H**OME TIME and tears on the tram to the train. That ferry crossing back to Dover, bodies lying anywhere and everywhere, supporters from the day and night before mentally exhausted, knackered and numbed. What a difference a day makes! The back page headlines... THE BACK PAGE HEADLINES at Victoria station in the early hours of the following morning. Putting pen to paper about certain times and matches I went to, brings back experiences and emotions and this is one. For a minute or two as I write, I dwell on those emotions, the emotions that I had that night as an eighteen-year-old. My brother Terry, Cousin Andrew, the friends I travelled with and the ones I came across by chance in Brussels, those who I still see or no longer see, and of course the thirty-odd hours or so that had been had, losing had never entered my head... **It hurt!**

## LEICESTER CITY (Away) League Division One 24/08/1977/St Johns First Aid Medics/No Attack or Missile Throw Incident/Gangway opened/Blood Flow Stopped

**I** WELL AND TRULY cracked my head at this one. We travelled to this match in Kevin's little Mini Minor but he was still learning to drive. It was me therefore being the qualified driver, who was to drive the car that night with passengers Steve Rees, Roy Chenery and of course Kevin himself. The match was to end in a 1-0 victory for Leicester but we were to come so close to a goal in the first half when Pikey (Geoff Pike) smacked a shot at the Leicester goal only for Wallington, who I'm sure, was the Leicester keeper that night to save. Pop (Bryan Robson) following up and running in had looked so likely to score that I jumped in anticipation of a goal and ended up smacking my head on an above lowly placed stanchion. I went down like a sack, instinctively holding my head with both hands; on getting to my feet I looked at my hands and blood was all over the place and my head was dripping buckets. I immediately found myself being ushered down the terracing with Hammers fans, on seeing my plight, opening a gangway and I was met almost instantly and simultaneously by what I recall St Johns First Aid medics and police officers. I was taken to a seating area close by for a quick injury assessment and at the same time answering police questions. On informing the officers my injury was not a result of an attack or missile throwing incident, I was led around the pitch by two members of the St Johns medic team passing West Ham manager John Lyall and team members seated in the dugout. John Lyall's "what has happened to him" looked expression on his face was a picture. Walking down the player's tunnel and then after a short while in the treatment room, the blood flow was stopped. I was head bandaged and allowed to return to the match about twenty minutes in on the promise I went to the Leicester infirmary that night after the match had finished.

## Leicester Infirmary/Alan Devonshire/Petrol Run Out/Seven Kings Train Station

**T**HIS I AGREED TO and with my fellow travelling friends we subsequently arrived at Leicester Infirmary at around 10pm. After cleaning, numbing and stitching, it just so happened that late in the match Dev (Alan Devonshire) had been carried off and who did we meet in the hospital?... Dev. We had seen John Lyall walk in a short while earlier assertively but at this time he was nowhere to be seen. On having a brief perhaps a little nervous chat and on reflection afterwards, we felt in unison that Dev had appeared shyer of us than us of him. Dev came across as a modest man who although only costing £5000 from non-league Southall, would always be in an all-time West Ham dream team of my selection.

With me driving home it began to get a little too much. I was feeling groggy and, what's more, an achy type of discomfort, having had injections also in the most 'upper part' of my rear leg. After having a consultation talk I pulled over and a friend took over the driving. It wasn't long, though, before we were back in the north of London and legal again. With all the distractions we now found ourselves facing another dilemma situation, created no doubt by naivety of running out of fuel. In this period of time petrol stations were very rarely open twenty-four hours and the inevitable happened. We ran out of juice just outside Seven Kings train station, Hornchurch (Roy) being our first drop off destination. What luck, standing just where we had pulled over by his three-litre powered Ford Capri and with the time somewhere around 4am, we asked this bloke if he knew of a garage open at this time of the morning and his reply was to prove beneficial, using the words to the effect of "What, with this petrol guzzler? I always carry a spare gallon!" Filling our little Mini with a gallon of juice was to be enough for our needs that morning. We gave him £3, somewhat over the top cost wise, we knew, but we were right happy with that and on our way we were.

## Fixed-In Vision

S ORRY FOR MUM coming downstairs, then walking in on me at about 7am, standing with my head bowed over the kitchen sink; she had caught me gently cleaning the wound with the sink caked in blood and Mum's poor upset face is a fixed-in vision memory 'laster'… After making my explanation I had to step up a gear and leave mum to her thoughts: train was at eight and work was at nine.

## BRISTOL CITY… League Division One… 17/09/1977

W E WENT to this one again in Kevin's Mini Minor. The little motor was feeling the pressure of four lads being chauffeured from pillar to post and the poor thing was getting no younger and here we were yet again, putting it to the test, but this time it was to the West Country and the city of Bristol. The radiator was struggling to hold onto water and on the way down from south east London to Bristol we had to top up more than once or twice. After the match and before setting off on our return, we made a point to top up the radiator knowing that a further stop or two at service stations or wherever would be required en route. Still in good social spirit despite the 3-2 defeat and travelling London bound on the M4, with complete surprise and no warning whatsoever, the motor started to accumulate smoke, then more smoke! It soon became a case of we're not having this, let's get out, the things gonna blow up.

On pulling over onto the hard shoulder and getting out the car, we stood to the rear but a good few yards away, looking towards the motor and allowing a few minutes or so for the smoke to disperse. It was then that we returned to the car and opened the bonnet; whoever had filled the radiator with water for our return journey hadn't replaced the radiator cap! We just could not believe it, but there it was, on top of the car being held on by the rim on the roof top. How on earth it hadn't fallen off will be one of life's mysteries and most definitely beyond me.

## The King's Arms, Eltham High Street

T HE KING'S ARMS, Eltham High Street, was most definitely my favourite watering hole around the period of the mid-seventies and eighties, if not of all time. The reasons for this are numerous and looking back on it no doubt an age thing and being more nowadays a controlled pub and drinking club socialite, it would be okay to say that over the Christmas period and New Year nights, behaviour became I guess one could say more 'enthusiastic' than the normal Friday or Saturday nights revelry and could even almost be classed to being as close as you can get to public 'acceptability'. The pub landlord Eric, manager or staff on duty, knew what we as a group were like and we were never the hardest to control should a calming down order be sanctioned.

I was fortunate to be involved with one super crowd, a crowd that was groups within THE GROUP. Lisa was a part of an about to leave school age group of girls and Lyn, Zena and Jane made up their foursome and it was in the King's Arms that I was to meet her. There were sets that would generally mingle together and buy rounds for financial sensibility, but everybody was by and large socially gelled. The football dances and the house parties, the crowd self-arranged 'early day Alton Towers' and coastal coach beano's, be it mixed or just the boys, the togetherness, the downright at times stupidity and even the odd fall out, the boy/girl 'relationships' and relationships with the progress of time even ending in the odd marriage. I'm telling you now it wasn't at all bad and it all directly led to the long-term friendships that exist today. The lads and lassies were a right mix; this was reflected also in chosen or non-chosen career paths, and this diversity covered the widest of spectrums. At work I have no doubt commitment was given but when we as a crowd got together, I can only say that ageing is a fact but maturity can be an option. I keep in contact with Chris Fowler from those years back and we had a habit between us of calling each other 'ugly'; in his case that may be true and possibly even vice-versa? I sent Chris a mobile telephone text message many years later that read, "We've had some laughs together me and you, remember when we were in the car and I stuck my bum out the window, you then put your head out and people thought we were twins?" This had touched a nerve with Chris and I know he showed it to many. On reading and then digesting my text amuser, Chris sent a reply text message saying, "That reminds me of us lot coming back from the Old Kent Road after Tuesdays 60's night in the Prince of Wales." Was Chris now finally acknowledging/admitting my bum, his face? Oh dear, he won't like that... lol... LOL

*King's Arms before hitting the King's Head, Margate 1978*

## Failed Journey SHEFFIELD WEDNESDAY/Bigger than Pussy Cat Cats and Climb all over your Motor Car Monkeys (Woburn Safari Park)

**T**HE JOURNEY and the travelling in the main always ended with getting to the match, but this second stand out attempted travel along with Southampton that never materialised was to be at Sheffield Wednesday. Looking back and taxing the brain, I have no precise idea of the year we had to abort but I do know it was mid to late seventies and that I feel for sure was with brothers Chris and Colin Fowler. We had stopped at Toddington services on the M1 just north of Luton and it was to prove a one right helpful pullover because it was here that we were told by other pullover Hammer travellers that the match had been cancelled. A waterlogged pitch springs to mind and that would I'm sure, have been the reason and cause at such a late stage. No choice but to continue heading north before 180 degree spin round for London at junction 12, but on seeing the sign for Woburn, 180 went straight out the window, suggestions of Woburn safari park and a few pints in a local had hands readily shook. Our day had changed from football in Sheffield to an animal safari park with shut your car windows bigger than pussy cat cats and climb all over your motor car monkeys. Obtaining a pub lock-in also was an added surprise bonus, and this simple improvising of day change around ended with evening beers in Shelley's dive bar W1.

## SUNDERLAND (Away) League Cup 4th Round 31/10/1979

**I** REMEMBER this one for four reasons. One being that Geoff Pike scored in a 1-1 draw; two, Ricky driving his two-door Ford Escort car saying at intermittent times "Yeh The Engine's Cooking" and then giving out a small giggle; thirdly, walking through my front door and hearing the alarm going off for me to get up and get ready for work; and fourthly, Ricky, who I have not mentioned until now, still having to drive home, but having the benefit of work location as will now be explained.

## NOTTINGHAM FOREST (Away) League Cup 5th Round Replay… 12/12/1979

**V**IRTUALLY all away matches I was now going to at this time was with workmate and Hammer nut-case Ricky Finnelly. We worked for Security Express employed as cash in transit driver/guards, with our division being based at Balfour Street SE17, a short drive up on the left from the commonly known Bricklayers Arms/Old Kent Road/New Kent Road junction heading towards The Elephant and Castle. This Security Express based depot was attached to a much larger based British Road Services (BRS) depot, from where the vehicles we were to carry out our daily duties were hired or leased from. After discussions with a number of lads from Eltham, Ricky and I jointly hired what we thought at the time was a small mini-bus that fittingly would take us to Nottingham for the replay of the League Cup 5th round tie against Nottingham Forest. The tie had been drawn at Upton Park 0-0 eight days prior and after completing our working day and going to collect the mini-bus for our travel, it became somewhat alarming and yet amusingly apparent that a mistake had been made, for instead of a mini-bus we were supplied a box lorry, not far off the size of a house furniture removal truck.

Not convinced our drivers' licences covered us but now being at a photo finish late stage in the day, we felt we had no choice and decided to "go for it", Ricky to drive up and me on the way back. We knew all the lads we were to meet would be at the Pill Box pub by now, a name so called due to its structural shape and visual appearance on the roundabout of SE1's Westminster Bridge Road/Lambeth Palace Road junction; we knew also they would with no doubt be raring to go and so for this reason a positive decision had to be made.

We had chosen The Pill Box for our gathering as all the lads had become familiar with this particular watering hole with the added reasoning of being conveniently placed to travel from south east to north west London and the M1. I had previously worked as an assistant to the accountant (PJ Watson) of BIS Market Research in York House and BIS (Business Intelligence Services) had three out of four subsidiary companies based within the building and Roy, who I mention in previous Hammers experiences and who I had met at Lep Transport, had followed me on and was now working in

York House as an assistant to the accountant for one such subsidiary company. York House was also the building that was actually attached to The Pill Box (later The Sir Geoffrey Chaucer and later still The Florence Nightingale) and this was the venue that the lads would meet for "last Friday of the month". The night when it was just the lads out that more likely than not as the night progressed, would culminate with finishing off at Shelley's dive bar on the corner of Stafford Street and Dover Street some two hundred yards or so from Piccadilly.

On meeting our ten or so fellow Hammers I explained to them the licence situation and that we had to pass The Houses of Parliament, travel through London and so to have a bit of decorum... POINTLESS, having had beer taken and no sooner going over Westminster Bridge it was 'Knees up Mother Brown' and so on. Ricky and I looked at each other ruefully, knowing we could/would/was in for one eventful journey.

At full time the game was level pegged. Very early on in extra time we're one down, then two and then three. The weather as it had been most of the game carried on teeming down, with the thousand or so Hammers fans standing on the open end terracing, soaked through to the skin and with game beyond repair, why not form a circle and do the Hokey Cokey—and that's exactly what we did and did to our thorough enjoyment. There were some Forest fans who, having already won the tie, were still a bit miffed though, in their higher covered stand some threw coins. On our return to "the lorry", we found brothers Mick and Joe hiding under it. They hadn't had an easy walk back from the ground.

The journey back home was so very different; the heater didn't work in the cab and what was a fun and games ride on the way up for the group in 'the lorry box', had now become the group in 'the lorry box' of very cold wringing wet geezers; getting home, getting dry and getting their head down was probably all they had on their minds! I drove the lorry back to Eltham but Ricky then had to drive himself home and he returned the lorry in the morning on his way into work. Ricky lived on The Aylesbury Estate SE17, not five minutes' drive from Balfour Street, the BRS (British Road Services) depot and our place of work.

## NEWCASTLE UNITED (Away) League Division Two 15/03/1980

**F**OOTBALL VIOLENCE during the 1970's and 1980's inside football grounds was probably at its height and for a time it was not unusual to witness supporters, fans or perhaps 'followers' of a said club, removing "heavy duty" work shoes or boots of steel toe cap type, before being allowed entrance through turnstiles of a match and then kept for reclaiming on exit. This decision was used as a preventative precaution of increased injury and to quell possible disturbance and/or hooliganism. Without being aided by such footwear, although this type of footwear was not worn by all associated, certain occupants would find movement and motivation probably a little deflated as such footwear could give a "lift" in the form of agility, aggressive and confident behaviour. This adopted method of crowd control by police and stewards was implemented until such footwear was rarely if not seen at football matches in the years that followed and it was a tactic that bore fruit very quickly. I had been witness to many violent disturbances in this period of time myself but what happened at this fixture was even a new one on me.

We had gone to Newcastle by car; Ricky was driving and alongside me were John Sweet, Kevin Dooley and Chris Fowler. We paid in as normal through the turnstiles and were in an area of the ground amongst Newcastle fans totally separate from other Hammer fan comrades. On watching the match I recall a flash being caught in my left eye; on looking round I saw what I immediately thought to be and in fact was a petrol bomb. It had been thrown into the West Ham section of supporters to the left and behind the goal posts from a section of Newcastle fans along the side stand. I could see quite clearly that a fan was on fire! The shock of this happening let it be known that where we had stood inconspicuously, the all around us Newcastle fans realised and became aware the five of us were West Ham Supporters and from London. At that moment they were so shocked also by this viewing that they too without any reaction to us, understood the immense despair and anger that we openly displayed. The fan was on fire to his waist and people around him were doing whatever they could to quell the flames. They succeeded and although burnt around the legs and other areas (as bandaged pictures in tabloid newspapers showed), I do believe that apart from possible scarring he made a full recovery.

On leaving the ground and isolated amongst thousands of Geordies, it was now a 'let's get to the car' situation and instinctively and with having past experience, we split up so as to be on our own and thus hopefully not draw attention. I remember this older and friendly man who came up beside me. Walking along he started talking to me about what had happened and about the scoreless game; much of what he was saying warranted a response but as much as I wanted to, replying to him was not an option. He must have wondered what I was on but after a very short while the penny dropped! He stopped talking to me but kept sociable by walking a little further beside me. This man had realised the reason for my apparent rude behaviour; a cockney accent may not have been well received by others walking close by in numbers. As we parted slightly to go on our respective ways, he tactfully tapped me gently with the outside of his hand on my leg and uttered quietly, "Have a safe journey home." The petrol bomber was of course apprehended and, given he probably had planned his action, I can't help thinking his comeuppance was a three year prison sentence, with his action reasoning being he wanted to put Newcastle United back on the map. But don't quote me, it was a long time ago—but I'm confident.

## EVERTON FA Cup Semi-Final Replay (Elland Road) 16/04/1980

**"THE BALL** came over; Frank fell over and scored the winning goal." This was a lyric song line that was sung at many West Ham home and away matches and for many years after this most memorable night. Dev had put Hammers 1-0 up shortly into the first half of extra time with Bob Latchford equalising for Everton. Why on earth was Frank Lampard, (you're our left back Frank) still in the box after a broken down attack? Whatever the reason—and I doubt even if you could give me the answer, Frank?—I Luvs Ya for it. That headed ball with just minutes to go took years to roll in off the post and I along with every other Hammer in the Elland Road ground, was leaning forward huffing and puffing as if blow football willing and forcing the ball across the line. I can still see you running over to the corner of the pitch close to where we were standing, holding onto the corner flag and then running round it doing one or one half circle.

What a night, the maturity and composure in the closing very few minutes remaining. No frantic rush of blood, no desperation, no kick the ball anywhere, just simple practical consolidation football. For me it was a team that was showing signs of being highly likely to be going places. Although eventually finishing only seventh in the second division in this season, the growth in discipline, strength and flair that John Lyall had created and instilled went hand-in-hand with the team and squad spirit that, for me, was now plain to see. This team was "getting there" and "getting there" in all departments; it was a team, also, containing many current or ex-international players along with possibly the most unfortunate uncapped in my time West Ham player in captain Billy Bonds. So much talent, playing football in the Ron Greenwood one touch, two touch, find space ideals way but now with the added John Lyall approach of being physically fitter and mentally determined. All this on show and yet playing in a second division side, there was only one place you lot were going to go next season… and you lot went there.

## Lisa and Ricky/Our longest Away Match… Hopefully Never to be Matched…

WE HAD GONE to the Everton Semi-Final replay match in Ricky's two door Ford Escort car; Lisa was now my girlfriend and joined us also on this night. Lisa was beginning to come to more and more away matches with the two of us now, and was becoming almost ever present at home matches also since we started seeing each other back in the May of the previous (1979) year. At home matches, however, it was a different scenario between the three of us; even though we had what I can only describe as much in common as people and almost ultimate passion for our club and team, Ricky never met up with Lisa and/or me (unless by a chance meeting along Green Street) at home matches. The reason for this is quite simple: at home matches we had our favourite places of standing, something that had been created through many years of habit; Ricky would watch matches with his father at the opposite end of the ground in the South Bank and I would watch matches from the North Bank, of which Lisa would naturally follow. The home journey from Elland Road proved to be our longest away, hopefully never to be matched match ever. On our return journey we were involved in an accident with all three of us spending time as in-patients at The Royal National Orthopaedic Hospital, based in Stanmore, Middlesex. The subsequent police report findings advised that our vehicle heading south had crossed the central reservation, skidding in an upturned position before colliding with a Volvo car travelling in the opposite direction heading north. The driver of the Volvo attended hospital but was allowed home after having treatment for shock. I had taken over the driving from Ricky some time before when we had stopped at a service station; I have absolutely no recollection of what caused the accident but can say that I was cleared of any prosecution.

The injuries sustained were of a serious nature. All three of us travelling in Ricky's two-door escort car had been thrown clear from the vehicle with both doors having remained closed. In my case I only became aware to what extent as the weeks went by and even to this day I don't know the complete story as I've never really asked any questions since; the questions that I did put to any family in hospital or soon after were often answered with a sense of not sure vacancy or of avoidance. The broken bones and scarring with a penetration that had been made by my ribs allowing a tube to a lung were both visual and evident, but I am aware there was more to my situation than my knowledge tells me. It broke my heart when I realised the upset, worry and concern I had caused, not only to my own family, work colleagues and friends, but of course to Ricky and Lisa's also. All this had been going on and I had been oblivious to all this, having slept through it all in the early aftermath totally unaware. The seriousness of my condition was such that my parents were offered living-in accommodation within the hospital grounds and this offer was accepted. Lisa, only being eighteen years of age, was placed in the ladies' section of the accident unit and Ricky in the men's. I was to join Ricky a week or so later.

The above was to be a major happening for all those affected. **(The Chalk and Cheese Women's Ward to Men's** Page 190)

## ARSENAL FA Cup Final… (Wembley) 10/05/1980

**D**UE TO THE HOMEWARD semi-final happening I was to miss this one and yet "I had a ticket". Having again as with Fulham 1975 been an Ever Present attendant to all home, away and neutral ground FA Cup competition matches, I watched the match from my hospital bed and never gave a thought to personal issues as a Trevor Brooking thirteenth minute crouch down swivelled header proved to be the only goal and winner. After the match, which to date is still the last time a club has won the competition from outside the first division cum Premier League top flight, I was taken down to the ladies' ward where, lying in my bed beside Lisa's at approximately 7pm and most unexpected, a small group of lads with my brother Terry who had been to Wembley walked in to briefly celebrate the Hammers win with us. One right nice full on surprise gesture, celebratory it was but toned down for sure; the hospital staff had no problem with this and this respect and decorum shown for other female patients was also understood and appreciated by staff, who had become with certain "long term" internee patients almost mates.

The Hammers group had met up with a younger lad, Simon Fincham, either outside Wembley or he had travelled with them from Eltham. Simon, an Arsenal fan, however, was not in possession of a ticket. Trying to remember those years back with complete clarity is not easy and asking Terry my brother proves his memory is a little foggy also. One thing he is clear on, though, is that on offering a turnstile operator five pounds, Simon squeezed in with Terry so the turnstile recorded only the one notch entrant. Simon was known to the group as he was a Boys Brigade member and had been associated with me for a number of years; he was also, up until the time of the accident, positioned as right back for my under sixteens' football team that I had formed previously and was in its second season. The surprise turn up was so much appreciated and as they ventured off for their journey home, I knew they were on their way to enjoy themselves and in the way I know and knew they would.

## "I Had a Ticket", "Too Right I Did"

**66 I** HAD A TICKET"—"Too Right I did," but was not to find out until some time afterwards. The same rule had applied for this cup final as in the Fulham final of 1975 re ballot vouchers. This time my number came up and Terry informed me of this and this was how he got "his" ticket. I asked him how long he had to queue up. "Walked in and walked out," was his reply. The reason for this simplicity was if having a winning ballot voucher, personal payment and collection of tickets could be made during a windowed time and on a set-aside date. I had asked him this question due to the fact on the two previous FA Cup semi-finals, queuing for tickets was on a first come first served basis. I had no experience of the Fulham 1975 cup final as I hadn't been successful with my ballot vouchers. This first come first served basis in my experience would mean getting to the ground at 6am-ish on the day of sale (always a Sunday) and yet still have many hundreds in front already queuing. "Happy days and Deep Joy"—1975 Ipswich, 1980 Everton, "Happy days and Deep Joy" again, as after playing at Villa Park on both occasions and both being drawn Saturday matches, this process, with me no doubt being 'full of the joys of spring', was to be a repeated requirement. In 1975 Godfrey, John Sweet's father I seem to recall, took me and John to Upton Park for the queuing process and in 1980 although not clear, it's possible the same pattern process took place. The ticket offices were to open for sale around the 10am mark.

## LIVERPOOL FA Charity Shield (Wembley) 09/08/1980

**I** CAN'T REMEMBER much about this game, only that I watched the match from an invalid area recovering from the car accident of the previous April. A 1-0 defeat at the hands of Liverpool was the result, having travelled to the match in John Sweet's little Ford Fiesta 1100—a motor car that was to do us proud over the next three seasons, taking us to home and away matches regularly up, across and down the country.

## SHREWSBURY TOWN (Home) League Division Two, 13/09/1980/Tannoy Announcement

**T**HIS WAS TO BE MY FIRST attended home game since watching the local east London derby match against Orient the previous season, a match that had ended in a 2-0 home win for the Hammers back on April 5th. John Sweet had got the tickets and we were to sit in the West Stand—a part of the ground that reminded me of when I sat watching the midweek tidying and cleaning up process of the ground, eight years more and less prior as a schoolboy during my school holidays. Shortly after getting to our seats in Block D, Row DD, Seats 33 and 34, John went missing saying he wanted to have a quick meet up with someone. Looking around the ground, I felt as if I was home from home, different of course from my North Bank terrace standing but home from home all the same; on his return John told me "everything's fine now" and he sat down beside me. John as we talked appeared 'distant' if not a little preoccupied, but then, interrupting me, said, "Listen." As I did so I heard Bill Remfry, resident disc jockey and programme columnist "Off the Record", make an announcement about me being at the match and in the ground after my recent experiences—that is where John had gone and it was also so typical of this man doing his best for a friend! It was so unexpected and I must admit it was quite a surprise, hearing my name mentioned over the tannoy.

I now felt as if I was beginning to get (although after only one game but of winning 3-0 proportions) back to being involved again, but I was aware that this would depend on the help of friends. The next Saturday on the 20th, I was at the home match against Watford that saw Bobby Barnes score on his home debut in a 3-2 win. This was followed again the following weekend, thus making it three consecutive Saturdays on the trot, but this time John had got tickets for the away match at Cambridge United. We were to be placed in a small hut cum invalid area and a picture taken by Steve Bacon, printed in the *Newham Recorder*, an East London and Essex newspaper for the following week's issue, shows the Cambridge goalkeeper pushing a screamer from either Frank Lampard or Ray Stewart around a post; in the background of the picture you can see me seated in my wheelchair at ground level but with John, comfortably positioned sitting on top of the hut with legs dangling. A 2-1 away win was to see the Hammers after eight games sitting pretty in 2$^{nd}$ place behind Blackburn Rovers. Attending home and away matches was beginning to become quite the norm again, but I was now to be going in the main with my brother Terry, John Sweet and the Lott brothers Mick and Joe. This was to develop into a three-season habit, but there were times when arrangements for a match, be it hardly ever, entailed the odd change in personnel or an empty seat due to an unavoidable commitment, reason or situation.

## LINCOLN CITY (Away) Milk Cup 3$^{rd}$ Round 10/11/1982 "Got Tickets Mick?"/'No Parking' Cone Removal/Good Beer Guide/Singalong Tapes

**O**NLY ONCE can I remember there being a hiccup; other than Lincoln City, a night match Milk Cup 3$^{rd}$ round cup tie on 10$^{th}$ November season 82/83, everything during these three year jaunts went swimmingly. We arranged to meet minus Terry in Dirty Dicks pub based in Bishopsgate close to being opposite Liverpool Street station. With time to spare we had that extra pint. John had sorted out a parking space probably through his work thus eliminating any problems with traffic wardens and therefore parking tickets, but match tickets we did have a problem with.

On getting into the motor I asked Mickey: "Got tickets, Mick?" Needless to say but back to Eltham we went and from being somewhat nice and relaxed it now became a proper let's get cracking job and no mucking about. On getting to Lincoln we could see the floodlights and time had become of the essence as kick-off time was getting unnervingly close. Drastic action had to be taken and parking sensibly was a No No: you just couldn't find a parking space for love or money. I jumped out the car and started removing two or three 'no parking' cones leading away from other parked cars so John could 'join the queue' and park. It takes no guessing who then turns the corner! Anyway, the transit full of our boys in blue jump out; explaining our story that had caused our stress and predicament, the boys in blue proceeded to return to their 'Maria' and turn a blind eye. We were only to miss the first five minutes or so at Sincil Bank with the match ending in a 1-1 draw. Paul Goddard scoring the goal for West Ham who were to run out victors 2-1 in the replay return home match some nineteen days later at Upton Park. The home match programme is dated 23$^{rd}$ November but beside is written or when played.

John's little Ford Fiesta 1100 was taking a city and motorway pounding week in week out but the motor never let us down. John of course kept on top of all things maintenance as he did with stop-off points, helped and aided by the most up-to-date issue of *The Good Beer Guide*. John and I were to produce what was to us, the most fabulous sing along tapes, be it of the sixties or songs more recent. After John's pre-match 'on the way' stop-off points being ably helped by this liquid bible, the belting out of our vocal chords with vigour was a natural follow on. With John driving, me as front seat side passenger, Mick doing his animal Muppet impersonation on drums sandwiched on the back seat between Terry and Joe giving out the odd guitar riff or lick; this had all but become expected if not customarily normal. It never failed; difficulty in controlled discipline of compulsive giggling was never easy for John and me for the first few minutes and would have been understood if the carnage going on in the rear back three seats had been witnessed by others. This three-season period of course brought about the odd happenings and situations, but most of all, it amounted to the fun…win, lose, or draw… the fun.

## Jim Steinman/Canet Plague, Andorra, Pyrenees Mountains and The Costa Brava

T HIS WAS ALSO the time I introduced the group to the songs and Lyrics of Jim Steinman, a man whose songs especially Meatloaf's album 'Bat out of Hell' was regularly listened to and blatantly played by many a tent occupant when I was camping in the South of France area of Canet Plague in 1982—pleasing moments and point scoring for me as the initial two lads I went with, Andy and Bruce but later joined by Mick Lott and Jason Barr 'hated' Meatloaf? Mick and Jason's arrival in Canet at the end of my first week was the most surprising. I was sitting in the bar by the pool and I saw their reflection in a window; on getting up almost with shock and awe, they told me, knowing where I was going for holiday and that I was travelling by coach, they had been sitting in The Kings Arms during this same week of their arrival and continued, "We just decided on the spur of the moment to catch a coach and come down and join you." This second week was a saviour for me, really; Andy and Bruce had different ways to me of enjoying the holiday, whereas me, I just wanted a good crack. That second week was such a different week from the first and was to include the three of us going by coach up into the Pyrenees Mountains and the tiny country (principality) of Andorra and then the next day, hiring a car and driving a similar journey before spending time and having an overnight stay in Spain's Costa Brave. I have never been one for a night club music venue or what is or can be associated around such premises; pubs are my custom or bars if abroad, and Jason and Mick shared that preferred enjoyment also.

## Clyde/Clint Eastwood/The Rocky Horror Show

**I**T WAS ALSO during this period I introduced this Jim Steinman musical style to a man who took no time in settling in with the Kings Arms' regulars. Clyde had so become known as Clyde (real name Steve, surname Harris) due to his shoulder swagger when walking into the pub that in his early days would normally only stretch to a Saturday afternoon. Clyde's arms when swaggering would lean down to between his thigh and knee joints, hence his walk resembling that of the orang-utan in the Clint Eastwood films 'Every Which Way but Loose' and 'Anyway Which Way You Can'. Clyde, aided by his shoulder-length ginger-ish hair and not shaven very often chin, showed why it was easy to see why this 'choice' nickname fitted. To date there are and will be people who believe Clyde to be his true Christian name, such was the strength of this nickname to catch on. Clyde's first wife Karen even once told me it was months into knowing Clyde that she first became aware his real name was Steve. Clyde liked the Meatloaf songs that Jim Steinman had written and agreed Meatloaf was also a man of musical and acting talents. Born Marvin Lee Aday, my first knowledge of the man was as Eddie in 'The Rocky Horror Picture Show' and a film that in the mid-70's was "hung on to" by a small group of us, then seventeen or so year olds at that time.

*Clyde, Holding Album covers with immense Jim Steinman Influence*

*A Day at Hastings 1975-76. Keith Unitt wearing his Rocky Horror shirt
and me wearing the Lep T-shirt I had on when
I got thrown out at Arsenal (20/03/1976).
Behind me is Andy 'Stoff' wearing his 'Kiss Me Quick, Squeeze Me Slowly'
hat and 'Age' Voce, shaking hands with the monkey*

## Wembley Arena and Stadium Tout Ploy/Cumberland Hotel Chamber Maids/Meatloaf Tickets for Free.

SOME MONTHS after our meeting and my introduction to Clyde of Steinman style music, Meatloaf was to play what is known now as The Wembley Arena, formerly Wembley Empire Pool, until 1978. A string of concerts was booked but having not applied for tickets ourselves we decided between us to drive to Wembley and "go for it". It was the European Neverland Express Tour of 1982.

Walking around outside the concert hall, tickets were readily available from would-be profiteering touts but who had come unstuck. Tickets could be bought at knockdown face-value prices, much to our benefit and amusement, and we were to see Meatloaf again the following evening taking up the same tactic—a ploy I was to use at Wembley Stadium for a Madonna concert that again worked for me, but in the year I believe was 1990. After the second night of viewing and driving from the concert, having had another one proper good evening, we saw two girls thumbing for a lift who had obviously been to the concert also. Stopping and asking them to see if they were going in our direction, their reply was Marble Arch. Perfect, no problem for us as Marble Arch and the drive down Park Lane was, as it happened, our already intended route and wasn't even taking us remotely out of our way. The girls got in and the result we were to have was of the highest order… if it worked out? The two girls were chambermaids at The Cumberland Hotel and they told us Meatloaf along with roadies and other members of staff had hired the top floor of the hotel for their time in London. Just a short time before their getting out of the motor time they said as a thank you if they could, they would do their best to get us two free tickets for the following night's show. Talking to the girls in the car, Clyde arranged to meet them at six o'clock the following evening by a side door they pointed out to us when dropping them off.

We drove into London the next day thinking if the girls didn't deliver, we would continue to the concert in the anticipation that getting tickets would be likely from "come unstuck" ticket touts anyway. I Stayed with the car, Clyde went missing and returned five minutes later with me not knowing by his body language if they had met him by the door or not. Even if they had they still may not have managed getting tickets. Getting in the motor and then putting on a big broad smile, Clyde pulled out two tickets from his pocket. The girls had kept not only their word but were spot on also on the time keeping of the arranged meeting by the side door. We didn't know if it was easy for the girls to obtain tickets for us or not, but by doing so along with the preciseness of keeping to the arranged meet up time and place, it told us how appreciative they were for the night before drive home lift and getting them back safely and quickly to their place of work and stay.

## Second Row/I'm In Control/Clyde was 'Just a Shot Away'

YOU COULD NOT have asked for better placed tickets, second row from the front and just to the left of centre stage. This placing was to allow and take a bit of a concert twist for Clyde and me and unusual you can say it was. Having had another vocal, jumpy sweaty night, Meatloaf during an encore came to the front of the crowd after entering the orchestra pit. He was openly appearing to encourage someone to take his microphone and so I did, leaning over and between the front row seaters who were now standing, I turned to the crowd and continued the singing of the Rolling Stones song 'Gimme Shelter' that Meat had now left me "in control of". It was some sight, I can promise, with a feeling of most definite amusement seeing thousands of concertgoers enjoying themselves and it was me dishing out the vocals! Looking at Clyde I could see he was right up for it also! I could see also that even though all around us there was a large crowd with body movement, stewards were making their way towards me. Choosing the appropriate time to perfection I passed the microphone to Clyde, who managed to get in a word or two before being relieved of his 'singing duties'. I'm sure Clyde would have enjoyed this moment more if a cameraman or a friend with a camera had been there. Clyde does like a picture and to think he was "just a shot away"!

## LIVERPOOL... League Cup Final... (Wembley)... 14/03/1981

THE ARRANGED MEETING POINT was from mine in Elibank road, a twelve seat mini-bus we have, all twelve seats being taken though thirteen turned up. Chris and Colin Fowler had brought Tommy, their third eldest brother of six along, but that was fine by us. On approaching Well Hall roundabout I asked my brother Terry, "You got tickets?" "No. you have," was the reply. What started off as a joke banter wind up soon became of an 'is he being serious?' nature, then to the 'no choice but go to the next level' of a 'please don't joke' matter. This banter had lasted no longer than a minute and a good job it started and got sorted it was, because we had both left it to each other to pick up the tickets. On our return there they were, looking proud and beautiful but still on the table. Can you imagine if we had got to Wembley and no tickets! We won't even go there as the thought doesn't even bear thinking about.

Stopping off at a watering hole somewhere on the way and getting back into the mini-bus, everyone was now feeling relaxed and so the singing started. Hitting a traffic hold up at the junction of A1 Falloden Way and the A406 north circular, there was a 53-seated coach two lanes across from us with travelling West Ham fans inside; they were at their coach windows in laughing convulsions and pointing at us as if to say, look at that lot! Tom who had bunked on board had stopped doing his Michael Crawford impression of Betty in 'Some Mothers Do 'Av 'Em' and had started singing 'When You're Smiling, The Whole World Smiles with You' (na-na, na- na-na). With everyone having joined in it was only when looking at our fellow Hammers and the singing mellowed, the wonder of their amusement was realised. Unknowing to us our little mini-bus transporter was literally rocking and rolling on its hinges to the movement of all of us singing and swaying inside.

Our travel was to continue on the north circular until we were close enough but still some distance away from Wembley but with the stadium in sight. On parking up we walked across the north circular road into The Pantiles pub (now a McDonalds and possibly not called the Pantiles then?) only to find the place to be occupied by quite a number of Liverpool supporters enjoying themselves. I started singing "Bubbles" with all the lads' semi-instantaneously joining in. What happened next is what to me is what it should all be about. A Liverpool fan said to me, "Until you lot came in we never knew West Ham were in here".... What he meant was among the scousers was the odd little group of Hammers who had mingled, probably in no more than two's and three's minding their own business having a pint, but had all started to join in with us when we walked in and started 'Bubbles'. These Liverpool fans were of the 'not looking for hassle' types and that was sensed the instant we walked in. The two groups became acceptable of each other with what amounted to immediate effect, and what was to happen next is what I mean by what it should all be about: with this acceptance and good spirit many Liverpool fans went to one end of the pub room as did most West Ham to the other. 'You'll Never Walk' was sung and then 'I'm Forever Blowing Bubbles' in turn; it was pure poetry, the way this impulsive happening happened. One overzealous Liverpool fan jumped on a table, pulled down his trousers and raised his arms and carried on singing. Not to be outdone, a West Ham fan got onto a table also and did the same during 'Bubbles Time' but went one stage further. Come On You Irons. There were handshakes and good lucks shared by both sets of fans on leaving....'Triffic!

Alvin Martin made the mistake, Alan Kennedy shot and Sammy Lee "ducked". His head would have been knocked off if he hadn't and referee Clive Thomas allowed the goal suggesting in his opinion Lee wasn't interfering with play. I had never seen Trevor 'Hadleigh' Brooking so reactionary incensed to a refereeing decision, or for anything else, come to think of it for that matter. With the match having finished 0-0 in normal play, extra time being played and a goal behind West Ham felt shouldn't have stood, Liverpool were to find themselves playing against a much wound-up West Ham team. In the very last seconds Alvin rose with such determination to head a corner kick towards goal, only for him to see Liverpool midfielder Terry McDermott push the ball over the bar for a penalty. Ray "Tonka" Stewart suddenly became so self-controlled, having spent the last minutes of the match running around headless chickened, agitated and visibly incensed, Ray now was to take the given penalty as well as having the compounded pressure and knowledge of knowing it was to be the last kick of the game. Ray "Tonka" Stewart? Na... Ray "Composed" Stewart for me, certainly for now. I watched as he placed the ball on the spot and for the first time I had ever seen him do this, he just side footed the penalty to Ray Clemence's left. Blasting the ball had been and was always Ray's penalty forte.

## LIVERPOOL… League Cup Final Replay… (Villa Park)… 01/04/1981

L OOKING BACK on it now and this is so not normal, but I really can't remember much about what we did on this day, so strange for me really and compounded by the fact we're talking about a League Cup Final replay here. I do know though that the group of thirteen that went to the final at Wembley eighteen days prior didn't all go together this time and those who went to Birmingham this night made their own purchase of tickets and travel arrangements. Our little posse was to travel to Villa Park by car and consisted of the normal fivesome of me, John Sweet, Terry, Joe and Mick, but where we met up or what time we left I'm clueless. Going 1-0 up through a near post Paul Goddard headed goal from a Jimmy Neighbour cross was possibly not a good idea on this occasion—why? Because Liverpool just edged up the gears and were to give West Ham a proper telling off by way of a football lesson for much of the remaining first half. Clive Thomas was to referee the replay as he had the first coming together at Wembley.

I remember reading in a newspaper soon after Liverpool's success that evening by a margin of 2-1 that hammers skipper Billy Bonds at the end of the first half had gone to referee Clive Thomas and asked words to the effect, "Can we have a new ball please?" Thomas' implied reply was that there was "nothing wrong with the one you're playing with". Billy inferred that there was and that it was Liverpool's ball and they won't let "us" play with it. This situation of dominance by Liverpool continued onto the second half as the first half had ended but began to alter as the match headed into the last twenty minutes or so. West Ham were for me finishing the stronger and if Billy Bonds hadn't headed high and over through stretching, or if he had known that Alvin Martin was strategically placed behind him with what for Alvin would have been a simple "meat and gravy" header, I can't help feeling that despite Liverpool's long periods of dominance, if extra time had been forced Hammers may have gone on to win their first League Cup trophy—a trophy that to date is still missing from their history success credits. So nearly a double with a difference also, with West Ham to finish the season runaway champions of the division two; should they have been League Cup winners, I can't help thinking that it may or even to date have been a first such double?

## Pat Holland/Legendary DJ Bill Remfry

**R**ETURNING TO WORK and resuming normal bullion security driver/guard duties after the car accident of April 1980 was not to happen until June 1981. I was "broken in slowly" and made up a four-man crew (normally three) to ease back into the swing of things and spent the first week either "on the Pavement" transporting a cash sack (only ever one at a time) from vehicle to bank or vice-versa, or performing "in the back" guard duties of the van, which would entail the passing or receiving of money sacks to or by the guard outside, be a lookout for a possible "happening" or radio operative in the event of an attack and therefore a mayday should such an incident occur. Other than said reason all other radio contact would normally be the responsibility of the team-led custodian.

I remember seeing Pat Holland in the National Westminster bank Limehouse branch in East India Dock road. Patsy, as he was known by many a West Ham fan, made 296 appearances for the Hammers that included the 1975 FA Cup final win over Fulham and, as mentioned previously, also scored one of the two goals in the European Cup Winners Cup final 2-4 defeat the following season at the hands of Anderlecht in Belgium. Unfortunately for me, on-going duties at the time were not to allow a quick hello nod of the head, eye contact, let alone a handshake. However, better luck was to come my way outside the National Westminster bank, Upminster branch, when I was to see Bill Remfry, our legendary DJ and 'Off the Record' programme columnist walking by.

With transitions from bank to vehicle having already been secured, I approached him. We were to have a jovial chat and I passed comment about his regular comical over-the-mike announcement 'mishaps'. Bill seemed to know exactly what I meant, suggesting these 'mishaps' were not in fact 'always mishaps'! At the coming to the end of a match and on more than one occasion and I use this as an example, Bill would ask the travelling away section of Stoke supporters "to remain for a few moments after the match so the ground can be cleared", when, in fact, the opponents were, say, Sunderland. Then there was his political correctness of which one announcement springs to mind, and that was when at half time, he asked a section of the crowd to refrain from throwing fruit onto the pitch and then proceeded to play The Banana Boat Song. I reminded him of the fact we had met before when attending a West Ham dinner/dance at the Heybridge Moat House "just a couple of years ago" and that we had a picture taken (Page 187); I mentioned also his mentioning of me and why at the Shrewsbury home match (Page 69) which obviously not knowing at the time of this encounter was to be eight months to the day after Heybridge Moat House. This was to be such an enjoyable two or three minute moment, full of amusement. We smiled and gave each other a hug, such was the enjoyment it appeared we had both had during this spontaneous, momentary and unexpected happening.

## Armed Attacks and Daylight Robbery

**A**RMED ROBBERIES and attacks on cash in transit security guards are more common than is let on and working for Security Express I became aware of this. It appeared to me that unless injury is sustained or an attack and robbery of major proportions has taken place, quite often a report will only be found in local newspapers of the area concerned or a small few fill-in lines put in place somewhere in a tabloid.

On the Monday of the following week of my return I was to be involved in my first armed attack. I made up the quota of a normal crew of three having had my first week's re-initiation. Phil being custodian, Simon his regular driver and me situated in the back of the vehicle as guard, I was taking the place of their regular guard Ron who was on leave. After passing Phil a sack from the hatch, he entered the bank door not three yards from our vehicle and I looked out a side window of the van as a viewpoint. Within a matter of not more than a five seconds, a man came running out from the bank entrance holding a hand gun and in his other hand I could clearly see the sack that I had just passed to Phil. Immediately moving to the radio to give out the mayday to control, Phil almost instantaneously banged on the shoot hatch and, trust me, can they be loud inside a security van when BANGED! He shouted just two words, "Mayday... Go!" I hadn't heard any shots and this told me Phil was physically unhurt; it proved to be that no shots had been fired and Simon was physically unhurt also. This armed robbery was the subject of Police 5, a long running five-minute program presentation that was sometimes extended for more involved appeals presented by Shaw Taylor, and this robbery was the subject decided upon that warranted such an extension. Police 5 was televised mainly on a weekly basis that appealed to the public in the hope of assistance to solve crime—a program that had its many successes, but as far as I am aware, on this occasion the bandits escaped and were never caught.

I was to leave Security Express officially in the early part of 1984. I had been in three more armed attack and robberies since my return to work after the car accident of April 1980 and the first attack in June 1981—before removing my "motorbike crash helmet", hanging up my work boots and handing in my now custodian security identity card and uniform. My last involvement had occurred a number of months before in 1983 but with thought in my mind, a pending trial scheduled for the Central Criminal Court (Old Bailey) and the happenings that had taken place but not before trial completion, I was to seek alternative, less hazardous work employment. Some time later and so unexpectedly, I received a congratulatory letter from R. B. Allen of Security Express dated 27th November 1984, referring to an enclosed letter sent to them for passing to me from G. W. Jones, then Deputy Assistant Commissioner, New Scotland Yard, for my actions on one such attack. On this matter and within these writings the subject is now closed.

## What Work?/Next Work Mayhem

O N LEAVING Security Express, work was to become a very mixed bag affair and any form of real settlement didn't occur until the formation of my small courier business some nine years later in September 1993. One of the offers of work after leaving Security Express however that I was to take up was as a financial advisor for a life assurance company based in Mortimer Street W1. Having taken a week's crash course at offices in Putney, "on-going" training was given to me in the form of obtaining answers to questions that potential clients would have asked and then reporting back to the client if not totally 100% sure having done a presentation. As a financial adviser I was to encourage financial savings for intended growth such as a ten year tax efficient policy, returning a whole lump financial sum or to take as increments to enjoy as chosen; alternatively, I would perhaps suggest a private pension plan if I felt it was the more beneficial for that particular or potential client's needs.

I was doing quite well and Terry the branch manager as a reward took me out for a trip in his single engine twin seated aeroplane. I so believed in the products but was not enthusiastic about doing the job and although 'with profit' and 'unit linked' savings schemes and pensions can take a battering from time to time, it is certainly my belief that with pensions the earlier you start and the longer you save, the greater the reward and the easier it will be in retirement years. Saving when young can be a chore but just that little bit to start with and then affordable increases as and when will help let the pennies take care of the pounds and the early contributions in general will be what makes the most pounds when taken. The bonus with pension saving also is not only the tax benefits that are added when contributions are made but when money does get tight as it invariably does, freezing contributions and resuming at a later, more convenient date or time is an option it holds.

Time does pass and quickly as we all know, but trying to play catch up through "putting off" is not at all easy; but saying that, there will be many in the "mind set" who will tend to be reliant on inheritance as opposed to being self-achieving through independent self-sufficiency as more and more parents and family possess property. Advancing years though can seem such a long way off and trying to talk to teenagers and many adults in their twenties about retirement and saving for the future, you might as well be talking to the key pad I'm typing on. It made me smile in later years when at a party a friend said to me, "It's April, where's the year going," and someone else said, "Yeh, soon be Christmas!" Then the icing on the cake was said by another, as he looked around the room, teenagers were dancing and appeared not to have a care in the world, he said "And look at this lot, they're still in January." It summed it up for me.

### True Friend Scruffy/Brief Peace/Social Standing Leveller/Pub Wisdom

I N SEPTEMBER 1984, taking Scruffy with us for the second or third visit in recent weeks, I went with Mum to the Vet in Passey Place SE9—but Scruffy was not to come home with us. Time and age had taken its toll and the vet's words only confirmed what we knew anyway. Mum said, "Shall we take him home for one more night?" The little Heinz 57 mongrel that had come into our lives those thirteen years before had been a true friend to mum and a massive comfort to her. So, saddened, looking eye to eye at each other, and then looking at our pet, the decision was simple—you could see Scruffy had had enough. We walked home and not a word was spoken. Dad came home and was told the news. For a short while there was peace in the house.

Dad liked his beer. Terry and Elaine had left the home and started families of their own. Nothing had changed "in house" since their departure, and why would it have? Describing dad isn't difficult but my assessment as for reasons for his behavioural patterns for now if not always will remain in my thoughts. An Alf Garnet type character in many ways, but then again, in many ways different. Dad "in house" chose words of a more aggressive, even foul-mouthed nature that basically was never needed. Ranting and raving was often exaggerated by alcohol, but intake of said substance was not always necessary. It created for uneasiness in the home and privately that memory exists and, although easier, is still too much in me today. For all his years of being a drinking man he never missed a day's work and was rarely seen not wearing a tie. It had also without doubt brought much wisdom. Public Houses are social standing financial levellers whatever work you do, however much money you earn or, if the case may be, as in certain employments get paid. Money is equal and self-dignity should be applied and in my view should be financially spent as so, not accepting a beer but drinking solo is an acceptable understanding. It is easy and likely over time to get into all sorts of varying people's company and at times no doubt different views of/and opinion arise, different work experiences, be it manual or professional is common and the collection without necessarily knowing of subconscious knowledge is an unaware factor. You could tell in conversation and mannerisms, dad had picked up very good adaptable social skills in whatever social or non-sociable company he found himself in, and because of this experience he was also a very good advisory. It would be privately but commonly known within the family, that my father was two different people from "outside house" to "in house" and it was kept that way.

## Lock Outs-Get Ins

**V**ERY RARE FOR ME, but getting locked out did happen. The North Bank turnstiles West Side would shut first but if you did a quick on your marks, get set…GO and legged it round the other side quick enough, you stood a chance of getting in the North Bank East Stand side as they shut those turnstiles a short while after. (Why? I've never known the answer to that one.) Other than further down the line cup runs or in the case of Hereford in FA Cup 4th round replay 1972, Portsmouth league division one 1990/91 and Aston Villa Premier League 1993/94, matches to be most careful of for a possible lock out were the three London derby matches Arsenal, Chelsea and Spurs and another would be Manchester United. I never got locked out at any time against Arsenal, Spurs or "The Mancs" but Chelsea I did, and twice it was and in the same season, the season that was to be the Oh So Close title season of 1985/86 with the second time lock-out being a lock-out/get-in as it was to be eight seasons later against Aston Villa 1993/94.

## CHELSEA (Home)….. League Division One…. 15/04/1986 (Lock-Out Get In No 1)

**T**HIS RE-ARRANGED FIXTURE had previously been called off on New Year's Day, but only after I had arrived at the ground and only a couple of hours or so before kick-off. Well, I didn't get in then and I certainly didn't get in this time either. Not until the closing minutes from the end, anyway. I was with Kevin Dooley who had also gone over to Upton

Park for the initial New Year's Day fixture and Kevin, like me, although not with each other on the day, had been locked out also and again like me, only found out the game had been called off after arriving at the ground. Tonight's game, though, being a night match so pubs would be open, we went to The Prince of Wales pub in Princes Terrace at the back of Queens Market; a number of other lock-outs we were to find out on entry had the same idea also. I sometimes drank in there at times before Saturday matches and would often see Cass Pennant (auto-biographer of his life and times as a West Ham supporter and subject of the Big Screen film Cass released in 2008) with pals over in a corner playing their customary game of cards. We were to be kept up to date of match information because a radio was put on the bar so all us lock-outs could listen to the match commentary. Together our plan was to wait until towards the end of the match when it was normal for gates to be open for early exiting leavers; this would then allow opportunist fans and on this occasion meaning us loitering outside to take advantage and to go in. Tony Cottee had scored first for West Ham before leaving the pub for the ground and our plan of getting in worked a treat as was expected; however, by the time of our entrance into The East Stand terracing at the South Bank end, Chelsea were 2-1 up and that was how the game was to remain.

Chelsea had one big say in the championship race and demise of West Ham that season and now, on the last full Saturday fixture list of the season, Chelsea were to play at home to Liverpool. A win for Chelsea would mean that the Everton and West Ham match, scheduled for Goodison Park just two days after on the Monday evening would decide the title, providing both Everton and West Ham got the results they needed on that same day. They both did with Hammers winning 3-2 at WBA and Everton trouncing Southampton 6-1 at Goodison Park. Liverpool's Kenny Dalglish however put paid to any hopes Everton and West Ham may have had for the title, scoring the only goal in a 1-0 win at Stamford Bridge. Everton subsequently beat West Ham 3-1 on that Monday evening with thousands of Hammers fans in attendance having purchased advanced tickets in the anticipation of…!

With Hammers finishing in their highest top flight position of third, this is a position I personally cannot see being repeated in my lifetime. The changes to the game financially has now produced almost leagues within the league that is now known as the Premier League; it is a bubble that will in my opinion no doubt burst but probably not for many years to come and not in my lifetime.

Kevin Dooley has been a friend since we were fourteen or fifteen. I met him at Eltham Park South when he was a member and training with a young football team known as Endeavours FC that I too, on that day of discovery was to join also. It is with great satisfaction that thirty-five years and more after that joining and after closure and then reforming again in 1978, many members of the team and club as with the Kings Arms crowd of which these players were a part of, in one way or another can still be contacted. The bonding, team spirit and friendship were of a most definite calibre and this would often show in determined performances in pitch adversity. I still meet up with Kev on a weekly basis unless a circumstance prevents. These meets have of course changed over the course of time, from the Mile End road days to the Old Kent road days, the clubs, the pubs, the parties, the football dances and the beano's, the Devon, Tenerife and East Coast USA holidays and being best man for his marriage to Carole. Dressing gown and slippers next?

## Season 1985/86 and How it Finished

|  | P | W | D | L | F | A | Pts |
|---|---|---|---|---|---|---|---|
| Liverpool | 42 | 26 | 10 | 06 | 89 | 37 | 88 |
| Everton | 42 | 26 | 08 | 08 | 87 | 41 | 86 |
| West Ham United | 42 | 26 | 06 | 10 | 74 | 40 | 84 |
| Manchester |United | 42 | 22 | 10 | 10 | 70 | 36 | 76 |
| Sheffield Wednesday | 42 | 21 | 10 | 11 | 63 | 54 | 73 |

## Eltham Pub Life Changes/Park Tavern/Hand Grenade Corner/Juke Box Installation

**P**UB LIFE had changed substantially in Eltham from the mid-eighties and has continued to do so. Closures, refurbishments, change in landlords and/or managers had not helped its cause but I still did local drinking in Eltham and was to continue doing so for many further years. The changes however were enough to notice not as many "faces" were out and about and this caused divisions in social beer drinking habits and gatherings as not everyone chose to go to the same change of preference. I was to spend most of my drinking time during this changing pattern and time in The Park Tavern, a hundred and fifty yards in Passey Place walking away from the high street and very different from The King's Arms. The pub consisted of being more fuddy-duddy and yet combined with distinct real life experience.

Colin Skinner was landlord at the time of my first regular dwelling, having used the pub previously on sporadic occasions, married to Betty with daughters Madeleine, Alison and Colette. Cribbage nights, quiz nights were arranged long before any other pub in the area took up the interest and the pub also boasted a golf society. The lead up to Christmas would see regulars and/or donators purchase raffle prizes; boards would be erected around the pub and on the railings over the bar that housed the drinking glasses with the names of donators and donated gifts beside them. Raffle tickets were then sold and all proceeds of such sale of tickets went to a designated charity. It was a wonderful pub but with change of landlords came changes in pub style and custom. Andy and Tom kept it very similar to the Colin Skinner regime but the main change came after their departure with mass exodus and a near 100% change in clientele.

John and Sally who had previously been in charge of The Man of Kent, situated next door to the fire brigade in Eltham High Street, were the instigators of such a transformation, having on the first day of official takeover a jukebox installed. This showed intent of diversity and also made it clear first hand that their intention was to bring in similarities to the Man of Kent in the form of a younger environment. John Dooley, father of Kevin, was to tell me he finished his pint and vacated the premises on viewing this installation. Doug the Box, so known due to his employment as a funeral director, and whose stature was most noticeable when walking in front of a hearse, along with Reg Walder were not to return again also. Standing at the end of the bar by the wall, hand grenade corner was how this trio were to be known as in the Park Tavern, a name so given by Tommy Ryan due to the fact that once beer taken had took hold, they would collectively reminisce about post 2$^{nd}$ world war conflicts they had or had not seen in action.

So many noses were put out of joint by this change! The Park Tavern was tucked away and had almost been a little oasis for many, but in my experience, this is a situation that can and does happen when change of pub governor takes place; but in saying that, this was a transformation of almost monumental proportions, though only in clientele as apart from the jukebox, no other changes of substance were made, be it internally or externally. I rarely used the 'Tav' after this changeover but began creeping back in on a Sunday afternoon early doors when the pub was tranquil, with the late George Peters. John and Sally were still at the helm, ably supported by Richard, Matt and Sally their offspring behind the bar. Six or so months after the return of my early Sunday afternoon beer in the Park Tavern, the partnership of Joe and Lindsey were the next to take charge and I then returned as a semi-regular until moving from Mottingham to Blackfen in January 2006.

## ASTON VILLA (Home) Carling Premier League 16/10/1993 (Lock-Out Get In No 2)

**I** **HAD LEFT** it late going to Upton Park, having socialised in one of the High Street pubs and had lost track of the time, so with yet another enjoyable time being had in wherever I was, I dragged myself away from this dinnertime session and got a mini-cab over to Upton Park.

Choosing to take my light and bitter with me, I asked the cab driver to return my empty glass to the pub when passing. I realised afterwards he was only humouring me, as asking a staff member that evening and the next day, I found no such undertaking took place. On arrival in Green Street the main entrance gates had been closed with people wandering around in the road or standing back on the pavement. I was knocked back at the fact I wasn't going to get in! At this time the then once all terracing South Bank was being redeveloped into all seats and therefore the capacity had been reduced somewhat; away supporters who were normally allocated an area in the South Bank were, during this period, given seating in the top corner of the West Stand, South Bank end.

## Kevin's a Brummie and I've just given him 13 Quid

**O**UT OF THE BLUE, this guy standing at the main gate entrance to the West Stand and on Green Street, picks on me when he had a choice of so many and asks if I wanted a ticket? He told me his mate couldn't make it and that all he was after was his money back. I accepted and through the main gates we walked. Chatting jovially, introducing ourselves and feeling well at ease and totally side tracked by 'this luck', it only occurred to me at the West Stand turnstiles that this man who had just introduced himself as Kevin had a different accent to me. Kevin was a Brummie and I've just given him 13 quid!

## Not Good Odds 400/1

**O**H WELL, I've done it now and so there I was, sat plum in the middle row V seat 052 of Villa's away boys. (The tickets still in my programme.) If I was a betting man I would guess 400/1 and even being a bit boozed, it didn't take much sobering up to realise this was not good odds and that decorum was of a practical essence. Kevin was as pleasant as could be; we talked bundles during the game but I made a point of keeping my voice down. A few Villa around cottoned on to me but they weren't too fussed. Kevin was a popular lad among the Villa fans and some (possibly from as many as five rows) stood up, shouted across and gave him good fun banter. I soon gathered that Kevin was an avid Villa fan and had been going to ALL Villa games for quite some time. Today though, he was getting stick as Villa were away in Europe that following midweek and he had told them he wouldn't be going. We went for a drink together at half time—now was the only time I felt uneasy.

Villa fans who were not sitting near had now picked up on me; they had seen I was with Kevin who in turn was known to them, but they still chose to whisper "nice things" in my ear, knowing Kevin was most helpful as I'm still here today to tell the tale, but then again, if I didn't feel confident all would be okay—I wouldn't have gone and been at the bar in the first place despite the desire for a top up. The match was to finish 0-0 and for sure, I did not want to be walking out the ground amongst The Villa boys; walking out with them at the end of the match would have been when their adrenaline would have kicked in and got going, aware and knowing that a possible meeting with likeminded West Ham fans could be a possibility. This was something I had no intention of getting myself involved in; the thought in itself was unnerving and I know I would have hated being caught in a situation should such a happening occur.

With minutes to go I lent to my right towards Kevin, told him quietly it was in my interest to leave, shaking his hand I thanked him. In return he showed his experience and understanding. As I went to stand he pulled me back forcefully and said discreetly, "Hey Graham, Don't listen to this lot, I've got my flight tickets." I liked it lots—everyone had been taken in, nice one! For sure after the wind-up and the surprise to see you at the airport, your Villa pals no doubt with a probable giving of more 'stick' would have been somewhat very pleased to have had you, their mate, with them and "on board".

### Behind the Post' Bob/Thick Skinned Denial Mode or Just WEST HAM Socialites?

I MET BOB back in May 1990 at a night home match against Leicester City. Bob, I was to find out, had a habit of standing behind one of the posts, to the right of the goal, "holding the roof up", as he once put it in the North Bank; he was later to be known by me if referring of him to others as "Bob behind the post". The final home match three days later against Wolves on the 5th May I did not attend and can't think why, but I hoped the next season I would see Bob again.

As always I was looking forward to the following season; summer month lack of football was a minus for me and the first home match was to be on a Wednesday night against Portsmouth. For me, however, it was a lock-out and I now can't be factual as for why as the attendance records show a crowd of less than 21,000. My next home attended match therefore was to be against Watford on Saturday 1st September. Standing in my normal place with the usual suspects, I would from time to time look at the area I had met Bob one day short of four months earlier; after a while almost to the point of not expecting to see him, he appeared. I made my way over to him and we re introduced. This was the beginning of a number of years West Ham association as for after this re-meet, any matches should I see Bob, a point of passing time with him was made. In the main however, I continued standing five or six yards or so to his right and a similar amount of terrace size steps lower with my other North Bank terrace regulars.

For the next four years this was how things stayed, but then came the closure of the North Bank for redevelopment to all seats in May 1994. For reasons I mention later (Terrace to Seats) about terracing meet ups, I can only assume that not everyone (if any) at that time had made any decisions as to what they were going to do regarding the next seasons football matches, or even discussed the possibility of upgrading to a season ticket, so to guarantee match entrance as ground capacity through North Bank closure would be reduced somewhat. I recall no positive congregated talk had been entered into although it was no doubt "hit on"; it was almost like a subject that was being put off and put off until all of a sudden it's upon you! It is my belief looking back that this is what happened and caused the unfortunate dismantlement of the remaining separate groups that grouped together to happen. The group gatherings had been no more than a natural development that started I estimate to be knocking on thirteen years prior and had remained until that final terraced match against Southampton.

Changes to personnel in groups through the natural course of time or circumstance happened, but people joined as people went and it was no more than a natural turnover. It could be true to say then that in the main, we were West Ham football socialites and not social socialites, although that in itself cannot be said as being 100% strictly correct because splinters as in my nights out with Debra and Mick coming to Tenerife with pals and lassies of mine in 1986 did happen. I can't remember the final parting moments of ways as we left the ground, now, or who was actually there that day, but it would no doubt have been mixed with the emotion of the end of "Our North Bank" as we knew it. I'm wondering now also if we were all in "thick-skinned denial mode" that we possibly won't see each other again, but it was just *abientot* and until next time; then again, could it have been that above all else we were in fact just West Ham football socialites?

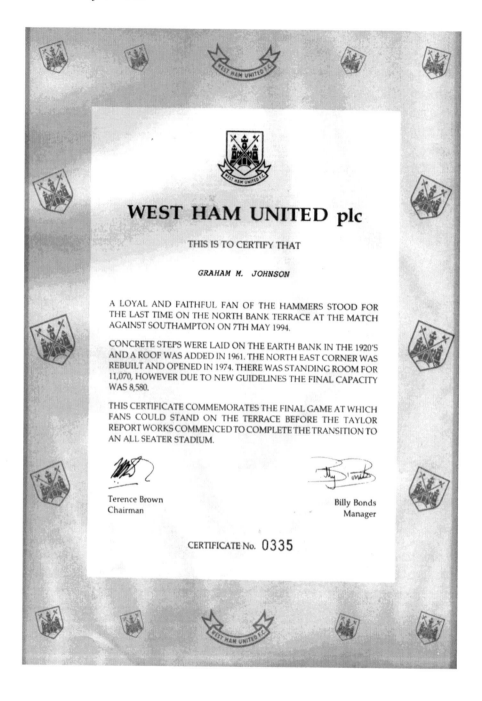

# WEST HAM UNITED plc

THIS IS TO CERTIFY THAT

*GRAHAM M. JOHNSON*

A LOYAL AND FAITHFUL FAN OF THE HAMMERS STOOD FOR THE LAST TIME ON THE NORTH BANK TERRACE AT THE MATCH AGAINST SOUTHAMPTON ON 7TH MAY 1994.

CONCRETE STEPS WERE LAID ON THE EARTH BANK IN THE 1920'S AND A ROOF WAS ADDED IN 1961. THE NORTH EAST CORNER WAS REBUILT AND OPENED IN 1974. THERE WAS STANDING ROOM FOR 11,070, HOWEVER DUE TO NEW GUIDELINES THE FINAL CAPACITY WAS 8,580.

THIS CERTIFICATE COMMEMORATES THE FINAL GAME AT WHICH FANS COULD STAND ON THE TERRACE BEFORE THE TAYLOR REPORT WORKS COMMENCED TO COMPLETE THE TRANSITION TO AN ALL SEATER STADIUM.

Terence Brown
Chairman

Billy Bonds
Manager

CERTIFICATE No. 0335

## Shared Season Ticket/Janet's Night Match Preference?

T HE SPLIT of North Bank togetherness at home match fixtures had now happened and this is where Bob from behind the post, over one or two soon after telephone conversations with me and in turn liaising with his sister Janet brought about the sharing of the following seasons' season ticket, an arrangement that was to roll on for eleven seasons culminating at the end of season 2004/05. It was a season-ticket arrangement that could have been made in fairy land.

In September 1993 I had started a small courier business and this is an industry that dictates working not when you want to work but when the customer wants you to. In the main but not always, the working days were Monday to Friday and would incorporated very long working hours that often meant early starts and late finishes. Starting a small business can also cause cash flow situations in early months and sometimes much longer and financial implications can be abundant and success is not guaranteed. Cash flow caused by late payments is a common reason for the demise of a small business when such efforts and determination could, should and would have brought rewards. Through my work commitments I was not to be able to guarantee attendance at night matches and forking out for a season ticket in one hit, however much I wanted to, was not practical but would have been achieved.

Bob and Janet now for different reasons were to come in so helpful for me. I had met Janet on a very few occasions on the North Bank when she attended matches with Bob and she was a lady who resided in Southampton. Janet had athletic sporting commitments at weekends and would have problems getting to a number of Saturday matches but in contrast to this, she could work flexi-time at work, and evening matches despite her living in Southampton were to be of no problem for her. I do believe, in fact, that night games were actually her preference? Bob spoke to Janet re my difficulties of guaranteeing night matches and so with Janet's weekend sport commitments season ticket predicament also, a practical and sensible solution was resolved re Janet taking night matches with occasional Saturdays and me the remainder.

Janet after the announcement of the coming West Ham season league fixture list would make a suggested breakdown of who was to attend what matches. This was always accepted by me without question as past experiences had proved that games against so called less glamour clubs would and could be just as entertaining and gratifying. Janet however was more than accommodating in her fairness of choice although a slight bias to watching a Southampton fixture at Upton Park was noticeable or imagined. Through the course of a season and due to individual circumstances, changes to this list suggestion would occur but I can't think of any time when a minor issue was not simply resolved. In fact I would use the words, the arrangement went swimmingly. Bob helped me out and eased my cash flow difficulties and paid Janet my half for the shared season ticket; I was in return to repay him as agreed in three monthly instalments. Using Bob as the hub, he would always keep hold of our shared season ticket and would meet up with whoever's turn it was to go before the start of the next match. Bob, should he ever knowingly beforehand have reason or cause to miss a forthcoming match, would then either leave his season ticket with me or Janet and that was the time, be it seldom, Janet and I sat together and saw each other at matches. It would also be the only time of communication between us as any changes in our circumstances re an up and coming fixture Bob would again do any necessary liaising.

## 7.30pm Evening KO's/Missing the first Twenty Minutes/Testimonials

**G**ETTING LOCKED OUT was not a regular occurrence pre-days to all seating and having a season ticket, but missing up to the first twenty minutes or so of an evening match was always a possibility. Evening matches generally commenced at 7.30pm and this would mean large numbers of people attending the match arriving from work anytime, say from 5.45pm onwards, but the majority within forty-five minutes or so before kick-off. Queues to the turnstiles in the North and South Banks along with the east and west side terracing would so often be choc-a-block. The North Bank queues would at times stretch fifty yards or so and on more "in demand" matches, I had known queues to lead into Green Street, which would be that distance again and twice over. Another factor to consider for late entry was that terracing accounted for the majority of people attending and payment was made in cash to a turnstile attendant on entrance.

In the main, night matches would be League Cup games or matches due to early round FA Cup replays, latterly league games due to extended FA Cup runs taking priority over Saturday league matches adding to league congestion or re-arranged cup or league fixtures due to weather postponements. In addition to these examples of night matches was the recognition but now getting less and less top flight player testimonial but not necessarily for players playing in a lower ranking division, a match traditionally granted to a player having served a ten-year loyalty period, or for unfortunate early retirement, say through injury. Amongst other reasons for granting a testimonial match may have included a long serving manager or high-ranking member of backroom staff.

These matches are of a non-competitive nature played against another club or a guest-selected team and depending on the prominence of the player, may have included past club greats or even a national team.

Geoff Hurst's testimonial in November 1971 was played against in invited European X1 and among many famous, prominent names of the time and recognised in football history if not since, included the likes of Portugal's Eusebio and Uwe Seeler, a player of distinction having played in four World Cup competitions (1958-1970) and captained West Germany as a World Cup final loser to England in 1966. Four years later he scored the 2$^{nd}$ goal against England that forced extra time (Franz Beckenbauer having scored the first) in the Mexico 1970 World Cup quarter finals, England having led 2-0 before being subsequently beaten by a third strike by Gerd Muller who in this 1970 competition, was to finish the tournament's top scorer with ten goals. Mordechai Spiegler was another player invited to play in Geoff's testimonial, a striker chosen four times as Israel's player of the year between the years of 1966-1971. Speigler was a player West Ham manager of the time Ron Greenwood made attempts to sign but was not allowed due to what my understanding was the restriction of foreign players in the British game, an alien ruling that now no way resembles the relaxation of such decisions and attitudes in today's world of football practices.

Player's wages had no resemblance to salaries that are paid today and money raised at such matches was to help the beneficiary in retirement, or perhaps help establish them in another alternative line of business or work. All proceeds were to go to the player and depending on which country such testimonials took place money raised would be paid tax free. Testimonials nowadays have become less frequent affairs within 'top flight' football and are more likely to take place for players established with teams that have greater opportunity of success. With the enormous rewards now paid to players throughout top levels of European football, I can only speak as I find and it would appear to me some players within the Premier League are less likely to stay with clubs through loyalty for extended periods as in past times if 'success was less likely'; these players will consider and take up a transfer onto an improved contract supplier even though success was no more likely on pitch and other than money, could and would prove to be no more than a side wards move. Another reason of exodus but on a far larger scale is in the light of relegation, where clubs are relieved of substantial payments through TV rights and so cannot afford to pay the contracts of players entered into. It is not uncommon now that should a top flight player testimonial be awarded, they have become in addition to the recognition of the individual concerned, a most likely financially charitable affair paid to causes that the player concerned now so chooses. An introduction of generosity and perhaps an admittance of player wealth I believe started for the first time by Niall Quinn when at Sunderland and playing the Republic of Ireland for his testimonial in 2002. A most welcome precedence that was appreciated, acknowledged and recognised countrywide.

With the emergence and introduction of SKY TV in the mid-eighties, all was to change and night match kick-off times were altered more commonly to 7.45pm or 8pm. Not only did this help the unintended late, very close to kick-off time arrival of fans, but also the paying armchair viewer who could now watch the full match, plus replays of/with varying angles along with analysis and opinions that go with watching football broadcasted live. Why was evening football not 7.45pm or 8pm anyway? I guess there must have been a reason???

## Seating/Songs/Atmosphere.....?

**F**OR TWENTY-SIX YEARS I stood on the terracing behind the goal at matches in The North Bank. Very rarely did I watch home games from the terracing in other parts of the ground but sometimes, though, through late arrival or a possible lock-out, it would dictate a rush and need to get in wherever. Before the coming of the Boleyn ground being totally transformed into an all-seat stadium and my shared season ticket in the West Stand with Janet, the only other times I watched matches from seating areas was through the choice and curiosity of the newly completed Bobby Moore Stand. I attended the matches against Norwich and Manchester United that saw the opening of the Lower tier on the 24th January 1994 and Upper tier 26th February 1994 respectively.

The North Bank has so many full-on memories for me but I hadn't seen a match from that end of the ground since closure in May 1994. Now, having my shared season ticket in the West Stand, I took the opportunity to sit in the North Bank newly named Centenary Stand for the pre-season Steve Potts testimonial that was played against Queens Park Rangers on 2nd august 1997. The only other time I was to sit at matches before now was aforementioned Shrewsbury Town 1980/81 and Aston Villa 1993/94 with both matches watched from the West Stand upper tier.

The all-seat stadium took away many terracing songs that unless they crop up at the odd away game (which I can't say I've heard when on my now rare travels) are now no longer sung? At away matches the travelling section of supporters generally would be the more vocal, being congregated together and in an area designated for visiting fans; at home matches vocal support is more spread around the stadium but it can be said the old North and South Banks as in pre being an all-seat ground still tend to be the more atmospheric parts of the stadium. Other than 'Bubbles' very few other songs are now sung and are for me sorely missed. 'The Bells are ringing', 'You are my West Ham', 'Who's that team we call United', 'Roll along Roll Along', 'There is a team called West Ham' (Ugly Duckling, to the tune of) amongst a number of others. Then of course the old favourite, 'Knees up Mother Brown'. Singing KUMB (there is a Hammers website) would often cause over-enthusiastic participants of song and movement to loose footing and scramble down the terracing before recovering their places. Also a possible surprise to many in more tender years, the singing of 'You'll Never Walk Alone', so associated as 'Liverpool's song' but was also sung regularly not only at West Ham, but at football grounds up and down the country. Do all seat football grounds experience the atmospheres they once enjoyed? Of course not... No Chance!

## Terrace to Seats

TERRACING you could stand in your chosen place, mingle, move about and vary for a better view if you wished, meet or even avoid, should that be the case. Because of this special friendships can develop, teracing allowed movement; groups due to geographical reasons met because it was likely they would only see each other on match days and enjoyed these football meets. If a group of ten or more as sometimes in our case formed, it was possible to move around so to talk to all and sundry at any stage, whether it be before a match, during a match, at half time or when walking out together after a match and saying goodbye.

Seating does not allow this—you can't mingle; basically you have your seat and that is your place. Seats create (in my experience) conversation in the main to the next one or two people either side of you and/or also the one or two rows behind or in front. I was very lucky in the sense that the surrounds I sat with firstly in the West Stand and later to be renamed the Dr Martens Stand where the surrounds became more firmly established were a nice bunch and match days were not spoilt by people of a biased opinion or used language of an unnecessary nature. Friendships can develop but it can also be said that should you get a seat next to an irritant it can be an enjoyment spoiler; if it's a one-off match and you're not or they're not a season ticket holder, so be it—it is a short term suffer; but if you are a season ticket holder and they hold season tickets also, then it's game in, game out and the sound of when you get a question wrong on the tele program— 'Family Fortunes' springs to mind—and that, trust me, is not good.

**HEYBRIDGE SWIFTS/The Boys of '86 Fun Day Fund Raiser
07/09/2003**

*Reproduced with the permission of Heybridge Swifts Football Club*

**A**T THE START of the season, ten points from the first nine games was no showing of how it was going to go, but look how it ended. That fantastic season brought the birth of the Boys of '86 and twenty-plus years or so later, members of that squad still get together or independently to host functions or play celebrity/charity football matches. I had not been to any such functions or attended any of these celebrity/charity matches prior to this occasion and had read about this one only when advertised in a Hammers programme as a combined fun day and fund raiser.

A Boys of '86' team plus Guests were to be playing at Heybridge Swifts on Sunday 7th September 2003 and the match had been timed as an 11.30am kick-off. As well as the match being played, a penalty prize competition, a football memorabilia auction plus other side show attractions as well as a BBQ and refreshments were advertised; but the main reason if not the only reason for my choosing to go was to take the opportunity to meet and mix with the players and I knew, yes I just knew, that this was and could be a distinct if not definite possibility.

On arriving and parking my van close by, I made my way to the ground just a few minutes' walk away and the relaxed, happy, family friendly atmosphere aided by a sun-pelting day gave rise to satisfaction even before entrance through a turnstile. I had still been deliberating at home whether to go or not just a couple of hours or so before my arrival and the match was already under way. On buying a programme my first thoughts was to look at the player listing to see who was down to play; as I walked into the small ground and looking onto the pitch I saw instant recognisable players. Phil Parkes was 'manager for the day' and standing on the side line. Taking Phil's place in goal was Allen McKnight. Allen never actually took part in any matches during the 85/86 campaign, in fact he wasn't to join West Ham until two years after and that was in the summer of 1988 from Celtic. Actor Perry Fenwick of BBC EastEnders' Billy Mitchell fame as well as actor/comedian Bradley Walsh, who at this time may have been about to/had or was appearing in ITV's Coronation Street had also taken to the field of play. I have absolutely no idea of the attendance that day but it was a day of people coming and going and spread over a number of hours. The proceeds achieved were to support the Heybridge Swifts Football Club themselves with what I understand was a substantial percentage donation being made to The Essex Air Ambulance Service also.

Once in the ground walking around was never to be a problem and I varied my viewing angles many times to confirm players on view. At half time the players went to their respective changing rooms with me standing not too far away. A couple of minutes or so passed when I noticed Tony Gale standing outside the changing room door on the open ground with nobody really around. With slight hesitancy I took my opportunity and went over to him. A quiet private talk ensued and until Alvin Martin joined us we had a proper one-on-one chat of which I relived what was to me, especially the last six weeks, a season that is so easy to relive, with thirteen matches from 29$^{th}$ March to 5$^{th}$ May being played over thirty-eight days. Alvin and Tony both signed my Boys of '86 book that I had taken with me before Tony Gale then out of the blue asked me my name and said, "Come with me, I'll introduce you." On hearing this I followed him into the dressing room to meet the players and in the space of seconds, I was in the same dressing room with many of the players who had given me the most enthralling West Ham United football season I had ever witnessed up until then and to date, although 1980/81 for me will be as close to par as you could get.

On looking back what had struck me that day was the fact that these men were so similar in age to me. This may be a somewhat stupid if not ridiculous thing to say, but when I watched them from the terracing, for some reason I had always imagined them to be older. It can be like that today: I sometimes forget I watch football from a stand played by young lads where some may only shave twice a week through youth; yet I still think of them as being older than they actually are. Now being in the dressing room and on reflection, it was to remind me so much of the days when I played—it really was no different to that. Boys will be boys and men will be 'boys', the chat, the banter, the misbehaving and the mucking about with one player prancing about with no embarrassment and I imagine he had done this many times before because nobody, but nobody took one blind bit of notice. It wasn't the best of changing rooms but then again it certainly wasn't Winn's Common SE18 either, where when I was still playing chairs were placed along the wall of the changing room for your clothes to be 'thrown' over and that was that. No showers, no running water taps (that I can think of), no nothing from what I recall.

Fantastic, over seventeen years had passed since that fabulous... FABULOUS season, and I could now/still see first-hand the friendship, team spirit, fun and laughter that had so nearly taken West Ham to the clubs first and only first division championship title. It plays on my mind even now to date; if the postponed matches through weather conditions over the Christmas and New Year period had been played, it's possible that without the fixture congestion so added to by an extended FA Cup run, terminated in the 6th round night match at Sheffield Wednesday (my only away match that season) but included three 4th round FA Cup matches against Ipswich Town and a replay victory at Manchester United, it could have been so different?

The home postponed match versus Chelsea on New Year's Day and the subsequent result of the rearranged fixture always springs to mind. Would it have made any difference? Did Orient and Spurs play their matches in London on New Year's Day? Were they at home or did they even have matches? I can't be asked to find out now—*Que Sera Sera.*

## Thirteen in Hand, Five to Go/Bobby Moore-John Lyall... I Won't Forget Where I Was

I WENT HOME that afternoon having thirteen signatures of the eighteen players (Alan Devonshire, Paul Goddard, Frank McAvennie, Ray Stewart and Steve Walford, all of which did not attend) that played in West Ham's league positions' finest season. Thanks Lads, and Thank You John Lyall, a most dignified gentleman who I had the pleasure to meet at a West Ham end-of-season dinner and dance at the Heybridge Moat House, Ingatestone on 13th January 1980, and who I spoke to that evening at great length (pictured page 186). I don't know what went on 'behind the scenes' for what to happen to happen but many are aware that when you 'went' in the summer of '89 we had just been relegated. For many that would be reason enough, but me, I knew you as a West Ham manager. YES... A WEST HAM MANAGER and in the true sense and tradition of. A WEST HAM MANAGER that I feel many Hammers fans but of course not all, from say ten years younger or so to me and then older will possibly if not probably agree and identify with my sentiments. I had hoped (as your predecessor Ron Greenwood had) that one day you would have gone on to manage England. Mr Lyall died on the 18th April 2006 at the age of 66 from a reported heart attack, with Ron Greenwood passing in February, just two months prior after a long illness at the age of 85. I was driving on the A13 just passing Basildon bound for London when I heard the news from my van radio. Just as with Bobby Moore back on 24th February 1993 (John Lyall's 53rd birthday), doing my collections of cable in Charlton and to be more explained later: **(Bobby Moore (OBE) What an Inside-Outside Football History/Always Smart and Liked a Lager**, Page 179). I will always remember where I was.

## Terry and Jean/Dennis/The Frankie Howerd Club

**2002** had brought my introduction to Terry and Jean Martin by Mickey Tye, a well-known figure around the pub and drinking club circuit culture in Eltham, a man I never had beers with in company at this time but if the situation had arisen previously, an amicably exchanged brief small talk momentary pass time chit-chat would take place. Mickey Tye was also father of Dale, a man I was to meet in this same set-up as Terry and Jean and who later was to become a very good and helpful friend, a friend who later was to join me a number of times taking in the Phoenix public house annual December beer festival weekend away in Canterbury, and who put me up at his for four months after the selling of my property when looking for another.

This introduction to Terry and Jean as with Dale took place in a wonderful little private members' club known as the Frankie Howerd Club and it was here that Mickey and me with then partner M-A first got involved in 'rounds'. A small organisation based not far from Well Hall roundabout on the old A2 Rochester Way, the club is a most friendly place, no bigger than the size of two sensibly sized living rooms; it has comfortable seats and offers a safe friendly environment and atmosphere that in the main is used by local residents living within a mile or so radius. The bar is of a size best suited for just one person working behind the bar, serving lager and Guinness, and has a small selection of ales complemented with a guest beer rarely not on show for selection. The club has its regular Sunday raffles of which tickets would have been purchased by members and guests over the previous weeks seven days or so before starting the system again.

The club committee throughout the year organises a number of functions that would include St Georges and St Patrick's nights, a beer festival, quiz evenings, race evenings and a coastal family day out. Other organised events take place but one that is not committee arranged and takes place on a twice-yearly basis with a small contingent of Eltham conservative club members, is the mystery country sixteen-seat mini-bus jaunts to various country pubs mainly in the county of Kent. A selection of pubs (four) only known to the organiser would have been visited and chosen (one of which would be the pub grub meal stop). This is a day that is disciplined by time slots as each pub management and staff to be visited would have been made aware of an arriving mini-bus and so be prepared. On arrival at each pub the organiser would announce a given time of departure. Morning departure time was consistently kept at 10.30am and return evening arrival to The Frankie Howerd Club of 7.30pm was always mandatory. As this was a non-committee club involvement, interested and/or participant members would take it in turn as a volunteer to arrange but two or three committee members always enjoyed the coming along also on this 'jolly boys' day out.

Now, having been introduced to Terry and Jean, I discovered within a matter of minutes that Terry was also a staunch Hammers fan and it is true to say having a strong common interest in early friendly meetings can be a major factor in friendship building if not bonding. Soon Terry and Jean obtained membership and during the winter months, if ever I was to see Terry and Jean, it would only be in the 'Howerd' club. In their early days of membership, they brought along a friend of theirs—Dennis, a friend they had known for many years and who was to prove to me time and time again what a loyal and trusted friend he was to both them, their daughter Laura-Jane and later to her husband Gary.

Dennis is a Manchester City fan and for all his talking of the Joe Mercer, Malcolm Allison management team and players Corrigan, Bell, Lee, Summerbee, Book and Booth etc amongst others of the late sixties and early seventies, I was, but only after taking some time before finding out, very much amused that for all his enthusiasm, Dennis had never, NEVER...EVER seen a live Manchester City football match at Maine Road. Over the winter and then as the summer months of 2003 kicked in, Terry, Jean and Dennis had introduced M-A and me to good friends of theirs. My relationship ceased with M-A on 11th May of this year, the day West Ham were to draw in an away fixture to Birmingham City 2-2, a result that saw relegation from the

Premier League to the first division on a record point's total of forty-two. Bolton were the team to finish immediately above West Ham having accumulated a points total of forty-four; the fact was if Hammers had won at Birmingham forty-four points would not have prevented their plight as goal difference was not in their favour. 2002/03—a season that promised so much that ended in relegation and by a side that could and should in my opinion have pushed for a European place. I feel many supporters, just as I have, will have their views and/or reasons for such a demise?

This introduction of new socialites was to give me a wonderful summer, because of Terry, Jean and Dennis they had all joined the 'Howerd' club and almost to a point of a regular basis BBQ's were taking place in turns of houses and garden with the now customary game of croquet. To add to the ease of relegation and other than the exception of Dennis' armchair support of Manchester City, these new-found introductions by Terry, Jean and Dennis were without exception all Hammers fans; they all coped with their individual feelings and dealings of relegation suffering in their own way and were West Ham... UNITED. They were also family and individuals alike; not all family members went to matches but those who did were season-ticket holders and renewing their tickets after relegation was not in question. Tony Goode (Tony G.) who later was to become 'Chair' of this anything up to 150 member club renewed his tickets with son Jack and daughter Kelly, Brett Portman same as with son William and of course Terry with daughter Laura-Jane. Dave Truluck as with all others renewed his season ticket and Dave like me, as a member of the 'Howerd' club, had been introduced parallel to me to this new unit of friends; it was also with Dave at his house I was to watch the final sealing of Hammers' fate at Birmingham.

## Dave the Post/Gary Curran/East Ham CIU Workingmen's club

WITH THESE new-found West Ham friends for me came a Brucie Bonus, as on a number of Saturdays there was it seemed and coincidentally, at least one individual who couldn't make a match when it wasn't my shared season ticket turn to go, I could and would then benefit from picking up a not to be used season ticket. This group contingent, although not sitting together, all sat within a matter of yards of each other in the East Stand lower, and as grateful as I was for this not to be used season ticket, I always preferred my shared seat with Janet—not because of the very low-down view of being almost at the bottom of the lower tier, so alien to my higher raised full pitch viewing in the upper Dr Martens stand, but also because of the points I mentioned earlier re the sound made on 'Family Fortunes' when a contestant gets a question wrong.

Since the completion to all-seat stadium and losing track of my old North Bank 'muckers', having a meet-up social beer before a match had become almost non-existent, I was now by and large travelling by van singly and apart from the odd time of meeting with Bob from behind the post before a match in the greasy spoon café at Queens Market. Parking up and going direct to the ground had now become almost same as same as. This was now to change as after my intro to Terry in the Frankie Howerd Club and my new-found West Ham mates along with the bonus of picking up a not to be used match season ticket, I found myself travelling with them mainly in Tony G's people carrier on match days and having beers with them in the East Ham CIU workingmen's club in Boleyn Road before a match. From here, and it was quite a nice feeling, I could with ease plainly see from the club's upstairs window and between the Bobby Moore Stand and the East Stand where as a group we would sometimes congregate, my Dr Martens contingent taking their intermittently timed seat places before matches. It was here also in the club that I was to cross paths again with Dave the Post for what must have been an over twenty year absence.

I had met Dave when as a twenty-two/three year old, I would venture in the early afternoon to The Kings Arms pub after having physiotherapy at the Brook hospital as part of my after-car accident rehabilitation. Dave had walked in with a number of postmen after finishing their early morning shift duties just around the corner in Court Yard and with them was Gary and Glen, two brothers and ex-primary school mates of mine and now posties also, but who I had not seen since moving to Eltham back in 1969, it was through my double brother recognition that these intros took place; this pub meet was to happen again on a number of future occasions and although I got pally with others from this post people play the pub machines and have a beer contingent, Dave and Nick Sargant (Arsenal) were the more prominent.

Dave was sitting down and I could see in an instant that he and 'my crowd' were familiar. Pulling Tony G to one side, I asked if the bloke they were talking to was named Dave and, if so, was he a postman? Tony G replied in the positive: "Who, DJ Dave? Yes, he's a postman." So it was Dave the Post to me, but DJ Dave (self-explanatory I'm sure) to the others. On moving in on Dave, recognition on his part, be it with a surprised expression, was instant, but with me and due to small world coincidence and all that, and having the opportunity of asking Tony G beforehand for confirmation, tackling made the re-introduction factual and therefore easier. If Tony G hadn't confirmed, a handshake hand held out would have happened because if it was Dave I wasn't letting him go.

It was also here in the club that I was to meet up again with Gary Curran before the home match against Everton in March 2006. Gary C I hadn't seen for what must have been, just like Dave the Post, twenty years plus. Gary C had been to a home match on regaining confidence after what must have been a couple of seasons or so after the League Cup Final Liverpool replay of April 1981, but after that one match, I really can't say if I saw him again until this now 'blow me down' meet in the social club. It was a fantastic feeling and although we never really knew each other, we knew each other and we had always been comfortable in each other's company. Gary C had been introduced by Joe Lott to me as well as 'the others' on the North Bank terracing in the latter months of 1980; whether they were work mates (likely) or just mates, fails me now. The fact was Gary C had become quite a regular with us lot on the North Bank and had travelled with us on the mini-bus to the original Liverpool final at Wembley but had met up with some misfortune at the Villa Park replay, where divided arrangements within groups for travel and purchase of tickets had been made. This misfortune had put Gary C off attending football matches for some time and it is a shame that like-minded football attendees don't just target like-minded attendees so they can 'get on with it' and leave non-likeminded supporters alone to travel and enjoy matches in peace. On seeing Gary this day, to say it was most gratifying is an understatement. To know also that he was back in the swing of things and had been for years was pleasing also. If I had not now been going to this CIU club, I would have had no idea if he had returned to The Boleyn, be it on a part-time or full-time basis. Full-time it was, and not only was he now a season ticket holder but his two boys of my absolute no knowledge were season ticket holders also.

## CRYSTAL PALACE Nationwide Championship Play-off Final (Cardiff Millennium Stadium) 29/05/2004

**I**T JUST NEVER FELT RIGHT. The tingle of match excitement was missing, apprehension was the order of inner thought and the feeling of "This isn't going to be our day" was never far away—but this was apprehension and just inner thought feeling and was in no way FACT... YET. So on with the day I got. With ten travelling, the fare was divided equally, although having two young lads with us in Jack Goode and Sam Jubb, both dads Tony G and Steve respectively were insistent on paying for their young lads' positions; so having hired a medium sized stretch limousine for £700 no one quibbled and paying £70 was generally accepted as fair play knowing getting there and back, Severn bridge toll, driver/fuel and the all-important selling point of being hassle-free was well worth the no responsibility of rail/coach or other forms of travel that had been discussed. A mini-bus was of course mentioned but the thought of treating the match also as a "let's go in a bit of style" occasion with a locally known Chauffeur hire company, the Limo was booked.

Terry's Jean with washed down on board supplies but unknowing before to us travellers on the day, had made enough sandwiches to feed us plenty. A parking space was found on an industrial estate close to the stadium, and having three or so hours to kill before kick-off, we headed in the direction of the stadium with the sole purpose of finding a nearby watering hole for further refreshments of the non-tinned or bottled kind. I was delegated to be the money whip holder and "I wish people would leave me to it" as some confusion arose with the beer and boys' soft drink order and we ended up with an extra pint of coke.

However, not a minute or two had passed and on looking out the pub window, I saw Eric and Liz, father and daughter who now sat behind me in the Dr Martens upper stand crossing the road outside with wife and mum 'Lin'. 'Lin' was not attending the match and had come down for their overnight stay at The Jurys Inn for what I personally assume was purely "for the fun of it?" On seeing them it was a quick hello and a photo take with Liz taking advantage of the incorrectly poured coke. Our next port of call heading towards the ground turned out to be a JD Weatherspoons pub known as the Prince of Wales. Weatherspoons public houses are in the main not known for being on the small side, and having a downstairs bar and upstairs socialising area is a popular design; this one was of no exception and although bona fide, it also had an upstairs bar thus taking pressure off the staff and hordes downstairs; it would be true also to say if a bar and or just socialising area are not upstairs then the toilets in Weatherspoons pubs generally still will be.

Chocked-full downstairs and packed to the rafters upstairs, but upstairs we stayed and no taking off the pressure for downstairs staff on this occasion was evident. I met up by chance with Sean and Sam Dooley, sons of Kevin and they with their fellow travelling pals were bashing an inflatable ball about with others as a fun "keep it up". The battered-around inflatable arrived over at our place of standing and one lad in our group, Phil Jubb, hit it with distinction before it landed on a ledge in the pub, and that's where it stayed, the fun having been put to an end and stopped with immediate effect. Sean and Sam without hesitation called out to the culprit jokingly shouting, "He's an Eagle, he's an Eagle!"—the Palace nickname, thus suggesting our party member was a party pooper.

*Liz taking advantage of the incorrectly poured Coke, seen here with Eric (father) before Crystal Palace Play-off Final 29/05/2004*

Bob from behind the post met me outside the pub having made contact via our mobiles about 2.15pm. Bob had my ticket but we were not to sit together. Janet had managed to get that all-important extra ticket, being a club member also, and the next priority for ticket sales after full allocations to season ticket holders was, for want of words, "swallowed up". My first ever visit to the Millennium Stadium and no one I'm sure could fail to be well impressed! My seat, just like all around the stadium, had no viewing impairments but like all "being on the rather large size" stadiums, my preference of being closer to the field of play is never going to happen and the higher in the stadium you are the further away from "The action" you will be, as well as players appearing just six inches tall!

After the sussing out of my seat location and plonking myself down for a few minutes digestion and taking in the all-round pre-match atmosphere and view, I chose quickly and out of seat 'what's your seat like' curiosity to track down Eric and Liz as she had told me their seat details. On contact and sitting with them to my shear surprise was Guy, a lad who sat behind me and next to Liz in the Dr Martens stand at home matches. I don't know for sure, but as this had not been a mutually arranged purchase of tickets between them and yet now sitting together, it's possible that ticket allocation to season ticket holders was intended to keep seated groups together as much as possible as if at the Boleyn, providing of course they had purchased tickets within the same price band; this is only my assumption as otherwise it is some coincidence. Guy is a home and away season ticket holder who by taking out this combined package, shows his intention of attending as many matches throughout a season as possible. Guy although rarely ever talking to me about away moments and experiences, would I'm sure have had many a story to tell. Guy lives in Northamptonshire and although this gives him a travelling advantage in distance to many 'away' matches, it must be remembered and taken into account that he, along with his travelling companions who I understand have the same such package, must be clocking an approximate 150-mile round trip each time an attendance to Upton Park is made.

Returning to my seat the match excitement was still missing; the apprehension of inner thought and the feeling of "This isn't going to be our day" proved to be justified. In my opinion even with Hammers having two (correctly) disallowed goals, I felt on the day Palace edged it and Neil Shipperley's opportunist goal from a parry by goalkeeper Steve Bywater in the six yard box from Andy Johnson's lowly driven shot two thirds into the match proved to be the score difference. Palace since the turn of the year had been the in-form promotion play-off team and had got into the play-offs due to an at the death equalising 1-1 goal at Wigan by Brian Deane for West Ham. This was to shelve Wigan's Play-off aspirations, letting in Crystal Palace to finish sixth by two points clear, although a win that day for Wigan would have reversed the fortunes on goal differences and possibly West Hams?

## PRESTON NORTH END Coca Cola Championship Play-off Final (Cardiff Millennium Stadium) 30/05/2005.

T**HE DIFFERENCE** in the feeling this time was so opposite to last year's Crystal Palace play-off; the match and day excitement was there, apprehension was not even a momentary contemplation or occurrence, and the feeling in the water of "This was going to be our day" was in me and being positively taken for granted. Was I building myself up for a big come-down and deserved fall for this inner arrogance? After all, it was true to say Preston had been double league fixture winners against West Ham in this just finished 46 match domestic season.

The day was to start by leaving Eltham at 6.30am with group member Phil being the driver in a hired for £10 only fifteen seat mini-bus, less than a pound each and of course sometimes it's not what you know but who and Phil knew that who. The only additional cost was the fuel for the day and Severn bridge toll and I was not to ask Phil how it came about to be just £10, why I don't know because I didn't ask and as curious as I was, I didn't ask and I still don't know even to now. Travelling through London with beers even at this unlikely time on the go and on the flow, the optimism for victory if not for the sheer expectancy of a good day out by all in attendance was clear for me and all to see. With no traffic hold-ups we found ourselves on the M4 just on the hour. What had seemed like no time at all, we were pulling in at Membury services about ten or so miles short of junction 15 and exit for Swindon. It seemed that Membury services was becoming a habit as we had stopped there the previous year on the outward and inward journeys when in the play-off final against Crystal Palace. A sight to behold, and just like the year before, the services had been completely taken over by happy and jovial Hammers fans present in there hundreds and bearing so much claret and blue. Scarves, hats, flags, deafening horns blearing plus merchandise stalls selling all this plus blow bubble containers and whatever in addition you can name. After having the tea, coffee, bite to eat and P-stop we were back on our way and with the beer beginning to take hold, the side door of the mini-bus was opened and the 'could be' premature party began.

With one or two occupants standing at the open door with music on and the mini-bus being of a high top model, air guitar playing and prancing could not be ruled out and wasn't. Our first sign of traffic so far was now happening since our journey set off and this was to be at the normal expected slow moving jam at the Severn Bridge Tolls that separates England from Wales. It was here that from another mini-bus about four lanes across and opposite from ours had a lad on it shouting across and calling out my name; seeing this but not knowing who I was to confront, I ran between the very slow predominantly moving West Ham traffic to shake hands and as I got close I could see it was Mick Pinard who, when I played football before the car accident of 1980, was goalkeeper of the Farmhouse public house on the Coldharbour estate in New Eltham SE9. I would run into him and Dave Hurt (Farmhouse team captain) in the Boleyn pub some years before this meet and prior to matches, but in my haste, quick retreat and return to our mini-bus before passing through the tolls, I had not been aware that Dave in fact was also on board and only found out when informed some months later. So much fun and banter was being had with other cars and buses in the slow moving traffic further down the road that on the one Preston coach we passed, the girls on board played up to us—so much so that although only gesturing, we felt they would have raised their shirts to us if circumstances were different; but we could see quite clearly their menfolk were keeping a watchful disgruntled and disapproving eye on them! We were on form though…

On arriving very close to the Millennium we just could not believe our luck as we found this 'one off' street parking space between other vehicles begging to be taken; what's more, it was large enough, albeit only just, for our mini-bus to slot in nicely and not more than a five minute walk to our intended port of call. With this luck and good fortune and having now had the previous years' experience we all headed off to Weatherspoons pub The Prince of Wales, but our luck was then to change; after what must have amounted to a good half hour queuing, the doormen told us they were not letting in people until the pub became less busy. The fruitless wait bore fruit for me though because as we were all waiting in the queue and before setting off for the stadium, a man I had met some seven months previously in Bournemouth on walking past recognised me, stopping and having a together getting focused remembering sort of chat; he took a couple of photos and I passed him my mobile number, since then and with Martin continuing to live in Bournemouth we have kept in contact and have met up a couple of times before matches at Upton Park.

So it was beers in the ground and to everyone's surprise at no time did we have to either hang about or wait for service. We had our tickets for the lower tier in the West Stand and could consume in an area well-placed for looking down on the river Taff. Picking up where we left off in the mini-bus, we began our rousing sing-song again in the lower tier concourse, with the high spirits, the volume and echo, everything seemed set. The feeling in the water was how it should be; all the boys had to do now was go out on the pitch and DO IT. A second half goal from a Matthew Etherington cross by Bobby Zamora meant that the boys DID IT! Throughout the match there was no water change and the game proved to confirm my inner match feeling and of the entire day.

With Premiership football secured after a two-year absence, it was now home, music on and party time again, Membury services for refreshments and in my case three pieces of chicken and chips from the KFC—déjà vu, you could say as I had the same on the way home last season after Crystal Palace. On returning to the mini-bus for the continued journey, the settling down now was taking hold on the group and with me now sitting, it was a stupid facial grin filled with content before being back home and in bed just before 1am.

*Dave The Post getting some fresh air breeze from the opened Mini-bus door with Steve Jubb, seen here leaning on the front seat back rests.*

*Happy, Pre celebratory Tony G, relaxed and at ease.*

*Queuing outside The Weatherspoons Prince of Wales pub before moving on.*
*Left to right Steve Rees with Phil Jubb (obscured), Dave the Post, Steve Jubb*
*(glasses) Tony G, me and Terry Martin. Front two are Jack Goode and*
*Bournemouth Martin*

## CHARLTON ATHLETIC (Away) Barclay Premier League
## 31/12/2005

I**T WOULD BE TRUE** to say that tickets for Charlton home matches at the valley amongst my movements and acquaintances were not often difficult to obtain, but other than a match involving West Ham, I was not one to take up any other such possibilities. West Ham at Charlton on New Year's Eve was a ticket I had been promised a month or so in advance by one of these acquaintances as they knew someone or had a relative who worked within the box office.

On having a conversation with Ray of management status at a company I arranged courier transport deliveries for and not long before Christmas, the mentioning to me that Genine the company administrator had four tickets for the Charlton West Ham match and that two were up for grabs touched an interesting 'I'll remember that' nerve, but I explained that I should be alright for a ticket as I had already been 'promised' one but thanked him for making me aware. A day or two after this brief bringing to my notice exchange of words and with still no ticket in my hand despite numerous "it's all in hand" acknowledgments, I made a phone call only to be told by this acquaintance that he was at the airport waiting to board a flight for his holiday and that he'd call me back with details of where to pick up the ticket; no undertaking took place and I wasn't even aware of him having holiday plans!

Things in life sometimes happen for reasons, albeit good, bad or indifferent, and it can congeal into coincidences. I made contact with Genine and she was to tell me she still had both tickets spare and that, yes, they were still available! I snapped both up and Steve Rees was only too pleased to take up the other offering. On arriving at our seats Genine was already at her seat with boyfriend Paul. A small world, we all know it can be and on talking to Paul I was to discover that he, too, was a season ticket holder at Upton Park; on asking him where he sat, he told me he sat in the Bobby Moore Lower, row X seat 60. I replied almost with astonishment to his almost astonishment that *I* sat in row V seat 60 just two rows directly in front! I had been in this seat since my change from the Dr Martens upper stand at the start of this current season in August and to this time, we had not until this introduction crossed paths even by recognition of eyeball and being just a few or so feet away from each other. After this introduction and now being aware of each other, passing quick hello's with the briefest of chats were the only exchanges, as talking through the lads separating our seats behind and in front was not always deemed appropriate. A poor game with a defeat for the Hammers by 2-0, but it was good in one way; travelling home was of local ease and of no real consequence.

## MIDDLESBROUGH FA Cup Semi-Final (Villa Park) 23/04/2006

**F**OOD from Tina's 40th, Dave the Post's missus' birthday bash the night before was to come in right handy, as with many functions, buffet food is left to waste for two main reasons. One is that too much is supplied and on offer for the fear of "running out" and therefore is wasted because of over-preparation; the other is guests getting so involved with the evening that "forgetting" the food was there for the taking and end up in a curry house or having a take-away doner or shish kebab, is and will be regular in occurrence.

The following day's match was never far from the thoughts of those in party attendance that night and with such good food through over-preparation destined to go to waste and with Dave and Tina's suggestion and blessing, why not take advantage? Smiling and putting on a voice, I joked with raised eyelids, "Fed up we are to be but not FED UP I hope we are not after the game!" With that I took the carefully packed grub home with me for consumption and safe keeping—for what was now today's travel and match.

### Fifteen Seat Mini-Bus/Driver Bernie/Hatherwood Bitter

**A**NOTHER FIFTEEN-SEATED mini-bus was hired but this time with driver Bernie and no £10 perk benefit as was in place with the play-off final win some eleven or so months earlier against Preston North End. We were to meet as two groups as opposed to the one previous pick-up point due to talks of convenience and geographical reasons, with the first pick-up point at the Woodman pub in Blackfen and the second outside the old, now derelict Odeon cum Coronet cinema at Well Hall roundabout. With fourteen on board our journey was to take us through the Blackwall Tunnel to the Redbridge roundabout and then onto the duel carriageways and motorways of the M11, A14 and M6. These mini-bus football journeys, even being only of the strength of two, were somewhat most enjoyable, with yet another proper good crack being had; with lagers and Hatherwood bitters from the German flexible store Lidl being over three hours consumed at a rapid rate of knots, we found ourselves approaching the vicinity of Aston.

## Traffic Police Pull Over/Very Own Private Escort

T O MAKE OUR JOURNEY that little bit more interesting we now get a pull over from the on the day on-duty football traffic police! After a brief chat of questions and answers and having been satisfied with what driver Bernie had to say and with us lot to the police, looking visibly harmless if not vacant and useless, I can't help thinking it may have been for these reasons, the police felt a little sympathetic to our cause as we then got the added bonus of our very own private escort to a subsequent parking space put aside "special" for travelling supporters, a parking area that we had no knowledge of and were oblivious. This was to prove well helpful because, quite frankly, parking was going to be a bit of a hit-or-miss situation anyway, as we never had a clue where for the best to park other than trying to find a place no more than a sensible within reason walk away from the ground.

Ten minutes' walk away was all that was necessary to Villa Park, but having talked on mobiles to Sam Dooley, son of Kevin and been given directions, I walked in the almost next to the ground pub whose name fails me now to be sociable, with a quick shake of upbeat hello and goodbye hands and then after minimal queuing, our contingent were in Villa Park and placed with not much more than a quarter of a hour wait before kick-off.

## From One Blue Moon to Another

N OT NOW GOING to many away matches in any way, shape, form or abundance, it is with good fortune that I tend still, on these now rare occasions, to run into people that I don't see from one blue moon to another. Running into Chris Lott who no longer lived in Eltham but Petts Wood was most welcome; Chris is twin brother to Joe who with younger brother Mick I spent many an away day out in the very early 1980's. I ran into Danny O'Reilly and Bobby Houselander also; Danny is a lorry driver who had worked for paper merchants in St Paul's Cray and who I had met through arranging their clients' late request urgent same-day courier deliveries. I had last seen Danny at Wigan away on that last league game of the season in 2003/04 when successfully pushing for a Premiership play-off place culminating into a defeat at the hands of Crystal Palace. With Bobby, I hadn't seen him since outside The Millennium Stadium after said Crystal Palace defeat and who though being more known to my brother Terry from days gone by through Terry's friendship with Bob's brother Alan; we had become more acquainted in time at Hammers matches. The first 'real' time though was when I had gone to Loftus road on my own for a night match against Queens Park Rangers in April 1977. I remember being to the back of the terracing having a good chant and cheer with what was probably a good few hundred Hammers fans when a strong arm grabbed my right shoulder from behind. On looking round this bloke was smiling, saying for confirmation reasons, "Are you Graham, Terry Johnson's brother?" The intro stopped there, the chat started and the match finished in a 1-1 draw with Bob "House" after the match dropping me off at Lewisham train station to help ease me on my journey home. Where Bob was living then I don't recall now, but I'm of the belief no doubt somewhere in south east London still?

On attempting to continue my journey back from the ground to the mini-bus, Wolverhampton Steve (as told of in pages 193 - 201) then got on the phone to me but, be it brief due to connection failure, this problem of communication was not helped by all the din going on around; but I managed to get Steve's words of congratulations and his enthusing about Marlon Harewood's well taken goal. After a 1-0 win and victory in place, this meeting with Bob 'House' and exchange of mobile telephone numbers was to culminate with him and daughter Kerry joining us on the mini-bus three weeks later to Cardiff, in what was to be West Ham's 3$^{rd}$ appearance at the Millennium Stadium in successive seasons. This time, though, it was not a contention for a place in the Premiership, it was to contend for the coveted FA Cup and it was to be against Liverpool, perched at this time comfortably in 3$^{rd}$ place in the Premier League and were to finish at the end of the season in that said position, 15 points ahead of 4$^{th}$ placed Arsenal.

## Villa Park Seven-Up

**A**FTER SEVEN VISITS, at last a win for me at Villa Park! One FA Cup 3$^{rd}$ round 1976/77 (0-3) and one league 1981/82 (2-3) defeat at the hands of Aston Villa themselves, then of course, there was the League Cup Final replay 1-2 defeat against Liverpool 1980/81, added to by the four FA Cup semi-finals of drawn matches 1975 (Ipswich 0-0), 1980 (Everton 1-1), defeat 1991 (Nottingham Forest 0-4) and now, that long overdue Villa Park victory over Middlesborough 1-0 2006.

## Frustration if not Juvenile Annoyance

**F**RUSTRATION if not juvenile annoyance for me that despite the initially massive finance agreements put in place, the operations for the new Wembley Stadium soon fell behind completion prediction for the second time of my knowledge and began to run well over budget; disputes became rife between those funding the project and contractors which inevitably brought about a well overrun completion date, making the original completion date and cost look almost like a mockery if not a fantasy. So no 'on time' New Wembley Stadium stops West Ham from opening said New Stadium with Liverpool for the 2006 FA Cup Final and thus prevents the commemoration of just what Hammers had done at the Old Wembley 'White Horse' FA Cup Final with Bolton Wanderers in 1923 some seventy-three years previous. A footbridge leading to the New Wembley however is known as The White Horse Bridge. Such trivia does, even if just for sentimental or throw-in conversational reasons, give rise to coincidental bragging rights, like Hammers being the last team to win at Arsenals Highbury and then the first team to win at their Emirates. Sgood tho'… innit?

## LIVERPOOL FA Cup Final (Cardiff Millennium Stadium) 13/05/2006

S AME AS before, hired vehicle, driver Bernie with pick-up points and arrangements as three weeks prior, but with three stand downs and three replacements. Terry and with daughter Laura-Jane were to be travelling to the final on the Friday and staying at The Jury's Inn hotel on my suggestion for location until Sunday morning along with Terry's wife Jean and Laura-Jane's husband Gary. Terry has cancer and had found the Middlesbrough day to Villa Park three weeks previously overtiring and therefore had chosen to spread the occasion over a two-night stay. Bobby 'House' and daughter Kerry were to take their seats and Dave the Post was joining us this time in place of Rob, who although a season ticket holder and for whatever reason that I can't now put my finger on was not to be attending.

### Vast Experience/Youthful Enthusiasm/It's 'What We Do'

N EEDLESS TO SAY but the beers were on the go again and with general chit-chat being bounded about, we found ourselves unison in agreement that with Liverpool's vast experience in comparison with West Ham's youthful enthusiasm and visual team spirit this match potentially could have all the ingredients for a very good football cup final regardless of outcome. The drive through London was again clear to the M4. A five-minute stop of necessity was held at Heston services before the familiar if not becoming ritual pullover at Membury services. Newcomer Bob 'House' made the comment of "Why we stopping here?"—meaning, why so soon after Heston, and it was gently explained that 'It's what we do'. After the 'come to be expected' pit stop we were on our way again. The services as with the Crystal Palace and Preston North End play-off finals again were rammo but as I saw it not quite up to the atmosphere of certainly Preston one year prior.

## Advance Party Butter Up/NEWPORT COUNTY FA Cup 3rd Round 78/79/Bobby Moore's 'Cousin'?

**P**HONE CALLS had been made where to meet up with the 'advance party', who it was to be established had done a good reconnaissance job; our meet-up was to be in a private members' club of political status or of CIU (Club and Institute Union) affiliation of which Terry and Gary would have had such membership. The advance party of four—Terry, Jean, Gary and Laura-Jane—had 'buttered up' the authoritarians of the club and so although not being members we were welcomed and accepted on arrival. The club was not a five-minute walk away from The Jury's Inn and that would mean not much more than a sensible walk to the stadium.

Draught beer now, not bottles or cans, I get talking to a couple of welsh lads who had been to the Hammers away to Newport County FA Cup 3rd round match in season 1978/79; they remembered it was 'Pop' Robson who scored for us in their 2-1 win and I took enjoyment recalling the well struck shot and goal that left 'Pop's' foot that night. These lads then introduced to us the cousin of Bobby Moore; although there was no given proof, it was quite clear no appearance of a wind-up was evident and what now doesn't help, I don't recall the name of "the cousin"—should I try to investigate a possible confirmation?

## The Millennium Stadium/Contingencies for Thousands

**W**ALKING to the ground viewing the streets packed with Hammers fans swigging beer, blowing horns and singing in packed pubs is something else—the eyesight is a sea of claret and blue, hats, scarves, shirts, flags and whatever! This fantastic atmosphere gave a feeling of immense on the day togetherness and friendship. The wonderful thing about a stadium such as the Millennium is that it has been designed especially for such an occurrence and purpose and can cater for an influx of tens of thousands in number. Contingences are all in place and from the motorways (and no doubt alternative routes) there are directions for opposing supporters, ushering them in directions of individual unity and so, of course, what I was witnessing in this part of the town and end of stadium to house Hammers' supporters, was similar behaviour patterns that were no doubt happening amongst Liverpool fans just a few minutes' walk or so up the road.

## Programme 'Issues'/Fortunes 'Not' Always Hiding

**W**ALKING AND GETTING CLOSER to the turnstiles, my attention is drawn to the fact I have not come across a single programme seller, but he who seeks will find and, yes, I find! I patiently queue with others but then within touching distance the programme seller's supply runs out. Concerned and inquiring where I can go to get a programme, the programme seller tells me he personally will be back in the same position with more programmes at half time. Half time comes, the score is in Hammers' favour by 2-1, happy for sure if not a little surprised, but this is Liverpool…. A Jamie Carragher own goal and a predatory goal from Dean Ashton had put Hammers into a 2-0 driving seat before Djibril Cisse was to pull one back. So here I am again with many others in the programme queue and viewing same said programme seller but again as before his supply runs out! Looking round with more concern than pre-match run out programme concern, I see another programme seller, so getting a shift on and joining new queue… yeah, you've guessed it, runs out. "No more left," I get told.

Looking around I approach an official/steward-type person about programmes only to get told "Well, we did have 60,000 printed" in a 'so can't be bothered matter of fact' way. This touched a nerve and I told him assertively in words to the effect that if that answer is meant to satisfy then I feel for you, as even with me having had a right good jolly up I could work out 70,000 plus in attendance doesn't go into…. What did he say?

As cup finals go this one I felt was one of the better ones, a match that went the full distance, six goals shared in a 3-3 draw at the full time ninety minutes with no added score in the fifteen minute two halved extra time period. Three good goals from Liverpool, fortunes were not always hiding with the Hammers' goals though with Carragher's own goal and Koncheski's wayward speculative cross cum shot, the resulting and deciding penalties went for Pool. On watching a taped video re-run of the match the following morning I can't help but remember an extract of what Steven Gerrard the Liverpool skipper said when being interviewed a few minutes after the match: "We felt our best chance was penalties."

## Pre-Prepared Text/Membury Services KFC/Summary Text

T**EXT MESSAGES** to me were flying around after the match as they do from friends and associates offering condolences. The result however had not affected me in anyway as in days gone by; adverse as well as positive results could and would take a major hold on me and my feelings, but the game as a sport and as a business had been changing and was having its effect on me, as well as being that much further down the line in years. The combination of win, lose or draw were now not having the impact that once I had little control over. After the first two texts I pre-prepared a reply freeing me a little of reply concentration, so providing it fitted with the text received, only the name of the person I received such text from was needed to be brought back up and the send button pushed. The text had read something like this: "On the day someone has to win and it wasn't to be us today, it's the beauty of sport and we can try again next year. It's been a fabulous FABULOUS season and you never know West Ham could still open the New Wembley next year as they did The New Wembley in 1923." A good travel journey home, although as expected, so much quieter and not much life going on, but guess what? Yes, you've got it, Membury Services for KFC and three pieces of chicken and chips! The mini-tradition was kept and probably only kept through tradition. It would have been rude not to. The following Wednesday I sent this text to a girl-friend who had earlier texted to ask me how I felt, what was my day like, what did I think of the game? Now having had the time to think, dwell and reflect, my reply had read: "I couldn't be sad Saturday, I'm thick skinned about results now, we played well in front of millions and that matters to me. At the beginning of 05/06, safety 17th would have pleased but 9th, a FA Cup final and with the way achieved... SUPER." Don't take me wrong, I wanted to win; you know that, but sometimes winning isn't everything. Credit and respect in itself is important. With Liverpool's mass experience and our boys' youthful enthusiasm I felt the match had expectations and I wasn't disappointed. Three good 'Pool goals, Deans was an opportunist's predator type goal and from where I was I could see Konckeski's cross-cum-shot was going to cause goalkeeper Pepe Reina problems. Gerrard paid West Ham a big compliment when he said penalties was their best chance. Were Liverpool not European champions last season? Were Hammers not in The Championship?

## Cup 'Superstition'/Live Sky TV Lure/Satisfying Self-Cooked Dinner/Jovial Lubrication

**E**VERY FA CUP MATCH I went to in this 2005/06 season except Manchester City away—was 'that' the reason we never won the cup this year? Football fans are well known for having superstitions and I don't really have any but was this my punishment? I had been to all FA Cup matches in successful triumphs leading up to Fulham '75 and Arsenal '80 finals and was teased this time to the point of victory until that last gasp Steven Gerrard equaliser in normal ninety minutes with four to be added. Was it that if Hammers were to win the FA Cup it had to be on the god not known to me promise that I went to all lead up matches to the final? Trust me, this stupidity did and does cross my mind even now, so perhaps in me there is, just is, a tinge of superstition?

I had delivered sacks of disguised credit card mail to the Chelmsford Royal Mail depot so easily seen from the A12. It was Monday 20<sup>th</sup> March and 2.30pm on the day of the match, Chelmsford to Manchester is not the most difficult of journeys and as a driver of many miles, the journey on to Manchester in no way for me was a put off. I pulled over to the side of the road, deliberating whether to drive to Manchester even though I had no ticket. The strange thing was there was a massive lure in me believing this could be another year for the final and this deliberating was a 'for some time' pullover and not just a five-minute ponder. Having recently bought a small house in Blackfen and being self-employed along with times could be better, going to Manchester would cost me, an issue that once would not have been entered into as going to West Ham would have been the paramount, and a weekend of stay-in or the normal cut down on whatever sacrifice I chose would be a small price to pay.

The overriding fact now, though, was football for some time did not have, or came anywhere near close to the almost uttermost hold on me that for much of my life it once had. I had let the change in the on/off pitch game and antics as well as the behind the scenes running of clubs at all levels within 'top flight' football affect me. I started my van and with an almost uplift of determined strength I decided against going; within this tough thought testing deliberation, I had weighed up every angle of plus and minus that I could think of and it was my at last admitting to myself long waning of interest that was probably the decision-deciding force factor. The fight for holding on to this, my relationship with West Ham, was all but doing me in, a relationship that I felt had become one sided, so perhaps I should have walked away three or four seasons before; but I remembered past times, and the reasons why I must/just had to carry on!

During this time struggle a change in me must have been noticed amongst my Dr Marten seated companions; it would be correct to say I wasn't getting so involved within match or social conversations and the economic climate was weighing me down a little also, two facts being major factors kept internal and not known to them. The thought and knowledge of the match being shown live that night on Sky TV, that a few lads were gathering to watch it at Plumstead Kirkham Street workingmen's club, was perhaps also helping my non-attempt of travel and possible 'not get a ticket' decision along, a decision no doubt influenced with the added bonus of knowing an already rumbling tum would have a satisfying self-cooked dinner.

Watching the match on the club's big screen was to end with a 2-1 Hammers win and throughout our viewing, our pleasure was added to and ably washed down during and after the game with jovial beer lubrication. The thought of non-attendance of the match and after such a good, GOOD away win was still to play on my mind that evening, even as I was socialising. A semi-final was next, one match away from the final, but even knowing this possibility and my feelings before the match and with the thought this could be a 'final' year, I really had to start being honest with myself. The truth was my main disappointment should we get to the final would have been I hadn't attended all matches leading to a final in my adult, being allowed to go and attend years when I could have. If and having reached three FA Cup Finals over a year span of thirty one, with the only non-attendance to the Arsenal final of 1980, for reasons I think excusable, it was a record now ruined, I would have still liked to have kept.

After a very bumpy West Ham managerial start and Alan Pardew's take-over as manager for his first match against Burnley on 18th October 2003, Pardew had now won over the majority of Hammers fans and I for one was looking forward to continued team building, bonding and development with what I felt could be better times ahead.

### The Boys of '86 20th Anniversary Dinner 17/11/2006

the **BOYS OF '86**

# 20th Anniversary Dinner

Friday 17th November 2006

at West Ham United, Boleyn Ground,
Green Street, Upton Park

7.00 for 7.30pm. Carriages 1.00am

**H**AVING OBTAINED thirteen autographs of the eighteen that played in 1985/86 at Heybridge Swifts some three years prior, a Boys of '86 20th Anniversary was to be held on the 17th November (my late father's birthday) at the Boleyn ground. I had made a telephone call to Mr Len Herbert of Boys of '86 Events Ltd at what I assumed would not be an inconvenient time but in fact caught him queuing at a checkout of a B&Q superstore. How I had his telephone number now for the life of me I have no idea, but perhaps it had been supplied in a West Ham home programme advertising the evening? Len could not have been more accommodating and talk we did re the forthcoming anniversary dinner, but with me in the comfort of home and he keeping his place warm in the B&Q checkout queue. Without being overly detailed due to being preoccupied, Len informed me all players had pledged to attend other than Mark Ward who I knew anyway, was spending time at Her Majesty's pleasure and possibly Steve Walford, who was now assisting Martin O'Neil and Aston Villa and who Len informed me would be playing that weekend. Having obtained Mark's signature in the dressing room at Heybridge, if Steve should be in attendance and every player pledge to attend was kept to, my thoughts turned to thinking I could end up with all eighteen players' autographs in my Boys of '86 book (The untold story), and do you know what? That for me was quite a thought.

Booking our return journey for 1am we arrived by mini-cab on the evening shortly before 7pm accompanied by Tony G and Brett Portman, Steve Rees and son Rob who made up our party of five and were already in attendance as they had booked stadium hotel accommodation and were to be staying overnight. We had a quick beer in the hotel bar before making our way upstairs before being shown to our table that was numbered nineteen. Our next objective was to sort out from the bar our on the table with dinner beers.

Matt Lorenzo of Sky Sports at 7.30pm got the evening underway by individually introducing players and special invited guests at their respective tables and this was soon followed by dinner. Tony Cottee and Tony Gale were comperes for the evening and on completion of dinner, went to the players' tables in turn asking a question or two relating to their recollection of the season. This was then followed by a tribute to John Lyall, an auction and raffle with our party member Steve having the good fortune of winning a 2006 West Ham squad signed football shirt.

On completion of the evening's order of events and then carrying on until 'finish', an 80's disco was to be played out to the dance floor. Now having the opportunity and chance to mix with the players, I chatted at the individual tables of Paul Goddard, Steve Potts, Geoff Pike and Ray Stewart, and the different subject discussions I had with each player is stored. On a more relaxed note and in a separate discussion I reminded the player about his prancing about in the changing room at Heybridge Swifts and saying to him, "So it's a myth then, what they say about...?" and we had a mickey-taking banter/giggle to his denial. I talked with Perry Fenwick of Billy Mitchell fame in BBC's EastEnders (I've never actually sat and watched an episode!) before exchanging beers at the bar. I looked around and on viewing, it was obvious to see the evening was going as well as anyone could have expected. Other than actors and sports personnel of which Kriss Akabusi (400m hurdler) was one I conversed with, in attendance also this evening were supporters of past fame notoriety, Bill Gardner (joint author with Cass Pennant of the book *Good Afternoon Gentlemen, the Name's Bill Gardner*) and Cass Pennant (autobiographer, publicist and subject of the big screen film 'Cass'). Talking to Bill that night I mentioned to him that a couple of friends had suggested I write about my life and times as a Hammer and he gave me his number. On my making contact some weeks later, Bill recalled our conversation and we arranged a meet up. On passing him my early stage manuscripts to mull over and any telephone conversations that came about as well as the meet for the return of my writings, I can only say with appreciation that any advice or suggestions he passed my way were listened to with gratified interest. Having now met with Bill but previously knowing him by name and reputation only, I can only speak as I found him: Bill Gardner came across as a most accommodating and helpful man, who I was to learn had a family business; he appeared very content and settled in life, a somewhat far cry from his football-fan involvement and activities of previous years. I was to pass time also this evening with Cass Pennant and I reminded him of ten pence I gave to him as did others to help him with the train fare for an away match at Leeds in January 1975, a match that ended in a 1-2 defeat that I recall well on account of the uneasiness of the walk back after the match to the train station. Cass gave me a pound allowing for inflation! He signed my Boys of '86 book as had Bill Gardner, adding in addition to a comment on me saying, "Ten pence went a long way!"

*Compere for the evening with the other Tony (Cottee) was Tony Gale, another firm favourite with the crowd who went about doing the business often in an un noticed way. TG has to be in my All Time Best West Ham Team that I couldn't do.*

*Mustard, Brilliant... That was Alan (Dev) Devonshire. A True Hammers Great and all round Nice Bloke. His understanding with Trevor Brooking was a joy; at times it would be so good that if talking to others, I'd describe it after as Brooking and Devonshire 'did their party pieces'.*

*Steve Rees showing off his raffle won 2006 West Ham signed squad team shirt. Immediately behind is son Rob, Tony G and Brett Portman.*

*Compere Tony Cottee with Frank McAvennie.*
*A firm favourite with West Ham fans during*
*his two spells as a Hammer.*
*Frank was to acknowledge in later times of his return that the crowd*
*reception given him that day was to be a most definite highlight of his*
*playing career. Between them Tony and Frank were to score 46 league goals*
*and 54 in all competitions in that Boys of '86 season. Frank is seen here*
*holding the microphone, with what looks like to me Ronnie 'Ticker' Boyce*
*being half hidden by his arm and elbow. All three get mentioned in my Best*
*West Ham Teams that I could not do one of, not over a four decade period*
*anyway. Could You?*

*A tight grip with Cass Pennant after giving me £1 allowing for inflation…….*
*"10p went a long way".*

*Bill Gardner, who came across as a most accommodating and helpful man, it*
*did not go without appreciation.*

## Mrs 'John' Yvonne Lyall/From Heybridge Moat House to Boleyn Stadium Hotel Bar

AS THE EVENING CAME TO A CLOSE and people made their exits, our contingent were to have the blessing that because Steve and Rob had booked overnight accommodation at the hotel, we could stay and continue our evening in the hotel bar using Steve's credit card as payment. The mini-cab driver had by now arrived and was parked outside in the stadium car park. A little talk was all it took and he was quite happy for time to drift by, knowing each minute was clocking up waiting time and as he was to inform us, "It's a quiet night anyway." I had chats in the bar with Tony Gale, Phil Parkes and Alan Devonshire, and they were the last of the players I spoke to that night, now the early hours of the morning; but before we were to leave, I was to have with the feeling of much affection a most welcome talk with Yvonne Lyall.

I recalled to her the chat and reason for my intended talk with her husband and then West Ham manager John at the Heybridge Moat House, some twenty-six years before and her prevented intervention of our talk by her husband. I went on to tell her my views and opinions that I had for her late husband, who I had only met once but gave her also my reasons for having those views and opinions. Holding her hand with both mine and of course with controlled weakness after so many beers not at a premium, dignified emotion was shared, but the caring look on her face of thankful appreciation of my now shared words with her was easy and plain to see.

## Come Forth Steve Walford

OH WELL, Steve Walford's Aston Villa commitments I must assume were unavoidable this evening and it is his autograph that is now the only all elusive one for my Boys of '86 book (The Untold Story).

## Season 2006/07... Yeh... Season 2006/07

**T**HREE GAMES PLAYED, home to Charlton 3-1, away to newly promoted 'play out of our skins' Watford 1-1 and an excellent away performance at Anfield, although only watching it through a television screen in The Three Blackbirds Sizzler pub Blackfen was to result in a 2-1 defeat. This start to the season of one win one draw one defeat was a prediction of somewhat ease for many after the finish of last season. Worth a fiver in the bookies, of course it was, but me not being a betting man, no undertaking took place—with the no doubt likelihood if a bet by me had taken place the prediction of ease would have gone skew-whiff! It's the reason you don't really see a poor 'bookie', for 'simple', 'obvious', 'guaranteed' results or 'bankers' is what they rely on. Football bets in their shop windows by turf accountants is now a norm, the sweetener of possibility can even convince from possibility to the likely so even without initial intention, a walk in will happen and the example bet on show is placed. I give as an example Wolverhampton Wanderers v West Ham. Devonshire to score first, £10 wins £150. I've no doubt over the few days before the taking place and kick-off of the match, an advertised bet such as this in a bookies window prominently placed, football fan walker-bys could and would be enticed to this 'distinct' possibility. Dev, should he have one of his better, 'more prolific' goal scoring seasons, would still only mean he'd knock in around the six mark (My, did he make a few though—what's the word used today, 'assist'? And of course I'm not forgetting those half to three quarter length pitch runs into the box and the subsequent penalties); but this put in your mind dangle of a carrot does and will work. I'm not the greatest lover of either dog or horse racing but even so I'm not averse to attending a dog track or horse race course meeting, and having witnessed six counters taking bets with only one paying out says it all for me.

West Ham had got off just to the start that was needed and perhaps even expected if sustained progress was to continue. At the time of the Liverpool defeat and the upcoming league televised match of Aston Villa on September 10, Hammers made a most celebrated coup in the double signing of young Argentinean 'phenomenons' Carlos Tevez and Javier Mascherano. With the progress made from Championship to Premier League 9th position and FA Cup finalists in 2006 and now, with a three-game new season start that epitomised the previous thirteen months or so, optimism and the taking for granted that the corner had been turned was rife among many a West Ham fan and perhaps even the neutral observer. However, a 1-1 draw at home to Villa was followed by five league defeats without the conversion of a single in favour goal. To make matters worse, defeats at home 0-1 and away 0-3 in both legs of the UEFA Cup 1$^{st}$ round again, without a goal to credit at the hands of Italian club Palermo, added to rumour of possible unrest within the player camp since the arrival of the talented Argentineans. Defeat at the hands away to Chesterfield (1-2) in the League Cup 3$^{rd}$ round towards the end of October compounded the belief West Ham had issues, but double home wins, firstly over Blackburn 2-1 and then Arsenal 1-0, gave lift that the rot, though prolonged, had now been stemmed.

### Icelandic Consortium Takes Over but Slide Continues

**T**WO FURTHER 0-1 defeats away to Middlesbrough and Chelsea was sidetracked somewhat with the announce-ment of a consortium takeover headed by former Icelandic football president Eggert Magnusson but financed by Icelandic billionaire Bjorgolfur Gudmundsson. This sort of revelation in my view is more associated with 'other clubs' rather than West Ham and was never far away from TV headline sports news or national newspaper news and, yes, it was happening at West Ham. At the end of the week a Saturday win at home to Sheffield United by 1-0 was then followed by three more goalless defeats of 0-2 away to Everton and the same score line at home to Wigan with the third a 0-4 reverse at Bolton Wanderers on December 9.

Pardew was tin tacked two days later on the following Monday after what was reported as being West Ham's worst period of results in seventy years. Appeasement was required as Pardew had now become a firm favourite with many Hammers fans despite this run of abysmal bad results. Tevez was getting a run of games but Mascherano was being used as very much a bit player, giving rise to speculation and rumour that should he play a specific amount of games for West Ham a payment clause was in place? The fact was nobody seemed to know what was going on and quite frankly, my interest was not of the greatest due to the game's changing face and I was allowing it to affect me in high percentage quantities.

## Alan Curbishley Takes Over Management but Slide Continues

**A**PPEASEMENT for fans came in the form of Alan Curbishley, a free agent since his departure from Charlton Athletic some seven months prior, and a placement for Alan Pardew within seventy-two hours if not forty-eight? This gave rise to obvious thought that preparation and planning had been put in motion beforehand and a 'done deal' had already been put in place? Alan Curbishley is a manager not known for controversy; he is dignified and composed in speech and had done a good consolidation job at Charlton Athletic, a position he had held in total, firstly as joint manager with Steve Gritt and then solely, for what I believe was fifteen seasons with many of these seasons being held within Premier League status. Not known also for a flamboyant management appearance in character or style, his dignified manner I felt would be accepted by the West Ham fan albeit with mixed and muted feelings.

Having had routes with the club as a young player, many a more senior supporter would remember first-hand his West Ham associations. Curbishley in my opinion was a manager of conserve, caution and method, a surprising perhaps even negative outlook of football expression having played under the free flowing management styles of Ron Greenwood and John Lyall. However, the game has changed and it's a most definite, different ball game now for managers from just twenty years ago. I can't speak of the reasons for different management approaches but sometimes the style managers adopt could possibly, or even likely be influenced by pressure and precaution of job security, as well as restriction of team development due to the lack of finance available, or perhaps just their way and approach, anyway?

Alan Pardew was back in management, coincidentally at Charlton Athletic within two weeks of his West Ham 'failings'. I had been saying for some time and before his West Ham coming of end that he had all the potential and prospects for a possible future England manager. I have no reason or grounds to change my mind or view and feel but perhaps not for a number of years, depending on how his career pans out and where it takes or sends him, I for one will not write this man or possibility off.

## READING (Away) Barclays Premier League 01/01/2007

S TEVE REES was to drive, Kevin Dooley and Chris Fowler were to come to mine and this was the meet up place. As friends together and all being lifetime Hammers supporters, we had been to numerous away matches over the years; but when the subject was brought up on this travel, we found it strange that this group of four had never previously been to an away game together as in this ratio. These days through life's natural courses getting together as a group was most rare, but these three lads to me have been fabulous friends over the years and it all stems way back to mid-teenage introductions. We'd all played the clown over the years and with reminisce and memory, youthful humour took no time to take its place on our travel. The journey to Reading went without any hiccup and after sussing the ground location we went to find a convenient watering hole. The Claddagh Inn was where we were to end up but at this time it wasn't open. On tiptoe and then with a half-hearted jump to peer through a window, I saw movement. Drawing attention by knocking on a window brought an opening of the pub door and the allowing of our entrance. New Year's Eve had taken place some close to twelve hours earlier and the resemblance of revelry was evident. The disco equipment was still on display as was beer glasses and crisp bags on tables and chairs placed in a sporadic manner; you could see the mopping up process had just been got underway or had been being done but not in the most industrious of ways. Beers were poured our way and we got chatting to a couple of the 'stay out' locals who had made their bedding for the night in the bar area. Sticking on the juke box, playing pool and being very socially welcomed had made the start to the day just as we would have wanted, and being with these three friends gave a good feeling and it would have been unanimous.

Reading 6, West Ham 0. It's my thirty-ninth season and I cannot recall such an inept (and there has been a few) performance—nothing constructive, no pattern, no passion, no idea or want for better and, put in a nutshell…

JUST NO NOTHING. And yet do you know what? The four of us as did the majority of Hammers fans on this day sang almost continually throughout this absolute horror show. For me I think it had something to do with the friends I was with combined with my disillusionment defiance with what was going on at 'my club' and football in general.

On our travel home the banter was still positive. It was raining and dark. Steve was in the wrong lane on the M25 during road works and had no choice but to come off at the M23 turn-off and head south towards Gatwick Airport. The chorus of "You're not fit to drive this car" erupted with Steve nodding his head in agreement before joining in and adding his vocals with, "I'm not fit to drive this car!" Using the Gatwick Airport slip junction as our turn around we headed back north (from where we had just come from…Steeeeve!) and returned to the M25 coming off at Junction 6, stopping off for an hour or two in Oxted Village before home—BRILLIANT.

The next morning however the reality hit, and the manner of result annoyed me; I wasn't a happy bunny any more by any short or curly. My friends had given me a fabulous day and that was what had distracted me from the match reality, but now they weren't here, now it was the result and the manner of the result that mattered. Hammers chairman Eggert Magnusson said with recognition and as an apology that he would give free coach travel to all those who went to the match for the forthcoming Aston Villa away fixture. I don't know all the away songs that are sung now but the one that touched a nerve that day at Reading was the one of centre half Christian Dailly. The words of being the 'Love of my life' and 'wanting curly hair too' amused me, but the middle line does not apply as I have no wife.

*Reading away 01/01/2007 and Mixed Emotions.*
*Three terrific lads, holding the Reading 6-0 defeat programme between Steve Rees and Kevin (DooBags D'Pooley)) Dooley is Chris Fowler, still looking content and pleased with themselves before departure from mine. With stark reality however, I wonder how they woke?*

## Who Really Knows?/Do You Know What Really Went On?

C OME JANUARY 2007, Mascherano had not and was not to play under Curbishley management and departed for Liverpool soon after his management appointment. Tevez however continued to get extensive runs in matches, be it as a start player or substitute. Mascherano pitch-wise had fallen into obscurity but in his time at West Ham, was mentioned in many a conversation mainly through speculation as to why he wasn't being picked and playing. Contract complications for both players became apparent and all was not as it seemed. A West Ham relegation battle was now in full flow and clubs sucked into the situation facing the same possibility, but in the main Sheffield United and Wigan pushed for the fact Carlos Tevez was an ineligible player and points should be deducted. An independent disciplinary committee was set up by the Premier League and hearings in April 2007 were to take place; irregularities in registrations for Mascherano and Tevez were acknowledged owing to a third party involvement and a £5.5 million pound fine was imposed on West Ham, but no three point deduction that had been campaigned for was docked or sanctioned. What's more, the decision was irreversible under FA rules and Tevez was cleared to continue playing for West Ham to the end of the season. Speculative rumours went round in circles that Hammers had not been deducted points as the feeling was their plight was untenable and relegation avoidance was not likely to be an issue. Coming towards season closure West Ham were to win all four of their last remaining games, 1-0 at home to Everton, 3-0 away to Wigan, 3-1 at home to Bolton and then the concluding game being a 1-0 away win on the last day of the season to already crowned champions Manchester United. Carlos Tevez, although not scoring at Wigan but having scored twice against Bolton, was now to score his sixth goal in a total win count of seven out of the final nine matches. He ended the season as player Hammer of the year and what I would consider a considerable cult figure for many West Ham faithful.

Unlike thirty seasons prior as written later (**Home Elation/Manchester United 16/05/1977 Page 168**) results elsewhere would count; Sheffield United was at home to Wigan on the final day of the season with a draw being their guarantee of survival regardless of the West Ham result at Manchester United. Sheffield United was three points ahead of Wigan but a reversal just by a single goal would leave Wigan with a superior goal difference by the smallest margin of one. Wigan won 2-1 at Bramall Lane and thus Sheffield United was relegated.

### Tevez Joins MANCS/SHEFFIELD UNITED go for the Jugular/Arbitration/Sir Philip Otton

**A**T THE END of the season but before the start of the following, Tevez left West Ham for Manchester United but Sheffield United would not let the case drop although now with Wigan having survived relegation, their interest appeared to have lost any previous momentum with immediate effect. In July and before the start of the 07/08 season Sheffield United forced a further hearing but failed in their appeal of the non-reversal of points and relegation was sustained; however with Sheffield United now feeling they had been dealt an unfair bitter blow compounded with the now loss of massive financial revenue, went for the West Ham jugular as a means of compensation. Due to what were probably unprecedented, most unusual circumstances, a private independent arbitration tribunal under FA rules was set up comprising of one member nominated from each club and one individual member acceptable to both parties. This hearing decision was agreed by both Sheffield United and West Ham to be final and binding and after all deliberations considered, the tribunal was to rule in favour of Sheffield United. The case of claim and counter claim between Sheffield United and West Ham had gone on for many months with Sheffield United now being awarded substantial damages. Conflicting reports suggested varying amounts of pounds from West Ham and anything between fifteen and forty million was thrown around, but the actual figure to my understanding was never disclosed? This at last totally finalized conclusion was to take place at a hearing in the month of September 2008; I understand the settlement figure was decided in October 2008 with payment to be made in March 2009? Sheffield United had 'won' a long drawn out 'victory' for sure, although the main aim before the start of the 2007/2008 season, if reversal could have been ruled possible, would have seen West Ham deducted points and therefore relegation with then their own reinstatement within the Premier League, a decision that sitting arbitration chairman Sir Philip Otton said he would have reversed and insisted upon had he sat on the original panel, a ruling if implemented would have seen West Ham United relegated on the last day of the season by means of goal difference.

|   |   | **P** | **W** | **D** | **L** | **F** | **A** | **Pts** | **GD** |
|---|---|---|---|---|---|---|---|---|---|
|   | West Ham United | 38 | 12 | 05 | 21 | 33 | 59 | 41 | -26 |
|   | Fulham | 38 | 08 | 15 | 15 | 38 | 60 | 39 | -22 |
|   | Wigan Athletic | 38 | 10 | 08 | 20 | 37 | 59 | 38 | -22 |
| R | Sheffield United | 38 | 10 | 08 | 20 | 32 | 55 | 38 | -23 |
| R | Charlton Athletic | 38 | 08 | 10 | 20 | 34 | 60 | 34 | -26 |
| R | Watford | 38 | 05 | 13 | 20 | 29 | 59 | 28 | -30 |

## I Don't Know (for sure) What Went On

I DON'T KNOW (for sure) what went on behind the scenes in the early months of 2006/07 that was to cause such a rapid decline in spirit, form and fortune after the progress of 2005/06. Of course you hear things from people 'in the know' and you read reports in the media, be it factual or speculation. Household living rooms, offices, building sites, bus, car, train, tram, tube, club, pub, walking down the road and everywhere else you care to consider or mention, would have had not just Hammers fans but football fans in general around the country having discussions and opinions as to what was happening and going wrong at West Ham? What I do know is that Alan Pardew after such a difficult managerial start at West Ham for me was getting things right, for what amounted to monumental early season 2006/07 changes for West Ham, things began going amiss from top to bottom at the club and all was not well. This long drawn out, wearing down, emotion draining and after serious mental comparing to other 'similar' type on pitch seasons deliberation, but never having such levels of dysfunctional internal affairs had ended up with it being my worst, most disappointing if not upsetting I had ever endured as a West Ham supporter and this saying, after such an impressive seven wins in last nine matches finale when relegation for many in March and April was all but a formality.

## The Changing Face of Football (This Man's Viewpoint)

**F**OOTBALL as a sport and business had been changing for some years now and continued to do so. As time passed I was allowing these changes to affect my enjoyment but it just couldn't be helped; sad, really, but my witnessing of players surrounding referees in manipulating and/or intimidating negative protest I considered, could and would deter future promising referees from taking up the profession, and dare I say it, this particular gripe of mine seemed to come from the clubs least justifiable to have reasons to complain and more likely to be financial and on pitch successful. On-pitch player cheating, theatrics, antics and behaviour would or could be copied by youngsters of an impressionable age or nature, and the witnessing of players kissing badges who also kissed a badge previously before transfer irritated me also. I was allowing these actions without any doubt to touch an annoying negative nerve with me and this, combined with inconsistency from governing bodies and officials was now, for me anyway, making the game almost unrecognisable from the game I grew up to like and love.

Players generally in past times tended to 'keep their feet'; they wouldn't necessarily go 'down to ground' by a 'mere contact' and I'm almost sure not through 'no contact' and as far as I can recall, they didn't lay down, roll about giving the appearance of being 'in agony', or walk around with exaggerated 'in pain' expressions as if injured, when everyone witnessing is aware they are not and let's face it, how self-embarrassing is that? Players in fact would do their utmost when it seemed impossible to keep their balance and George Best is perhaps the easiest example of many. If players did get injured it would be quite common for them to 'get on' with the game and keep any pain suffered as a private matter.

What invariably saddens me also and in addition this is without even venturing on the social and domestic lives of players that pick up certain well publicised adverse media attention. Should they be seen as role models or 'are' they role models? Manager bias in pre-, post-match interviews compounded by the public criticism of officials taking away an element of self-dignity would again frustrate and annoy. The England national team, due to having so many foreign players now producing their skills in the Premier League, will give rise to less opportunity and development of home grown talent and some players even then, now having the compliment of being picked for representation, do not appear to have the passion, commitment, dedication or even desire that past players would devote to their country's interest. We also now in higher percentage rates have players retiring prematurely for reasons that are not injury related from international duty, where for me players should want to play or be prepared to play for their country until no longer selected. These personal examples I give are my thoughts, my feelings and my opinions and are a major concern of mine for any future national team success.

We now have buy-outs and business take-overs by certain multi-million or billionaire owners who seem to have very little knowledge of the rules of the game; with this being attached to little or no idea of the history and tradition of clubs, they purchase, aided along also by their possible looming interference in management team control and this no doubt and of course, will be most worrying and unsettling for any manager having constructive ideas and building plans already in place. All this was fuelling my waning of 'top flight' football enthusiasm and I knew that watching lower division football or even semi-professional football, can often supply a surprising 'for some' very highly skilled, committed and entertaining standard and shows little sign of the issues my opinion states that have changed in 'top flight football'. What's more, the cost including beers, travel, and programme etc etc etc can come to less than a Premier League football match entrance ticket.

In saying this, I know it could just be an age thing of mine if not just an opinionated viewpoint. Many would and will not let these changes affect them and will in fact move on and accept it as 'just a sign of the times and the way it is'. Supporters and fans also of less senior years may not be even in a position of knowing the difference in changes and will feel as if it's 'how it's always been' or have an 'I couldn't care' attitude. Could this, therefore, cause rifts in opinion between generational football supporter age groups? Attendances with exorbitant entrance prices still seem to be maintained, as does the purchase of merchandise excess and so, even with the ever (my) changing views and attitudes towards 'top flight football', would I be correct in sensing a marked decline? Many may say it is 'an age thing', a West Ham fan, just an "Any Old Iron" and no more than his opinionated view?

Telephone : **01-472 0704**

# West Ham United Football Co., Limited

*Secretary:*
E. CHAPMAN

*Manager-Coach:*
R. GREENWOOD

*REGISTERED OFFICE.*
**BOLEYN GROUND**
**GREEN STREET**
**UPTON PARK**
**LONDON, E.13**

Your Ref. _____

Our Ref. _____

13th June 1969.

Mr E. Johnson,
4, Cranemead,
Reculver Road,
London. S.E.16.

Dear Sir,

I wish to thank you for your letter of the 5th May in which you were kind enough to include a recommendation from your Son's Sportsmaster and we do appreciate your interest. I am sorry to say though Mr Johnson, that we do not stage trials for young players of such tender years as 11. I do hope that you will fully understand.

May I suggest that you let me know when your Son starts playing again so that I may have one of our representatives come along and have a look at him.

May I also convey to you my very sincere apologies for this late reply to your letter, due to Tours etc. I hope you will forgive me.

Hoping to hear further from you.

Yours sincerely.

W. St Pier.
W. St Pier.    Chief representative.

*The caring side of football 1969 style (even if name detail has been sent to Mr E as opposed to Mr G). A personal letter from Wally St Pier, West Ham United chief scout for many years and who discovered with the help of 'his team', Moore, Hurst and Peters amongst countless others.*

## Hi- Tech Sky TV/Club £Millions/Player Agents

S KY TV now had a major hold on live Premier League and cup football, albeit not necessarily cup final or international matches. In conjunction with this massive new hi-tech change came a complete football fixture turnaround. In the coming years football was to be played on what could be any day of the week that would include Sundays, and played at times of the day that were not previously recognised. Football so acknowledged by most as a 'Saturday sport' had ceased.

With the coming of this new televised monopoly, Premiership clubs are rewarded with payments in the millions of pounds bracket as part of a Premier League and sky television deal. Players now employ agents to advise, negotiate and at times vigorously obtain their most lucrative property and financial share of this deal possible, and I wonder if the agent acting sees it also as a time to take advantage of their own best interests also and not just the player(s) they represent? Costs to attend top flight football matches rocketed and with non-season match tickets now being purchased some weeks before date of play for guarantee, it is not uncommon for Sky and alternative established TV rivals to change the dates and times of matches should they feel fit, thus and of course with the season ticket holder included, preventing the fan (possibly a dad treating and taking a son) to have the pleasure of being able to attend on a specified date, which can be compounded if say a birthday present or treat?

Not having a dish, aerial or cable for satellite broadcasting, I found myself (and to this day) having to go to a pub or political/workingmen's/ Servicemen's or any other drinking social club to watch football, and this was alien to me. I've never enjoyed watching televised football in people-populated surroundings that have no common interest as distractions inevitably occur; a distraction can of course be caused by likeminded people just adding a verbal input or opinion, but it is more off-putting when it has nothing to do with why I'm actually there in the first place. For these reasons, if possible and if on 'normal tele', I will generally watch 'indoors'.

## Sundays are not Sundays/Convenience/Inconvenience

So... Football on a Sunday! Then again, Sundays are not Sundays anymore. High streets are like Saturdays. Pubs are open all day and these distractions for many, started the slow death of the Sunday roast dinner and possibly the Sunday afternoon travel for family social gathering get-togethers. Such changes have happened widespread but is still a generational tradition within my family, visiting mums and dads and therefore grandparents on a Sunday afternoon. I am most pleased to say for me this tradition still continues.

With developing times come changes; inventions for convenience or enjoyment more commonly known as luxuries can bring about materialistic but not necessarily needed desires; the feeling of pleasure with what you have and not wanting what someone else has brings contentment and is for me richness in itself although peace of mind can add to the contentment and take it to another level. Wonderful inheritances if not abilities, though not necessarily related. Missing a train or train cancellation even with the help of being able to inform family, friends or associates with a mobile phone is not the 'end of the world' although I've seen it appear so. The convenience of a microwave oven can prevent the preparation and time waiting of food when feeling hungry and the flick of a button can give warmth and hot water. Is it that with such easiness creeps in a spoilt expectancy, and inconvenience for a growing number of people is a 'mental' swear word? Should I not say I sense it's possible to have an effect on social and domestic lives as well as a work "I want to get paid as much as possible for doing as little as I can for it" attitude? But can I say I tend to be a traditionalist, have faith in long-standing laws or rules and established values that these days certainly as regards to rules and values to my disapproval, seem to be easily moved around for the benefit of whoever depending on their positional status and/or circle, and that to enact disciplined/tough love say from parents of children or similar is not a crime? Over time, for whatever different but imaginative reasons, alteration in common meanings of words that existed for past generations have changed also, and for me this comes with interest if not also with humour in mind.

## Same Word, Different Meaning

**I** HAVE THIS WRITING at home and a selection from this writing I have chosen to share. Let's see: "Big Mac" was an oversized raincoat, "Sheltered accommodation" was where you waited for a bus. "Time Sharing" meant togetherness, a "chip" was a piece of wood or fried potato, "hardware" meant nuts and bolts and "software" wasn't even a word. "Stud" was something fastened to a collar or shirt and "Going all the way" meant staying on the bus to the bus depot or terminus. Cigarette smoking was "fashionable", "grass" was mown, "coke" was kept in a coal shed, a "joint" was a piece of meat you had on Sundays, and "pot" was something you cooked in. A "gay person" was a happy, jovial, good-humoured or laughing person, and "aids" was a beauty treatment or help for someone in difficulty.

## George and Daughter Pauline Pearson

**O** NE OF THE MANY over an age group who would relate to all the old and yet new wordings and meanings of our 'modern' social culture would be George Pearson. George is married to Rose who I had met through their daughter Pauline, one of four siblings and who I have known and been friends with for many years. Pauline has very much been a lady of free spirit and during her having boyfriend times and then marriage to Alan, has always expressed her loyalty and friendship to me in a way that they have all accepted and given their trust. Never, not on any occasion of either visual, hearsay or comment have I been aware of dissidence. Over the years we have met up together but independently of others in the full knowledge of partner or husband and their trust has always been justified. Pauline was having her 40th birthday party. Having come from a past tense East End London family and herself being born in Mile End Hospital, Pauline had lived in Eltham since the age of eleven although the family before then had moved across the water from Stepney to Greenwich when she was five. Pauline's 40th was to be held at the Butterfly Lane Club, Eltham SE9 in the April of 2003.

I would get together with dad George whenever we met up as we would always make a point of a chinwag. Through common interest we always ventured on to West Ham and on this night we got into a deep conversation about "The New" Boleyn Ground. I told him about the changes, about it now being an all-seat stadium and how he wouldn't recognise it! I promised that at some time I would take him over so he could see for himself. George was in his early to mid-seventies and hadn't been to West Ham for many years. It is true to say that some time had come and gone but the promise of taking George was always in my thought; eventually over a purpose-made phone call to him one mid-week evening, the following Saturday was booked and that was that. On picking George up mid-morning, I took the most direct route from Eltham to Upton Park travelling through the Blackwall Tunnel explaining the changes he could expect to see on the way that would also include a hotel.

## The 'New' Boleyn Ground/Stadium

**D**RIVING along the Barking road, passing Prince Regent Lane towards the Boleyn pub, I sensed George looking forward with his head angled but slightly raised left and then slightly right by an inch or so... think of it as looking at number eleven on a clock face and then one o'clock. This slight swaying of head was due to a low rise block of flats that would have been blocking noon or midnight. I could see the old West Stand, now known as Dr Martens Stand, so I knew what I was witnessing, George was witnessing also. I sensed and felt his inquisitive excitement but it was only as we turned left into Green Street at the Boleyn pub, travelled for a further couple of hundred yards and then looking to his right, could George now see The Bobby Moore Stand attached to The Dr Martens Stand, then The Dr Martens Stand being attached to The Centenary Stand that the ground transformation and full view size really kicked in and took hold. How different in size and comparison this was to the old South Bank, West Stand and North Bank. I had seen the development and transformational change for a number of years and had got accustomed to it, but for George...

Once parked in the grounds' car park we walked into the reception area of the hotel—and at this point you could knock George over with a feather! There were two young lads on reception, and I asked if it was possible for them to take George for a quick look at the ground from inside and explained as to why? That 'why' is George hadn't been over to Upton Park for possibly in excess of thirty years! A polite apologetic "no" was given with the explanation that a tour of the ground was in process. Fully understanding, I asked if it would be okay if we went to have a pint in the hotel bar.

With both of us walking to the bar deliberating over the selection of beers on offer, we were taken aback by one unexpected surprise and having not even had time to choose our selected beer to make an order, one of the reception lads came to the bar to tell us that the tour had ended early; he smiled and from two or three yards away waved a set of keys at us. Happily following the young man we became aware within no time of this unexpected treat, that from just asking for a view from the stand of the transformation of the ground for George, we had fallen right on our feet and this was to be a bonus way above our expectations—expectations we never had in the first place but through an instant spontaneous request without thought or practice to the reception staff, brought about a happening that just moments before hadn't even been dreamt of.

Walking along a corridor housing doors to hotel rooms and being shown one or two interiors, entering one of the supporters/corporate boxes and looking over and across the pitch to The East Stand, then looking to the left and right to The Centenary and Bobby Moore Stands was one thing, being inside the West Ham home team changing room, then looking from the entrance door into the away team changing room was another, but what really hit us was walking out of the players' tunnel and onto the perimeter of the pitch. The size in comparison from the old to The New Boleyn Ground or Stadium as it is now known is breathtaking. We were the only three people within the ground/stadium area and… the silence! I think that was what did it for me—THE SILENCE.

The current bun was out and the ground looked spot on. The playing pitch was in excellent order, the stands were swept and clean, the claret and blue colours were a sight to behold, and it was totally empty. This was one right unexpected result. I looked up to the area to where I now sat as a shared season ticket holder with Janet in Row B, Band 2 Dr Martens Stand and with the congregated group of Bob, Colin, Guy, Eric, daughter Liz and not forgetting the man who sits between Bob and Colin and who I spoke to many times but whose name I have never known. I was for the first time appreciating just how big the stand really was, how big The Stadium to the 'ground' once really was, then the wandering thought to what it ONCE was. It may be progress but the before terracing, atmosphere and memories will last for ever. I didn't possess a camera then and I don't now, but I remember thinking, "Oh for a throwaway!"

George was over the moon and I felt as if I had jumped over it with him. The idea initially was to just drive past so he could see the ground changes. Life can be about moments, some you take, some you don't; it is more to do with how on the ball you are at the time and/or how quick thinking. We elate, despond or even regret those made or missed decision instances. The hotel reception lad declined our offer as he was working, but it was the least we could do to invite him to join us in the hotel bar after his gesture. Sitting and drinking a beer I could see George was in cloud-cuckoo land and we both felt as if we were the cats that had got the cream. Most adults in my opinion, given the environment, are privately only grown up teenagers anyway. Holding a fictitious microphone, pumping arms up and down to an imaginary drum or prancing round a living room or bedroom playing an air guitar comes readily to mind, but I can't think why?

## Flat Cap/Ron and WEST HAM Deb/Entertainment was My-WEST HAM'S Defence

**H**AVING NOW REFERRED to the Dr Martens congregated group of Bob, Colin, Guy, Eric, daughter Liz and not forgetting the man who sat between Bob and Colin who I spoke to many times but whose name I have never known, it is impossible not to reminisce about the people I knew during my North Bank history that was had when standing in varying periods on the North Bank terracing prior to May 1994.

In my early twenties I was always to wear a flat cap; it had been bought for me by Lisa from Faith Bros in Lewisham, the same shop where my mum and dad bought my one and only school uniform back in 1969. We were in Lewisham one Saturday early 1981 and Lisa bought me the cap simply because she thought I would "look good" in one. I ended up wearing it everywhere, setting a trend amongst others who were part of The Kings Arms pub "Monkey Club", a name so given to "our crowd" by Scooter (Dennis), but to date I still don't know why, and Clyde was still some months away from being known to the 'group'.

Standing on the North Bank terracing with all the boys from Eltham at home matches was always socially good. Winning was important to me but playing well and being entertained by the team was of importance too. Coming from the days of managers Ron Greenwood and John Lyall, the style of football no doubt had made a lasting impression on me, though don't think it was all rosy; attached to individual matches or periods of total entertainment and fluency that often did not result in a result, was many a dreadful performance, teasing relegation battles and going nowhere in the league mediocrity almost felt like a norm and, of course, we must not forget the two eventual successful relegation seasons of 1977/78 and 1988/89 as this was basically all part and parcel and the ups and downs of being a 'Hammer'.

If and when West Ham ever lost and the match had been televised for Match of the Day or the Big Match, when it came to taking my "ribbing" on a Monday morning from other than West Ham school friends and even in later years from whoever, the way Hammers had played could be a fundamental attack in 'My' West Hams' defence! I remember through many of our jovial fun moments at the ground noticing over a number of games that this man and girl when l looked their way would be looking my way and we would often make eye contact. It was all such a social thing as from the beginning of this eye contact looking away was delayed and smiles in my direction and returned didn't falter.

One home match after West Ham scoring and with the crowd celebrating, on impulse I made my way to them and smiling away as we were we celebrated the goal together; as things settled I asked them why was it when I looked their way, they were looking my way? They told me they had noticed me some time before and said to each other that when they were on their way to a match they wondered if the bloke in the cap would be there? They were standing very close in those days that I can't help thinking being 1981/82 season to the post behind the goal in The North Bank where I was to meet Bob from behind the post some years later.

Ron and West Ham Deb, as she was later to be known, became part of our crowd from Eltham. Years went by and the friendships grew. Deb would often meet up with us in The Boleyn pub before matches. Ron would do the same or meet us inside the ground, depending on time as I can't help thinking he may have worked odd Saturday mornings. Deb (Debra she preferred to be called, never Debbie, but Deb was the closest she ever got to her preference and it was always West Ham Deb if we spoke of her in her absence) would know one or two others in the Boleyn because she had, on occasions, travelled on a football special with West Ham fans to an away match. One of these lads was Mick who with his younger brother and friends were from Erith. I had met Mick also through travel on the away match football specials and the first time he saw Deb and me chatting in the Boleyn pub his first words were "What, you two don't know each other as well?" before taking the surprise in his stride and briefly joining us. Deb throughout our association and for all her commitments and travel to see West Ham never flinched on her insistence she was in fact actually a Manchester United Fan!

Ron worked for Jaguar—or was it Mercedes or was it Dagenham Motors? I'm not sure now but it's possible I'm wrong on all accounts and had struck up a business cum friendship association with Alvin Martin. Ron through this friendship with Alvin would at times ask if it was possible to obtain the odd pair of away match tickets and as far as I'm aware, Alvin managed to fulfil this request more than once although I was never to find out if they were complimentary or if Ron had to pay.

In the lower terracing of the Park Lane end at Tottenham one evening match and at the end of the game I was looking directly above at the seating area set aside for Hammers fans, although up top so many people were standing and making their way to the exits as they were, Ron and Deb stood out. I had not been aware they had tickets and despite all the noise, shoving about, movement and bustle in the lower terrace, Ron and Deb by chance looked down, saw our little group and it was all smiles and waves. Ron and Deb were not a couple in the relationship sense of the word, but were good friends also outside attending football matches. It's a long time ago now but I'm thinking that Ron was married and had a son. Ron was protective towards Deb for all the right reasons and it showed. They were both very well liked; if and when they should be mentioned even now, it is noticeable they are still very fondly remembered and thought of.

*Flat caps were a 'Fashion' amongst the King's Arms crowd; this picture shows me and Clyde at a party in Julie Jones house. Julie later married Keith Unitt, The Best Goalkeeper of any team I played with.*

## Bob, Gerry, Mick, Peter/North Bank Regulars

**A**NOTHER GROUP we stood with for a number of seasons, and again it was something that just came about in the North Bank, were the four lads, Bob, Gerry, Mick and Peter who I can't help thinking came from the Harrow, Middlesex area. Peter was a London black cabbie and looked the part, and it was Pete's black cab that took the lads to Upton Park on match days. Gerry was the quietest of the group but he contributed in his own way and I never saw Gerry without a small smile. Bob and Mick worked together as council colleagues on the dust. Bob also did a bit of weekend mini-cab work and wasn't short of a story to tell. This was also employment that I had taken up during the early to late eighties and for sure I knew what he meant. Mini-cab stories can/will vary, certainly from day to night shifts, but by and large there are those that will intertwine. "Scoops", "revelations" and/or "scandals" so often reported of on "profile" people and "celebrities" in the media naturally happen in all walks of life and I was, before becoming "thick skinned", shocked and surprised by the comings and goings on what can/are happening actually "on your own doorstep". Depending on the subject concerned being discussed or visually viewed, in-depth detail can be obtained and tact, diplomacy, consideration, discretion and even being of an opinion advisory or contributor became all part of the job. It is true to say with local area mini-cab driving, picking up the same customers on a regular basis is most common; not only in my case was a relationship or two formed but also a trust in a driver can develop and I learnt in time that certain customers would want a confidante or if what was to be a 'one off' fare, just someone to talk to. Mick was also just like the rest of their group, one likeable bloke, and we ended up sharing a room on holiday one year in Tenerife. Mick, only knowing me and not knowing the company he was joining, soon settled and fitted like a hand in a glove with the dozen or so mixed group of lads and lassies that stayed at the Las Aquilas Sol Hotel, Puerto de la Cruz.

In January 1995, just eight months after the North Bank terrace closure, West Ham were drawn away to play Wycombe Wanderers in the FA Cup 3rd round. Bob from behind the post lived in Ashford, Middlesex. I drove to Ashford from Mottingham SE9 via the A20 and M25, then in towards London to Ashford on the M3 before coming off at Sunbury and the joining of the A316. On arrival at Bob's and after a cup of tea, the arrangement was then for Bob to drive to the match. Having parked a twenty or so minute walk away from the ground, not at any time did we pass a programme seller. Programmes are my way of keeping a record of matches attended and to date this programme is still missing from my collection, and is one of less than ten in total covering a period of forty years (and yes , * marks the spot, I did get my Liverpool 2006 FA Cup Final programme at the Millennium, thanks to TPS Dean).

On entering and walking on the first part of terracing we came to but still not settled, Bob and Peter from Harrow called to me. I was made up, "Well pleased", one could say. I remember Bob the dust saying to me, "I said to Peter we'd see someone from the old crowd today!" We had the normal catch up of how is and who's doing what questions, but did not stand and watch the match together. All was the same in their home and work lives, but I seem to recall I was told that Mick had got married? What Gerry was up to I'm not sure, but I had asked how he was and I know he was okay.

## Turnstile George and Bootsie

**W**ALKING THROUGH the North Bank turnstiles west side and on most occasions, George would be the man we would pay our entrance money. It just so happened his was the turnstile we entered via at most home games. Trying to think back now but not totally sure, my mind tells me there were three adult turnstiles and one for under 14's, or was it 15's or was it 16's that had a rail separating adult to juvenile?

There was this 'stunner' who walked around the perimeter of the pitch on match days, selling scratch cards or whatever and she used to do this before kick-off and then at half time. Having never spoken to her, it was noticed that at each home match her dress code was to wear blue denim jeans with boots of the high thigh leg type. 'Bootsie' became the name for her amongst us boys in the North Bank. We would regularly see notes and verbal comments passed her way from men in the crowd and we all assumed these notes would contain anything from name and telephone numbers, compliments, feelings of devotion, the please will you marry me types and no doubt the odd note containing basic, blunt comments of testosterone normal running away with themselves male fantasy behaviour. Bootsie always appeared to deal with this attention in the most dignified and charming way and you would see her exchanging words of brief conversation or comment when doing a job everyone could see she thoroughly enjoyed doing. One Saturday home match in late 1980 and as a small group we were all taken back when paying to walk through the turnstile because there she was! Bootsie was here and she was helping George in his turnstile. With myself and the lads having come from The Boleyn pub and full of that confident feeling, I gave Bootsie banter and in doing so it came to light that George was in fact her father!

We began to see Bootsie regularly with dad George at the turnstile; at that time other than banter no other communication was made until the Liverpool League Cup Final replay at Villa Park in 1981. Having gone by car we stopped on the way back at Corley Services on the M6. George, Mum and

Bootsie were at the services walking over the motorway footbridge and that was the first time, albeit only briefly, we talked and not bantered; the conversation was no more of nice and polite with no substance and perhaps even clouded at having just lost the League Cup Final 1-2.

One match Bootsie wasn't there and George told me she wasn't well and in hospital. I had always assumed she had chosen to give up selling what it was when walking around the pitch perimeter to help out her father at the turnstile through preference, but it came to light that this wasn't at all the case and my assumption was far from the truth. As matches and weeks went by I always made a point of asking George how Julia was. In the passing of time and with the easing of familiarity, Bootsie had now become Julia to me, and George told me on more than one occasion that I would be most welcome to visit her in hospital. Julia was being treated in Herbert Ward at The Brook Hospital in Shooters Hill Road not two miles from where I lived with my parents in Eltham. It was an offer I was not to take up for already committed reasons at the time. Having finished that particular period of hospital confinement but with future returns necessary, Julia would be with or not with George as her illness was an on-going condition that gave good, and then not so good days; but whenever it was a West Ham 'good day', we always had our very brief few seconds of 'humour time' at the turnstile before I passed through.

Some considerable time was to pass and on leaving the North Bank and walking towards the exit of the main gates in Green Street, a chance meeting with George, Mum, Julia and other family members after a night match led to Julia coming for a drink with me and pals to The Park Tavern Pub in Passey Place. Julia, as I was to find out that night, was living on our side of the water in Barnehurst and not in East London or Essex as I had always assumed. This coming of awareness pleased me bundles as Barnehurst at a guess is about seven miles and a twenty-minute drive depending on route of travel. With this unexpected convenience we met the following night at Barnehurst train station and a short while after Julia took me to Elm Park, or was it Hornchurch where George and mum lived (Julia's mum's name fails me now). They were a nice family and although not having seen them for many years now, I do hope all's well. Julia was one brave girl and I witnessed in the time we knocked about together more than one painful moment for her, but she was a girl who never complained, not in my company or to my knowledge. I said to her one night friendly, gently and with the hint of smile that she was getting lines around her eyes, mockingly, because she was still in her early 20's. Julia's reply was "They're laughter/smiling lines"—and I believed her. It was a fact that Julia always smiled.

George worked the North Bank turnstiles, west side entrance for a number of years in the eighties and possibly before and for those standing in the North Bank during that period, was the gentleman who often wore a knitted Claret and Blue jumper with his name blazoned across his chest.

I remember West Ham Deb telling me that Julia went to the same school as her and was in the same year but not in the same class and because of this she said, they had separate friends so never really got together or socialised. Julia after finishing her duties and with the match into the second half of play would come onto the North Bank and stand with me to watch the remaining stages of the match. Julia was a social girl but once in the North Bank would stand by me and not necessarily get involved with all and sundry in our group(s). Looking back I can't recall Julia and Debra talking together but it's possible that although Debra remembered Julia from school it can't be said the reverse was realised. Debra was from Upminster.

## Yearly Lingfield Horse Racing/BB Boys and Football Team Friends Remain United

**O**VER THE YEARS but prior to the North Bank groups coming together in the early eighties, I went to home matches with various friends, mates and acquaintances. I also enjoyed taking a Boys Brigade lad or a friend's son to a home match. Each year and normally in the month of May, Colin Lake who first played for my football under 15's side I formed back in 1978 but not a BB member, organises a trip to Lingfield horse racing, a trip and day out I am a criminal of not always attending. It is a mark of the bonded friendships built by the Boys Brigade boys' initial, pushy encouragement of the forming of a football team those years back and now with former team members and invited friends, this trip and day out is almost paramount in the diaries of those who attend on a regular basis.

These lads, by now men, work in varying employments and amongst others would include white collar, qualifying trades, driving or manual and no doubt work of the 'out in open spaces' fresh air types. Many have families of their own and together with the 'unattached' as I now saw it being much travelled, experienced and socially skilled. It's true to say age differences in younger, youthful years can feel as if worlds apart and five or six years' difference between twenty/twenty one year old to a fourteen/fifteen-year-old, can be seen as a 'large gulf between'; but of course it doesn't take long to catch up in behaviour and joint discussion can take on a different and more 'together' level.

On my last trip to Lingfield (was it my last trip?) Robert Saunders ex-BB boy, now London black cab driver, Arsenal fan and family man, said to me on the coach to the "for more refreshments" stop off point after the racing, how he remembered and therefore reminded me of taking him to West Ham for the first time and sitting on my shoulders so he could see. On my shoulders? I'm not so sure for people behind, but being lifted to my eye level is a possibility, but shoulders he insisted. His recollection was that West Ham had lost, (Come on You Irons) but he couldn't say for sure who it was and I'm not putting my head on the block by speculating or committing, Oh alright then Rob, it was Derby County Feb '76 1-2. Another lad I took but more on a semi-regular basis was Richard Ferguson who, like Robert, became an Arsenal fan. Somebody tell me what's going on here? Richard also being a part of this Lingfield set-up was also to play for my under 15's and then under 16's side as goalkeeper and was also a keen Boys Brigade member. It's always nice when once young boys who are now men remember things you did together with a smile and appreciation, and it's easy to slip into fond memory mode.

I missed many a Hammers home game as a boy through playing BB football on a Saturday, and in latter years night matches also due to a Boys Brigade week evening commitment as a senior or officer; but even with these involvements and at varying age stages, my mind would always drift to "How are we getting on?" At the time I really missed not seeing West Ham, but looking back it did me no harm. Youth organisations of whatever type can have for many, long if not always and forever lasting memories with psychological rewards, and it's a personal thought of mine but no doubt shared by many that it is a shame it seems to be a dying trend. Videos and DVD's, TV games, computers etc etc are fantastic inventions, but could they not also be interventions? How nice for parents/guardians if children and teens were to take advantage of the happy medium; not all youth clubs are too far away and in spare time amalgamating both enjoyments could be richly rewarding. Having FRIENDS FOR LIFE (and I don't mean just knowing people a lifetime) is PRICELESS and it wasn't invented!

## Overnight Stays/'View Places of Interest'

**A**T THIS STAGE of my football following and changing attitude to life, should I ever attend an away Saturday match to a city or town, the likelihood is I would now make it a 'weekend away match'. Perhaps preferably with a girlfriend or girl-friend as that in the main would help me (and her) in viewing places of interest in and around the area; with another male accomplice, a bar-propping action could and would be the probable course of action. To make a one- or two-night stay and get a feel of the town or city would make a proper football weekend away. It is true to say that if not for the football, people would probably not visit or have reason to visit the town or city in the first place and unless they have a prior commitment or busy schedule that weekend and affordability is not a concern, why not make the most of it? You never know, it may even be a place that gives reason to return and go back again, football or no football? When going with mates it's often been a beer on the way and a beer on the way back; nothing wrong with that and I've done it time and time again and won't knock it. There was one exception though.....

Bob from behind the post and me went to Wigan away in season 03/04 and stayed in a Travel Lodge the night before the match. We had a bite to eat and a little mooch about pub crawl before finishing off only a short distance or so away from where we were staying in a pub called the Ben Johnson. The pub had live entertainment in the form of a singer/guitarist and was to give us unscheduled extended hours; having been given the nod, staff let the pub quieten down first at closing by allowing those not in the know to leave before the singer/guitarist kick-started the night cum morning again. If a headache was to be obtained, it was mentally relaxing knowing that next day the Wigan ground was only a mile or two away and we had all morning to poodle about and get our act together. A sensible distance away match with overnight stays were much more likely for me now.

## Boleyn Ground Atmosphere/Elation/Home and 'Away' Entertainment/Exhilaration/Woe and while I'm at it, Why not Throw in The Weather as Well?

**A**FTER **40 YEARS** of Laughter/Crying/Despair/Elation/Excitement/ Fear/Frustration/Disappointment and Near Heart Attacks of watching West Ham, I can only put the above emotions together, jumble them up and come up with one word... LOVE, or if stretched to two words... 'LIFE SHORTENING'. Having previously 'hit-on' the subject within titled Seating/Songs/Atmosphere (Page 97) and Terrace to Seats (Page 98), I will be giving reasons 'for first past the post' my Upton Park crowd atmospheric moments within this heading, but for now, and after watching so many games at The Boleyn, my home on the field of play chosen moments are as follows. Please understand me when I say I am fundamentally aware just how problematic it is and not just for me, but the many supporters who have experienced a lengthy period of time spread over a number of decades following a football club with feeling and passion, and of course just how difficult it is or can be to ascertain the reasons for remembering and prioritising particular fixtures, together we would agree, I'm sure, how it is SO not easy?

Yet in saying this, the selected home matches I now give as my choice examples actually came so readily to mind and no doubt, will fuel much debate from anyone choosing to discuss and/or compare my selections. But select I will, and at the end of the day these are my individual memories and personal feelings, though even with the ones I now select to/or prioritise, there will have been many other matches that would have bordered on the minute closeness in comparisons. This is such a dilemma for me as over the years memories can be exaggerated or even deflated, but that is what the passing of time does or can do and no one is an exception!

# HOME ENTERTAINMENT SOUTHAMPTON League Division One.22/09/1981

**T**HE LAST home terraced match I viewed from the North Bank was the closure match for redevelopment into seats played against Southampton on 7th May 1994, and it was again to be a fixture against Southampton that stands out for me for entertainment reasons alone, and compares to any I've seen at Upton Park. It was a match not for West Ham anyway or now, come to think of it, for Southampton either, that was to have any bearing on future outcomes such as a possible Wembley cup final appearance or important placing in the league. It was in fact just an early in the season evening league fixture in the September of season 1981/82. Over the years many an excellent match has been seen and witnessed at Upton Park and in this fixture, West Ham showed their continued development from FA Cup winners of May 1980, to then run away champions of division two with a record number of points based on two points for a win over forty two games the previous season.

West Ham were playing what was probably the most entertaining football I had up until then from past seasons ever had the pleasure and joy of seeing them play. Southampton boasted players of the likes and calibre of club captain Nick Holmes, England regulars Kevin Keegan and Dave Watson as well as England fringe player Dave Armstrong, these players being complemented that evening by having World Cup winner Alan Ball also in attendance. England's Mick Channon was with Southampton but I can't recall him playing. A 4-2 victory in Hammers' favour with goals from a Paul Goddard hat trick and a glorious move finished off by a Geoff Pike slot in had made it for me. It was a match for the purists, and for entertainment value alone stands out in my memory without the need to deliberate.

## LIVERPOOL 14/05/1977
## BB Snooker/The Royal Albert Hall/Transistor Radio

WEST HAM have always been a club and/or team that knows how to keep their fans on their toes; mid-table anonymity would happen but generally in the first division or now known Premier League, and on the very odd times it has happened in my lifetime a push for a top 5th place, (exception 1998/99) or 6th place (exceptions 1958/59-1972/73) has with disappointment, faded away with a number of matches to the end of the season still to play although of course, the 1985/86 3rd placing of, will always be the exception until…?

Relegation battles in said period since 1958 have included last-ditch survival matches but have also in unison factored the dreaded hatch being opened and the fall through the fatal drop down door to the 2nd division or now known Championship being unpreventable. There is however the most memorable match when before kick-off it appeared to all that a win was the only likely way out for survival, and that was in season 1976/77 and that "must win" game was a Monday evening night match under the lights against Manchester United. Hammers had played away to Liverpool just two days before on the Saturday and my nerves had got to the point of racking. The London Boys Brigade had their annual display and The 22nd West Kent Boys Brigade Company of who I was now of Warrant Officer ranking, were performing at The Royal Albert Hall on what was the last full weekend of the football league fixture calendar. A novelty item that all company section boys totalling seventy-two in number, regardless of rank and without exception had some role to play.

I was to have no involvement in the organisation or structural displays of this huge sized novelty snooker match the boys were to perform spread over three shows covered on the Friday and Saturday evenings and sandwiched by a performance on the Saturday afternoon. The boys from the company gymnastic team were the snooker balls wearing appropriately coloured track suits, with company section boys holding green boards around the edges so to form the rectangle table shape with netted pockets being placed in their relevant corner or centre side positions. Green floor matting was laid and this completed the very large snooker table setting that was most dominant over the arena 'stage' floor. Two overly large snooker cues in an organised manner would push onto the white "ball" before rolling and knocking colours into pockets until the adapted allowing for 'time permitting' game came to completion.

My responsibility along with other more senior ranked members was purely as a "keep control of" on-hand helper and for boys to be ready and positioned at the precise moment of arena entry. It was to be the third year in succession the 22$^{nd}$ West Kent company was to be involved at the RAH with a fourth added the following year, a pigeon that was solely mine with organisation and arrangements made with the captain of a West Norwood company; this was again to be a novelty item incorporating a volleyball match but with the twist of table tennis rules scoring between the two companies.

*The Boys Brigade Royal Albert Hall London District Display 1977*

*And again at the same venue and for the same reason 1978*

With the thoughts of Hammers at Liverpool never away from my mind (although I'd like to think multi-tasking and Boys Brigade responsibilities was not hindered), it got just too much so after our BB company doing their Saturday afternoon "snooker bit" on the arena stage, I took it upon myself to go missing and made my way to an exit door.

Having taken a hand-sized portable transistor radio for the sole purpose with me and now having it in my grasp, I sat on the step just three or so feet from the exit door I had just passed through. With my back against the wall, facing the pavement and outside perimeter road, I listened to the closing twenty minutes or so of the second half of the match. The nerves switching on the set not knowing the score was traumatic to say the least, but then the relief of hearing the match was still 0-0 was like an Everest mountain lifting from my shoulders. Listening to a match on radio—I've come to realise that although the commentator gives description of play, player positions and positioning of on the pitch goings on amongst other commentator information, should the match being commented on be shown at a later time on television, I've found my positional pitch bearings in mind and thought have no resemblance to the picture I had envisaged from the commentators wordings in my head! Arousing moments of possibility or even despair were in fact not worthy of a sped up heartbeat or even a concern as later viewing would so often prove. Could a radio commentator be charged with manslaughter?

West Ham at Liverpool and then at home to Man United just over forty eight hours later is daunting by any standard but last two games in a relegation battle… In excess of thirty odd years after this time it is a measure of these two clubs that each season general pre-season predictions of at least one trophy win of whatever nature be it cup or league is profound, not only in early fun small wager predictions amongst friends but of course with the bookmakers. The match was to finish 0-0 and Liverpool were crowned Champions that day. Yes, that was West Ham's obstacle of Liverpool and away at Anfield at that. Turnstile gates had been closed way before kick-off time with thousands locked outside. Liverpool fans for celebratory reasons of another possible championship and thousands of travelling Hammers fans in the feeling of the same emotion of concern and worry as I was having when sitting with the transistor radio outside the RAH on this same day and time. West Ham lived to fight another day and fight is what they had been doing; the Liverpool draw had now seen Hammers only lose once in the last twelve league matches and that had been a 0-3 reverse at Newcastle. Liverpool this season were also FA Cup finalists and could now look forward to a possible domestic league and FA Cup double, an achievement previously held only by Preston NE (1889), Aston Villa (1897) Tottenham (1961) and Arsenal (1971). Liverpool's opponents… Manchester United, the team that now stood in our way of either survival or relegation.

## HOME ELATION/MANCHESTER UNITED 16/05/1977

I **'VE ALWAYS REMEMBERED** the crowd attendance that night. The simple reason for this was my bewilderment at the 'comfortable' space around me on the terracing. Having now stood being pushed, barged and not being able to lift my arms without a struggle in many a "full house" or "a very close to" I was baffled that for a match hanging so much in the balance and after the magnificent lifeline result at Liverpool only two days before, an attendance of only 29,000 + was the reward for a match that prior to kick-off and looking at all the statistics hinged on survival or relegation.

Manchester United at Upton Park since Hammers promotion of 1958 from division two has always been a match that had drawn a full-house or "a very close to" attendance, with the exception of seasons 1962/63-1963/64 when the attendances were below the 29,000 + as on this evening, and the season of our cup final win over Fulham 1974/75, when the attendance was zilch as Manchester United had been relegated in 1973/74 and were playing in division two. A season that so almost had the Hammers joining and suffering the same fate as the Mancs due to having precariously hovered around the drop zone for basically the entire season, the results of mid-week re-arranged matches that 73/74 season not involving West Ham had meant superior goal difference in Hammers' favour would mean another season in division one, regardless of their own result at home to Liverpool or results elsewhere in the final full calendar schedule of Saturday fixtures that coming weekend, or to be played two days later on the following Monday. Six points from the last six games was enough for Hammers as they took three of those six points from relegation rivals Southampton (two at home and one at the Dell) and these were the all-important matches that reversed who stayed and went between West Ham and Southampton with Manchester United and Norwich City.

So... Manchester United, last match of the season at home under the Boleyn ground lights and despite having suffered only one defeat in twelve, remaining league matches showed on the night that a must-win before the match with other teams dragged into the mire playing this night and on the coming Thursday was the only certainty of relegation avoidance; Manchester United although having a cup final to play just five days away took the lead in less than thirty seconds through a Gordon Hill clip over the diving at his feet goalkeeper Mervyn Day and showed throughout the match that no favours were heading West Ham's way, an equaliser by Frank Lampards thunderous shot low in off a post from a Brooking corner on thirty minutes and then a missed penalty by Geoff Pike just before half time pointed to the fact that this was one full-on match, nothing was guaranteed and Man U were replying by hitting Hammers at every opportunity and playing football with no concern or thought of an FA Cup final that coming Saturday.

Half time saw the fans' nerves, excitement and encouraging optimistic expectancy of a favourable Hammers' result but no one in the ground could be sure of what lay ahead in the second half and the forthcoming forty-five minutes. Pikey was to score early in the second half and that would have made him feel better and the crowd easier after his missed penalty, although pondering on the missed penalty earlier was probably not an issue with Geoff because this was in the truest of words, a match for West Ham of nail-biting and then down to the elbow proportions, getting on with it was all that mattered. Bryan "Pop" Robson a top...TOP footballer and goal scorer by anybody's standards who along with Billy Bonds, so unfortunate not to be capped by England scored goals three and four, these goals aptly sandwiched by Stuart Pearson's looping shot over Mervyn Day is for a West Ham supporter, so typical, and I'm sure West Ham do it just to keep their fans dangling on the edge, and because it has happened so many times you wonder whether its deliberate... Na, they've never been that good.

Hammers finished the match relegation free, Manchester United finished placed sixth in the league and went on to win the FA Cup final beating Liverpool by two goals to one thus preventing Liverpool from being only the fifth club to win the coveted double League and FA Cup acclaim and what would have been only the third club up until then within the 20th century.

Tottenham having already been relegated were joined this evening by Stoke City who lost away to Aston Villa. The last place to be taken on the coming Thursday evening was between Bristol City, Coventry and Sunderland. Bristol City were to play Coventry away at Highfield Road but with Sunderland having the better goal difference, a draw at Everton would mean survival. The table below gives you the outcome as well as the answers:

|  | P | W | D | L | F | A | PTS | GD |
|---|---|---|---|---|---|---|---|---|
| West Ham United | 42 | 11 | 14 | 17 | 46 | 65 | 36 | -19 |
| Bristol City | 42 | 11 | 13 | 18 | 38 | 48 | 35 | -10 |
| Coventry City | 42 | 10 | 15 | 17 | 48 | 59 | 35 | -11 |
| R Sunderland | 42 | 11 | 12 | 19 | 46 | 54 | 34 | -08 |
| R Stoke City | 42 | 10 | 14 | 18 | 28 | 51 | 34 | -23 |
| R Tottenham Hotspur | 42 | 12 | 09 | 21 | 48 | 72 | 33 | -24 |

## HOME WOE/LIVERPOOL League Division One 29/04/1978

**G**REAT DISAPPOINTMENTS and upsets were to happen over the years, as it does for all supporters whichever their club of choice. The defeats by Stoke City League Cup semi-final of 1972 at Old Trafford and Anderlecht in the European Cup Winners Cup Final of 1976 at The Heysel Stadium will always be forefront in disappointment cup memory as will league matches for positional importance. Another reason for not wanting a disappointing adverse result would of course be for rivalry purposes and feelings of pride. If someone was to sit me down and put me on the spot and ask me "What really was my most upsetting moment?" then I would have to say Liverpool at Upton Park in the final league match of the season 1977/78, only one season on from which we had salvaged the most precious of points at Anfield to help stave off relegation almost twelve months prior. This match was to be the final nail in the coffin of the first of four relegations I have had to endure with so many other Hammers' fans since my first West Ham match attendance in 1968.

Having listened to the radio after Boys Brigade table tennis club situated in the print room, and winning away 2-1 against Middlesbrough just four days prior through a double strike by "Psycho" David Cross, a win at home to Liverpool would have seen Hammers stave off relegation. David Fairclough was the so known and called super sub for Liverpool and was villain to West Ham this day as he scored twice in a 2-0 Liverpool victory, although I can't help thinking in this match Fairclough played from kick-off? Seeing Billy Bonds give chase before his second goal is about all I remember of the actual match itself but remembering the stark reality of relegation and second division football the following season, with dozens of fans standing behind the North Bank goal and terracing almost in defiance is something I find easy to recall. 'Hi Ho Hi Ho We are the West Ham boys' was the song repeated over and over, but as I stood and looked at the sizeable group and then around the ground at the many, many stragglers either standing around or slowly making their way to the exits fifteen minutes or so after conclusion, I too found myself not being able to make my way to the exit also, and what's more I just could not join in on the defiance. How I felt it just was not my song and for that moment even if they had then changed and chosen to sing "Bubbles", even a muted "Bubbles" from me was probably not achievable… I was empty.

The following day on Sundays, the Big Match—I watched the "Highlights" and it showed captain Billy Bonds saddened face at the phasing out closure of the programme shaking his head after Fairclough's second goal; in football times but more so if involving your own team it's moments like this you don't forget. Billy Bonds is/was SO West Ham.

## HOME 'AWAY' Boleyn Ground ENTERTAINMENT/DINAMO TBLISI (USSR) ECWC Q/F 04/03/1981

THIS WAS PROBABLY the finest away performances I can ever recall at Upton Park. As European matches go, it compared to the sheer class by who I'm sure was Red Star Belgrade when playing and winning at Liverpool. If I'm correct about the club I still couldn't tell you what season it was, but I can't help thinking they managed three goals with only one or even without reply and what's more they came at Anfield, an away goals tally that in those times and at Anfield was not thought or even heard of? Dinamo Tblisi in football terms on this night "peaked", because in my layman's way of putting it over, if this was a normal display for them, then everyone in any kind of football circles would have recognised, been aware and heard of them before. Tblisi were simply stupendous and West Ham although not a first division side, boasted a number of international players or of sustained recognition and although in the second division were to be the proud winners of the 2$^{nd}$ division title a couple of months later by no less than a thirteen clear point margin, a total that would have increased to twenty-three if using the current three point for a win system.

The score line could have been a little more flattering for West Ham had the Tblisi keeper not saved a Ray Stewart penalty that saw Ray after having his spot kick saved; carry on running towards the keeper waving his wrist with his index finger raised and pointing at him approvingly. A showing of respect that I can't help feeling players in the West Ham team that night was thinking also for their opposition and most likely without exception. There were standing ovations from all areas of the ground at the final whistle and after such a performance against a West Ham side that had no real answer, how could anyone not stand up, show their respect and then join in on the appreciation?

John Lyall, like his predecessor Ron Greenwood, doted on the European style of football. What or how much access John Lyall had of Dinamo Tblisi's football calibre I don't know, but they were a Georgian side and they were from "behind the curtain". I have no doubt it's possible that this factor would not have helped in his or the team's preparation. The return leg ended far more favourably for West Ham as for now having played against and watched Tblisi at Upton Park, I can't help thinking with extended prior knowledge and therefore preparation, would that not have been the key to a closer result? I don't know, but then again nobody does and one thing is for sure, no one can take away Dinamo Tblisi's brilliant performance in the first leg at Upton Park. Stuart Pearson scored the only goal in front of a reported 80.000 attendance to make the two-legged affair finish on a 2-4 aggregate. Dinamo Tblisi went on to win the trophy. Why was I not surprised?


## HOME WEATHER/Mike Oldfield/CAMBRIDGE UNITED 21/12/1979


N OT BEING A WEATHER MAN myself, Dinamo Tblisi from what I understand came from an area known for having very cold weather and if that is true, they would have been accustomed to the bitter winter weather experienced during December 1979. Weather then was winters were winters and summers were summers. The winter weather of recent years to me has become milder but this, of course, does not mean that we don't get shallow or many inches of snowfall at intermittent times, with sustained freezing, bitingly cold spells along with of course the rain and the damp that winter months invariably bring…

It was a Friday night and a home league match was to be played against Cambridge United—AND IT WAS. The pitch was frozen, as was the terracing and of course all surrounding pavements, roads and streets not only around Upton Park or London but at this time it was a most definite countrywide situation. It was weather of proportions that in days closer to the period of these writings and with pitches more likely to be playable through developments in ground staff equipment as well as under soil improvements; a fixture cancellation is now more likely through around and inner ground supporter safety rather than an unplayable or dangerous pitch.

DJ Bill Remfry at half-time played Mike Oldfield's single record release 'In Dulci Jubilo', a song that had first been released as a Christmas issue in 1975, and it isn't difficult for me to recall people standing and doing whatever body movements they chose just to keep warm. Attendances at football grounds around the country tend to drop toward the lead and build up to Christmas and more so, as the festive season draws yet closer. A number of factors combine to form this decline and one main obvious reason would or could be a lack of funds, added by a running out of time situation perhaps caused by non self-organisation and then of course, we have Christmas work parties, of which this match was a Friday night. The build-up to Christmas is a stressful time for probably the majority until it gets to the point of "I've done it now, whatever I've got they'll either have to like it or lump it". Today with the benefits of late night and seven-day a week shopping being at a premium, the build-up to Christmas should be easier, but it is of my opinion that even with such convenience, leaving "much of it" to "the last minute" is a fact that won't change. West Ham won the match 3-1 on this night with a crowd figure of below 12.000; it was the lowest attendance for a competitive first team match since the 1950's

## HOME ATMOSPHERE/EXHILARATION/EINTRACHT
## FRANKFURT 14/04/1976/All but Biblical... Trevor Brooking

**H**AVING HIT ON the subject of European football and weather conditions, the mention of the European Cup Winners Cup Semi Final against Eintracht Frankfurt that Wednesday night in April 1976 must be said as a definite when it comes to one of my West Ham at home all-time high points; top of the steeple if not close, this match is up there in the clouds shading and hovering around the pinnacle. The weather for much of the time before, during and after the match, was rain of torrential proportions and the football pitch was a "football pitch", so different to more recent times where pitches resemble snooker tables or bowling greens. The British Legion Band played loud and proud that night and did the one thing I'd not seen them do before, and that was to come out and do again at half time, the long extended amalgamated jazzed up version of 'Bubbles'.

The soaked to the skin British Legion band was matched by the soaked to the skin all around the ground Hammers' fans and their German Eintracht 'Frankfurter' counterparts either standing on The South Bank or sitting in their allocated West Stand seats. Every Hammers fan without exception or 'I want a letter' must have given their all that night; looking around the ground and seeing the East Stand lower terracing swaying side to side to the tune of Bubbles meant so much, but then to look over and see the West Side lower terracing now doing the same WAS JUST AMAZING, and plus thirty years on this reminisce can still bring my/an admitted weakened emotion. Amongst other songs, many a neck jugular was raised to the wonderful tune of 'I'm Forever Blowing Bubbles' this night and with the North and South Banks throughout adding their most considerable and undeniable might it was the most atmospheric game I had ever been to, or been to since, and that is saying something when there has been so many "under the lights" evening Boleyn ground matches that can be justifiably recalled. I feel also that it is unlikely to be surpassed in the future with the introduction of an all-seat stadium.

The Ipswich home Championship play-off semi-final in May 2004 was for me probably the loudest I've heard but the new stands and roofs now cover a greater area of people thus retaining volume; however, in the main this is people sitting and stretching their vocal chords with the exception perhaps of the Bobby Moore and Centenary Stands lower who tend still to have a habit if not preference although seated of standing. Eintracht atmospherically had everything, 1-2 down from the first leg and having gone 3-0 to the good, West Ham have to do it, they have always done it and although it must be said Eintracht Frankfurt were well worthy opponents, Hammers just couldn't/wouldn't put the game to rest and a late goal with less than five minutes to go scored by the Frankfurters, and it's a match that has gone from excitement but not jubilation, to nerve-racking emotional irrational talking, added to with incoherent shouting towards the pitch with nervous body movements for many—all the ingredients for a rapid aging process that West Ham, be it the club or team over the years and as prior mentioned, have got off to a fine art. Did Hammers not then concede an indirect free kick inside the penalty area after this massive nerve raiser? Let in another goal and the away goal rule would favour the Germans but was not forthcoming, but my, did they go for it!

Brussels, here we come! Heroes all that night, and I mean both teams, so full of fluent attacking football in conditions that showed true football ability, a match that at times certainly towards the end required full-on backs to the wall spirit and could so easily for West Ham have gone so bum about face. I like listening to the nice, good social wordings and go to church sometimes, but would not class myself as religious; but I rubbed my eyes that night just to check Trevor Brooking was not walking on water.

## The Supporter/Trevor Brooking/Geoff Hurst and Billy Bonds Return

**T**REVOR'S FINAL MATCH for West Ham was to be against Everton in May 1984. It was also the closing league match of the 1983/84 season which West Ham lost 1-0 and in my opinion Trevor was the best performing player on the park that Monday night. Trevor had announced from the outset that it was to be his last season; to retire playing at the top of his profession was his choice and for many, that was the right decision to make. The match finished and the players left the field but the crowd stayed. I looked time and time again at the exits and there appeared no or very little movement. This is what the West Ham United supporter is all about. The Hammer fan/supporter, like many fans up and down the country, can be varying in view and opinion, but one thing is for sure and consistent and that is if loyalty is shown, loyalty and respect is returned and strongly given: do your best, show effort and if it doesn't come off, it doesn't come off but what will come off is fan and supporter respectful appreciation. West Ham are very much a "man's club" and yet with such parallel a family club, a combination I hope will remain for always. Since my starting and of course before such time, supporters and fans alike at West Ham were brought up on FOOTBALL, VIEWING FOOTBALL, good for the eye and so appreciating the wonderful game without the rewards, their play often so richly deserved. The Hammer fans by and large are a football knowledgeable lot and this would have been fused and encouraged by the football often expressed and of course, the passionate involvement often displayed and shown by the in the main East London and Essex supporter in attendance. The West Ham fan however also has a long memory at the cost of not too many but certainly a few, and the names of these players do not require a mention as both fans and players alike will know who they are. I can't help thinking though, it's possibly the truth and full reasons of departure of one or two such players may not have been explained with total correctness in certain circles or in the media, and the "stick" the player got or now receives may not be as deserving as many a fan may think; so with this doubt in my mind, on the fence I sit.

**Geoff Hurst** returned as a player with Stoke City and on his return to Upton Park was warmly acknowledged when touching the ball or in possession of it; he then scored the opening goal at the North Bank end and yet the chant of 'Geoffrey, Geoffrey', a chant so familiar to him as a West Ham player be it somewhat muted compared to past times from the North Bank faithfully happened. I remember when **Billy Bonds** came back as a manager with Queens Park Rangers and the Rangers fans sang an identical song that West Ham supporters also sang when Billy was a Hammer, basically a mock that implied that "they have him" now, only for The Hammers' fans to join in on what was THE West Ham song for Billy from times past and completely drowned out the Rangers fans with the same song and words. It doesn't matter where or what Billy does within the realms of football, it will always be my opinion that he will always Do His Best no matter what, because that is Billy Bonds as a honest football person and man;

in Billy's heart, when it comes to football, from a Hammers' fan and supporter point of view, claret and blue blood truly flows.

Trevor Brooking was always dignified and in addition was a true example on or off pitch throughout his West Ham and international career. When it was thought he could or would be leaving after the relegation of the 77/78 season, many a song was sung as always at Upton Park, but amongst them 'Don't go Trevor, Don't go' was always never far away. He nearly left in his early years for Newcastle United but the £90,000 asking price banded about by the media was apparently judged too high by his would-be employers. I was already enjoying Trevor's unusual style of 'letting the ball run' as opposed to 'going to the ball'; this 'difference' would often wrong foot an unsuspecting player and as well as this 'difference'—his devastating if not subtle feints were in more mature years to develop into such a fine art that despite having done it so many times on the pitch and televised for all to see, somehow he would still leave opposing players bewildered before they'd 'pick themselves up and get on' with the game.

Derby County came to Upton Park in the November of the 1969/70 season under the legendary management team of Brian Clough and Peter Taylor. Derby County had just returned to the first division as division two champions and early form was sustained throughout when as a newly promoted team they were to finish a most creditable fourth. West Ham won that day 3-0. Geoff Hurst scored his second and West Hams third and Trevor "had done the work". I clearly remember saying to Terry my brother that "Brooking is going to be a great player"; his reply was, "It's too early to say"—semi agreeing and yet not committing. Trevor Brooking had made his debut two seasons previously on the opening league match of season 1967/68 away to Burnley.

A short while but what seemed like ages, Trevor emerged from the West Stand player's tunnel, he slowly jogged towards the South Bank acknowledging applause, scarves hats and what else I do not know were being thrown on to the pitch in what I would describe as adulation with Trevor picking up all and sundry. The crowd was shouting at and applauding an ambassador of the beautiful game; he got to the North Bank after trekking past the East Stand, and I witnessed that on every instance he diverted or went back showing supporter/fan respect and appreciation should he see an item that had been thrown his way having passed. On successfully getting three quarters round the pitch, approaching the goal posts North Bank end I was sorry to see the "Please don't" look on Trevor's face as young fans began to encroach and then enter onto the pitch. With young fans now physically impeding his lap of honour, such impairment caused Trevor to drop much of what had been thrown as gifts to him. It would have been impossible for him to hold on.

Trevor after being so adoringly mobbed went to the director's seating area situated in the West Stand upper and made a speech to the spectators which included a glowing appraisal of the West Ham fan and supporter. Liz who sat with her father Eric behind me in the Dr Martens Stand saw the now Sir Trevor Brooking outside Tottenham Court Road tube station when on her way to university. 2004 was the year, she told me she just 'had to speak to him' and after making her approach did speak to him albeit briefly. Sir Trevor I am assuming was making his way to the FA Head Quarters at Soho Square, not more than a five minute walk away where he held the position of FA Director of Football Development. Although never seeing him play, Eric her father no doubt told her a story or two, not only about Trevor the man and player, but also the teams that played in those earlier times. A young girl/woman who had only been told stories and yet so wanted to talk to the wonderful man. This for me was just an example of the deserved legacy left by the now Sir Trevor Brooking. I have a personal thank you that I would like to make to Sir Trevor Brooking myself and I hope one day to have that opportunity. I have a cutting taken from the *Sun* newspaper dated 28th April 1984 sixteen days before the hanging up of Trevor Brooking's professional boots; it shows a picture of Colin Hart and beside it is written, Colin Hart 2nd row, B Block, West Stand, Upton Park, a seat row and block that was to be the same for Colin Hart when the West Stand was to convert to the Dr Martens Stand. How many years Mr Hart had sat in this area of the ground I do not know, but he was to be the same Colin I sat just three seats from after taking up my shared seat in 1994/95 season until I moved to the Bobby Moore Stand for season 2005/06. This newspaper cutting is a tribute to Trevor Brooking and the title reads 'He's a Genius and a Gent!' (With these words in smaller letters but underlined, placed underneath: 'Just magic, Brooking.')

I wasn't one for keeping newspaper cuttings as a general rule, but this one I kept as it echoed my thoughts of admiration and respect for a man who, I believe, was an exemplary example in every aspect of the game be it in playing, training, behind the scenes, TV in front of the screens, talking at functions, in authority or as importantly, just plain socially. I have kept many complete newspapers and of various publications leading up to and for a week or so after the FA Cup Final of 1975, I have no doubt the same habit collection would have been self-enforced if not for hospitalisation for the 1980 FA Cup final against Arsenal although I do have some that family and/or friends saved or gave me at a later date or at the time. Other newspaper cuttings I have are of the Stoke 1972 League Cup 2nd Semi-final replay, Anderlecht European Cup Winners Cup Final 1976 and also the staying up Manchester United last game of the season 1977. These are notable newspaper cuttings I use as examples, although there will be a number of other match report cuttings folded and tucked away in appropriate match programmes.

## Bobby Moore (OBE) What an Inside-Outside Football History/Always Smart and Liked a Lager

**I** **MANAGED** to go to the openings of both the lower and upper tiers of The Bobby Moore Stand when firstly playing Norwich (Lower) and then Manchester United (Upper) in the months of January and February 1994 respectively. Matches I was joined with by brother Terry and Bob 'from behind the post'. It was a tribute to 'Our' Bob that a stand should have been opened in his name. I had the great pleasure of watching him play on numerous occasions away from and at Upton Park, with the added bonus of on my first visit to watch West Ham as a ten-year-old, seeing him score for West Ham in a 7-2 win over Fulham. In 1975 by the skin of my teeth and then having four tickets, I saw him play at the age of 34 for Fulham in their defeat against West Ham in that year's FA Cup Final and for sure, I would need some convincing if ever there was another football club he'd rather have played, won or lost to. Bobby had departed from West Ham and joined Fulham in the March of 1974 for a reported £25,000 and in the following season, but the same season as this FA Cup final defeat, Fulham had come out on top 2-1 in an early round League Cup tussle at Craven Cottage.

Bobby Moore—what an inside-outside football history! He was a World Cup Final Captain and Winner and in addition Voted Player of the

Tournament, a FA Cup Final Winner and Loser. European Cup Winners Cup Winner, League Cup Runner Up and achieved 108 England caps, ninety of which were played as Captain and a proud record jointly held with Wolves legend Billy Wright. In comparison to some modern-day footballers with roll on successful clubs, other than the captain and caps tally, this may not 'sound much', but it doesn't tell the whole story as not only was Bobby Moore a football leader, he was in alignment liked and highly respected by so many. He is the holder of the Officer of the Order of the British Empire (OBE) award. Bobby Moore was a family man but still one of the boys, always smart and liked a lager beer. Pele described Bobby Moore as the finest defender he had played against, and THAT said by Pele, the soccer legend widely acclaimed by many football fans of his generation as the best player in the world if not all time. An opinion certainly respected should it come from a person of very senior years with football as an organised sport commencing more so in the 1870's and the first World Cup inauguration in Uruguay (subsequent winners) of 1930. Bobby Moore was never knighted: "Sir" Robert Frederick Chelsea Moore should it not have been, if having lived into latter life one day, would it have been?

In February 1993 I was working for an overnight distribution company based on the Northfleet Industrial Estate, bordering Gravesend in Kent. Late each weekday afternoon I would collect reels of cable, be it wrapped on ply or drums in a 7.5-ton lorry from companies Cable Factors and Winstonlead; both companies operated out of the same premises in Anchor & Hope Lane SE7 not a stone's throw from Charlton Athletic FC and their home ground The Valley. These collected consignments via the overnight delivery network, in this case based at Dudley in the west midlands, were then to be delivered either the next day or on a two-three day service to various destinations on the UK mainland. I remember waiting to talk to Alan Grubb, the departmental manager who at the time was speaking on the telephone; out of the blue he goes: "Na, what, Bobby Moore?" At that moment precisely I was distracted into the warehouse. A few minutes afterwards Alan emerged. I had been waiting for this and I called across, "Al, what was all that about Bobby Moore?" His reply knocked the stuffing out of me: "He's dead."

'Our' Bob, Brown Bread, Bowel Cancer—I can't recall if I knew he was ill now but it was one hard, bitter pill to swallow. I was always surprised even as time went on that after retiring from the field of play and trying his hand at management, Bobby Moore was not offered (I can't say he wasn't considered) a respected post within the FA, or was he, could it be, that a position was declined? Bobby Moore was known throughout the football world, an ambassador of the game and his views would be held with high regard I'm sure. Was Bobby Moore the first real football celebrity, and is it possible that this did not help him, or was he not that interested anyway? Someone may have the answers and if they do they will know if it was personal.

On 11<sup>th</sup> May 2007 a bronze statue of Bobby Moore was erected by the main entrance of the New Wembley Stadium commemorating his effect on the game and in time for the forthcoming FA Cup final between Chelsea and Manchester United, 19<sup>th</sup> May. In august 2008, fifteen years after Bobby Moore's untimely death, West Ham United officially retired the number 6 shirt as a mark of respect, with back four centre back Matthew Upson being the final wearer of the coveted 6 numbered shirt.

'Our' Bob was to give me my on the professional field of play funniest ever moment; it was in the early seventies and a home match that I always thought was against Leeds United. I had read in a West Ham programme fan article many years later re this Bobby Moore incident that it was against Wolves, speaking to car accident Ricky at a meet up with him in February 2007. I'll happily accept it was Wolves. The opposition is not really that relevant to the story but after having doubt put into my head and having thought it was Leeds for so long, curiosity got the better of me. Having brought up this reminiscence and asking Ricky if he could recall who was the opposition that day, his reply without any hesitation, prompt or hint was a resounding "Wolves!"—and that, coming from Ricky, was good enough for me.

These writings I do are based obviously on levels of research but also very much on memory. Having made this mistake that had been for many years so firmly set in mind, please, should there be one or two further mistakes that I'm totally unaware of, please accept an in-advance apology.

Bobby Moore almost on all corners defended the goals near post and on this occasion the ball was crossed hard and low; it was hurtling towards the near post Bobby was protecting and he headed the ball away with force. The referee was standing a number of yards away but on this occasion was one slow mover. The ball hit the referee on the side of the face and he went down like a sack. It was hilarious—I know I shouldn't admit this, but it is how it was, added to the fact he didn't get up straight away (sorry ref) seemed to add to the amusement. The ball was cleared and I may be wrong, but I think it was Peter Eustace who was with the ball and running away from goal to start a quick on the break attack. Bobby without hesitation took instant control; he walked towards the referee, picked up his whistle and blew it to stop the game. I rolled up. I looked around and saw many others who had seen the funny side also. I looked also directly behind and then up, I saw this man with a short beard and a harmless looking face who had seen the amusing side also and I was looking directly up his nostrils. He was rolling up too. I was still in my early youthful teens, not of any great height and still standing near the front of the terracing.

In November 1970 a testimonial was held for Bobby Moore and West Ham's opponents were Celtic. The South Bank was full of Scottish fans and the match although a friendly was played quite competitively. I remember thinking to myself what fantastic support these Scottish fans are and that they'd all come down from Scotland just for a testimonial; being young it hadn't crossed my mind that these were Scots that probably lived in or around London and an opportunity to see Celtic be it their club or not was an opportunity they did not want to miss. Celtic had many of the famous tartan army players on show that night: Tommy Gemmell, Bobby Lennox, 'Little' Jimmy Johnstone and John Hughes, who on the night from twenty yards or so hit a 'stonker' in off a post amongst them. The game finished 3-3. Johnny Ayris scored and so did Clyde Best, a bullet like header that if my memory serves me correctly was the equalising third goal. I don't recall who scored the other West Ham goal but I know it wasn't Bobby Moore. In the last few minutes 'Our' Bobby went up front in search for his testimonial goal but, alas, it was not to be.

## Photographs of my WEST HAM UNITED MEMORIES/TIMES are Few and Far Between

**P**HOTOGRAPHS of The Memories/The Times are very few and far between. I have many pictures of friends that I attended matches with but these are more in line with domestic socialising than football days out and the football experiences experienced. Some examples of photos I hold or held dear are those taken outside the offices of Lacey's coaches along the Barking road, where as an eighteen-year-old on the 31st March 1976 and no doubt buzzing, I was looking forward to an away trip which was for me an away trip with a difference. I say examples of photos held dear due to the fact I had taken and handed personally my early manuscripts with photos to West Ham; these were used in a four-page spread for the home Everton league match programme of season 2006/07. To my dismay and disappointment and after repeated requests for our agreed return of property, no return of pictures or manuscripts was forthcoming, worsened by the fact the article had an embarrassing amount of errors.

The European Cup Winners Cup run of season 1975/76 had taken Hammers to the possibility of the final, but before such a high, a visit in the first leg semi-final to the city of Frankfurt and West German representatives Eintracht Frankfurt was to see travel by coach to Dover and then ferry crossing to Zeebrugge, before continental coach continuation on what proved to be marvellous clear roads. In these pictures with Chris Stone (one in hand and one copied from Everton match programme) we are seen waiting outside the offices of Lacey's Coach Travel before coach arrival, and then in another picture we are seen again with our 'not too small' Union Jack flag walking along the streets of Frankfurt.

I have a picture of me taken with John Lyall and his wife Yvonne at a West Ham dinner/dance (13/01/1980) that was held at The Heybridge Moat House, Ingatestone, Essex. I had gone there sporting a beard with girlfriend Lisa and good brother friends of mine Chris and Colin Fowler. Other photos taken on the night are with Stuart Pearson, Geoff Pike, Paul Brush, DJ Bill Remfry and David Cross.

David Cross was THE 'original' West Ham PSYCHO and for that although he won't care one hoot I apologise to Stuart Pearce as he, also, was West Ham's 'Psycho' for the Upton Park faithful in his two seasons at West Ham 1999-2001. In the late seventies and early eighties 'Psycho' was the chant from the North and South Banks for our 'Crossy'. Attendees in these years, like me, will remember many a 'Crossy' goal and one of two he scored this day that comes to mind, purely for from edge of the area, curl it into the corner artistry, was at Watford in the 2nd division championship winning season of 1980/81. However of all his scoring achievements for West Ham that I remember most must be the four goals he scored at White Hart Lane in season 1981/82, a night game where one of the goals from the most purists of four pass moves went in on full volley from just inside the Tottenham penalty area. IT FLEW IN, but after and when looking at the tele re-run the ball had actually come off his shin. In all fairness the move for move's sake deserved a goal finish but on re-viewing, the brilliance turned to laughter; but whatever way it was looked upon and for whatever choice of reason, this was a goal to be appreciated.

David Cross was injured at the time of this dinner/dance and had 'relaxed'. I clearly remember him at the end of the evening when the mini orchestra (or was it a band?) played out the night with 'I'm Forever Blowing Bubbles'. West Ham staff, players and guests formed a circle and gave a rousing chorus, but standing a yard or two within the circle 'relaxed' with arms aloft, singing to 'Our Tune' was David Cross.

Sometimes 'Crossy' would have a beard, sometimes he wouldn't. As mentioned, I had gone to this evening having what was probably a month's growth around the chin; this bloke came up to me and asked if he could have his picture taken, thinking I was David Cross. Smile I did, thought about it I did, but I just never had the heart. Can you imagine if he DIDN'T find out on the night and then showing family and friends his 'I've got pictures with David Cross' and then realizing what had been done, what his reaction would be like? Laugh, cry, take it on the chin? We'll never know because it didn't happen! With discretion, no public embarrassment was caused—just self-embarrassment and pride dented, was all, maybe? I explained his mistake and pointed him in the direction of the REAL David Cross. I hope he got his pictures.

*Shaking hands with Stuart Pearson. Stuart scored one of the two goals in the
1977 FA Cup final 2-1 win over Liverpool, just five days after that before the
game MUST win Elation MU Monday night match (Page 168) that would
guarantee West Ham relegation safety, but who in fact scored against West
Ham that night also.*

*Lisa to my right with Paul Brush and Chris Fowler. Hammers were to get to
the FA cup final in the May of this year playing Arsenal and Paul (Brushy),
having played in all rounds leading up to the cup final but missed the WBA
3rd round 1-1 drawn opener, was then to have the disappointment of being
the chosen and then not used substitute.*

*Chris and Colin Fowler take end positions, Lisa puts an arm around and David 'Psycho' Cross with Geoff Pike are happy to oblige a picture. Pikey was runner up Hammer of the year in 1981 to Phil Parkes, a positioning that would not be questioned by those who watched the matches that season and who in agreement I feel, would have also accepted if the positions of winner and runner up was reversed. It WAS between the two.*

*John and Yvonne Lyall, Chris Fowler is far right.*
*Wonderful…… Just Wonderful.*

*Bill Remfry....DJ and Programme 'Off the Record' columnist 'Legend'*


## THE MEMORIES/THE TIMES


**T**HESE ARE THE INDIVIDUAL GAMES and days gone by as well as the happenings that readily came to mind when flicking through my West Ham programmes and then entering them onto home and away listings for my own reference. There are of course memories that just can't be written or described; it is a case of "You had to be there" or "Not there" as probably preferred in some instances. I think of so many people who I hope are happy, healthy and well, but also have no idea if in fact they are still alive and kicking. After Dave Radisic and Tony Goode's suggestion of writing about my stories I couldn't help but be sent down my very own memory lane, be it in most instances still attached in one way, shape or form to West Ham United if not football in general. This is a writing I can only hope will be informative, be of enjoyment and interest to those of more tender years than myself, as I hope those of similar and more senior years will more likely relate with me and to my memory lane, and not just for the West Ham United and football association.

## 'All Time Best' WEST HAM "A" Dream Team but JUST CAN'T DO IT, Oh Well… Have to settle for Team "A & A"

**D**OING A PERSONAL ALL TIME BEST WEST HAM 'A' DREAM TEAM is difficult. I'M DOING TWO. Which proves for me "Doing an ALL TIME BEST WEST HAM 'A' DREAM TEAM is DIFFICULT"? All time best A and B a, or is it two A's? Two A's is what I'm sticking to and I've chosen two 4-4-2 'A' teams for composure, balance, flair and imagined together understanding; cross over in playing times is apparent as not all players would have played in the same West Ham team or era. I can only choose players from the years I have attended and please, should you analyse my selection, remember it is of my opinion and that football is about opinions. So long as there is football, the family heated/friendly disagreement, the on-television debates and of course the heated/friendly pub discussions will always be. There are of course, players that would have pushed hard for places in my two "A" X1 and substitute line-ups. But I thought LONG AND HARD and what I eventually came up with is what I came up with after thinking……………………………LONG AND HARD.

**WEST HAM TEAM "A"**

PHIL PARKES

| RAY | ALVIN | BOBBY | FRANK |
|---|---|---|---|
| STEWART | MARTIN | MOORE | LAMPARD |

| MARTIN | BILLY | TREVOR | ALAN |
|---|---|---|---|
| PETERS | BONDS | BROOKONG | DEVONSHIRE |

GEOFF HURST        BRYAN "POP" ROBSON

Sub…Mid-Field RONNIE "TICKER" BOYCE and why not!.

**WEST HAM TEAM "A"**

LUDEK MIKLOSKO

| TIM | STEVE | TONY | JULIAN |
|---|---|---|---|
| BREAKER | POTTS | GALE | DICKS |

| MARK | GEOFF | GRAHAM | PAOLO |
|---|---|---|---|
| WARD | PIKE | PADDON | Di CANIO |

TONY COTTEE        FRANK McAVENNIE

Sub…SLAVEN BILIC because you can't play five in a back four!

Terry Martin as referred Terry and Jean/Dennis/the Frankie Howerd Club (Page 103) and Liverpool FA Cup Final/Cardiff Millennium Stadium 13/05/2006 (Page 121) passed on 8th August this same year. For me our friendship of four years was too short. One month and nine days later an obituary was published for Terry in the home Newcastle United programme 17th September. I will always remember Terry. God Bless.

## The Chalk and Cheese Women's Ward to Men's

(Continued from Page 66)

**T** **HE WOMEN'S WARD** to the men's could not have been more different. The women's ward mainly consisted of much older ladies to Lisa and who may have had falls or hip replacements. It was also unfortunate for all concerned in whatever capacity that one or two deaths in the ward took place during Lisa's confinement, something that during my stay was a situation experience I did not have to endure. This made it so much more difficult for Lisa; we were fortunate in one way, though, and that was on most days the nurses would push my bed down the corridor and place my bed beside Lisa's so we could spend an hour or two together. On the very odd occasion it would be the opposite way round but it was generally preferred that I should be taken to Lisa. I mention that the ladies ward mainly consisted of older ladies and that is most true to say, but there was one very memorable exception and that was Jacky, a young girl a year or so younger than Lisa and whose beds was placed directly opposite each other. Jacky was a young police cadet and had been taking her courses at Hendon Police training college. During Physical Exercise she had landed awkwardly between protective landing safety mats after climbing a scrambling net. Jacky's misfortune resulted in paralysis and cost her the use of both her legs. Julie was a friend also from the same training college as Jacky and visited her friend regularly; this was good company for Lisa and many months after us all being discharged from confinement to hospital, we were to meet up one more time, and that was to celebrate Jacky's eighteenth birthday held in her family home, which I recall to have been in the area of Gerrards Cross. Middlesex.

The men's ward was so much the opposite to the ladies, consisting mainly of motorbike, car or sport related injuries and there are so many stories that I could tell in the weeks that were to follow. From a social point of view it was so much easier for the men and their stay in hospital; we were mainly of an 18-30 age group and despite the fact most had to withstand the frustration of being bedridden and nil by mouth on constant view, we had one heck of a crack with Paul Bladen even marrying Heather, one of the nurses. On a Tuesday and Thursday all senior, including the most senior of team members and leaders, Mr Wilson and Mr Trickey, would each come round with their teams to all individual beds to discuss treatments and progress of each independent 'client'. All those capable along both sides of the ward whether in armed, leg or wherever Plaster of Paris would, as the teams entered the ward, all start doing their bed (not given or given) exercises, patients' neck turning, arm pushing in different directions, or leg raising and lowering—all this was to go on and simultaneously. The medic teams kept self-control but participants found it very amusing.


## Thank You, Yes You... Families and Friends


**F**AMILIES AND FRIENDS were fantastic in the weeks that lay ahead and I don't recall a day that went past when either Lisa or myself went without a visitor or visitors. It would be different at a weekend but even more so on a Sunday though, with the Endeavours football team that I captained playing in the morning, with pub afternoon opening times of twelve till two, it was not uncommon for a number of cars to do the not so easy journey from Eltham to Stanmore and join us in the afternoon. Ricky who, having a broken pelvis amongst other injuries had been "released" in the earlier days after the accident, made return journeys of support a number of times but would often choose weekdays for his visits as opposed to weekends as these normally would be times of a more relaxed nature. Lisa had sustained a compound fracture of the femur along with a multitude of abrasions and never made a whimper of note to me or to anyone that I was aware. Lisa was in traction and bedridden for in excess of three months before the beginning of her physiotherapy. John and Rita are Lisa's mum and dad and never, not once, was it heard that they placed any blame on me. We're talking here of an eighteen-year-old girl and their only child. I could not have asked for more. From friends we had support from all angles and we could not have been more fortunate, although a special mention of Steve Rees, John Sweet, Jason Barr and Neil Wallace I don't think anyone will mind. The get well cards, the presents and the wishes, even a signed by West Ham players who played in the 1980 FA Cup Final football. After the accident which had taken place in the early hours of the 17th April, the next West Ham away match was to be at Cardiff City on the following Saturday 19th April; other than the Wrexham match first game of the season Ricky and me had gone to all away league and FA Cup matches that season. The next home match was to be against Birmingham City on 22<sup>nd</sup> April; it was to be my first absence in all competitions since Everton 24<sup>th</sup> August 1974. I apologised to Lisa for what had happened, and her reply was, "It was worth it, I had never seen you so happy." Help me out here—what sort of reply was I to say to that?

## Scotland/Prince Charles-Lady Diana/Mrs Grant/Paul Bladen/Aviemore Phone Call down South

**I WOULD SPEAK TO LISA** and in return she would often, while in hospital, speak to me about things we'd like to do "When all this is over". One of these "When all this is over" suggestions was to go to the Highlands of Scotland. In the last week of July 1981, a week or so and some fifteen months after the accident, this was to become a reality. I collected Lisa from the family home in Westcombe Park around 6.30am and drove to what was to be our first night stopover in the Scottish town of Perth. Lisa was quite happy to go along with my suggestion of travelling along the A9 northward towards Aviemore and the Cairngorm mountains; our furthest north point of travel was to be the city of Inverness. It was at Aviemore that we were to stay for two nights at the guesthouse of Mrs Grant. Mrs Grant was the most wonderful lady and I know Lisa will remember her fondly no matter how many years pass. We watched as Mrs Grant took pictures of her television screen as the marriage of Prince Charles to Lady Diana Spencer on 29<sup>th</sup> July at St Paul's Cathedral unfolded. I recall thinking as I watched Mrs Grant take her photos how much I hoped her pictures came out okay and now, as I'm writing, wonder if in fact they did? Mrs Grant's excitement of the day was plain to see—you could sense how much she would have liked to be in London for what was to her such a memorable occasion. The outcome and quality of those pictures would have meant so much to her.

It was also in Aviemore that I was to make a telephone call to hospital in-patient pal of mine Paul Bladen. How I came to have his number originally I do not know; I don't recall ever asking him for it either, but I do know I had taken it to Scotland with me for the sole purpose of making contact with another in-patient pal of mine, Steve McCormack. I was aware both had been in contact with each other but for Steve I had now lost touch. I did know though that he with wife Julie resided in Ilfracombe, North Devon. I called Paul down south to ask if he had any idea how I could make contact with Steve. Watching the pennies literally disappear on the telephone call box money meter and Paul not having a pass on telephone number, he told me the name of the housing estate Steve was living on in Ilfracombe but he could give me no road, door number or name of block building. We exchanged compliments and "how are you's" with brief bringing up to date of "what you been up to's" before the money I had put into the telephone box disintegrated before my eyes. Having spent a night (or was it two?) in our uppermost northerly part of our tour drive, Inverness, we drove down the side of Loch Ness on the A82 visiting The Loch Ness museum before spending time at Fort William and taking in the stupendous sights and scenery of Ben Nevis, Glen Nevis and Glen Coe. It was from here that the joint decision was made to track down Steve.

### Scotland to Somerset… Success was just a Hotel Night's Sleep Away

**O**N LEAVING FORT WILLIAM I drove directly to Taunton in Somerset some fifty-five miles or so short of our intended destination of Ilfracombe. Getting late and no doubt dark, we stayed overnight in a small hotel before setting off the next day on our tracking down mission. Finding the estate did not take long; knocking on doors, describing a man in a wheelchair with his wife and a Staffordshire bull terrier dog, meant finding Steve did not take long either, so a knock on his door was not too far away, or was it? Knocking on the door with a feeling of mixed nervousness and excitement, a lad of similar age to me opened the door. This vision of unexpectedness momentarily deflated me. I was expecting Julie, now his wife since their marriage in November 1980 shortly after Steve vacated hospital, but there was no sign of her. On asking for Steve I half expected to be told I had the wrong house. This lad, who also had the vacant look, an expression of "Who's this?" on his face, told me and Lisa with a slight hesitancy in his voice to "Go into the living room, he's in there". We walked into the living room and, sitting in his wheelchair, looking out of the window, was Steve! Turning to face us and with his face motionless, I can recall vividly Steve saying to us, "Look what the cat's brought in! You're just in time, we're just waiting for a lift to the pub." It was Sunday morning around 11.30am. Steve had many things in common with me and one most definitely was our liking for "ale". In hospital it was the 10th of June and the taking away of certain medication that now allowed me to have a beer should I so want. This welcome news could not have been better timed, even if I had made it up as it was also Steve's 24th birthday. Julie had arranged for friends from Ilfracombe and Wolverhampton to visit the hospital along with taking treasured Staffordshire bull terrier dog Duke as a surprise for Steve. The two small groups could not have been more different by nature. Amongst the visitors from Ilfracombe two or three were of the hippy type and had guitars. They sat around his bed playing music, and the ward all bar none appreciated this treat and the music was enjoyed by all. The lads from Wolverhampton were more of the Steve McCormack breeding as I was to learn from in-depth discussions as time went by. Having had a beer thrown my way I can't help thinking I may have forgotten whose birthday it actually was.

### Ilfracombe/High Street Pub Number Three

**P**ETER was the lad who had opened the door to me and Lisa in Ilfracombe, a friend of Steve's from Wolverhampton visiting for a couple of weeks. Julie turned up later at the pub and it was she who was to take us all back to their home. Steve soon after returning was put to bed; tiredness crept up on him back in those earlier days of hospital discharge. It was then that Julie brought out an Ilfracombe local newspaper cutting of Steve as an amateur footballer; the report told of him scoring a goal in a cup match for Ilfracombe Town against Minehead. This put my mind into a mind-set, thinking what was now and what was then and it upset me, although my composure took hold quickly, for my feelings had openly showed. Steve and Julie's home wasn't the biggest; Pete kindly offered to vacate his bed for me and Lisa and slept on the settee. Over the next week we spent much of our time as a group together in Ilfracombe, mainly in the pub known locally as 'number three' but whose actual name was The Prince Albert. Malcolm, an ex-Para, was manager (landlord?) and it was he who mainly kept us supplied with beer and top shelf liquor. Malcolm was not averse to joining in with us himself either, and his tipple enjoyment would be from the top shelf in the form of a whisky. The ale of the locals was Taunton Natural Dry Cider or "A pint of natch" as it was commonly known. The Prince Albert was known locally as 'number three' due to having a huge number three on the door and that was also its high street address.

Steve and Julie had moved to Ilfracombe in 1979. Steve had been working as an apprentice aircraft engineer in Wolverhampton and had seen men on the shop floor that had been there for in excess of twenty years. He visualised this could be him in the future and although he was offered a full-time job and well paid too, he was restless. In a conversation that no doubt was repeated on more than one occasion and with more questions being asked and then answered by a friend's brother, Steve found himself becoming more than just interested with what he was being told about Ilfracombe and the lifestyle—so much so that when this friend's brother said he could get him a job "flipping burgers" in a greasy spoon with a staff bed-sit thrown in, Steve made up his mind and upped and went, but not on his own which was his original plan. Julie, seeing Steve was most serious, then packed in her job also, went with him too and waitressed.

## "He Had a Ticket", "Too Right He Did"/WOLVES-FOREST League Cup Final 1980

**S**O IT WAS TO BE The Royal National Orthopaedic Hospital, Brockley Hill, Stanmore, Middlesex, that through unfortunate if not strange circumstances was where I was to meet Steve McCormack—a meeting that was to build into a firm friendship bonding that still exists today. Steve had his Wolverhampton Wanderers colours hanging from his bed and I had my Hammers. Steve had travelled north from Ilfracombe by hitch-hiking on the Thursday to see his mum; on the Friday he was to meet up "with the boys" as Steve would refer before travelling to London for the Wolverhampton

Wanderers Nottingham Forest League Cup Final match due to take place at Wembley the following day, the following day being Saturday March 15th 1980 and a match Wolves were to win 1-0 by a 67th minute goal from Andy Gray. It was also a match that Steve and his friends were not to see, not in live form anyway. They had travelled down on the Friday as a friend of theirs, Toddy, worked in the Hendon ex-servicemen's club and had the night off. Steve was introduced to others and after a few drinks their white Ford escort van was involved in an accident and flipped after clipping a curb. Steve made the point to me that no speed of note was involved. Five adult males were in the van with four sustaining injuries. Three of those had injuries combining a broken leg, two broken collar bones and one punctured lung, the driver being the most fortunate coming out of the accident unscathed. Steve had injuries that were to form a different story altogether. Having been thrown clear of the van through the back doors on the Edgware road, it is debateable whether the helping Irish couple on picking Steve up, had actually made the spinal damage he had sustained worse? Although not always advised, it is a natural compassion for people to offer assistance in making a person or persons more comfortable in times of illness or injury adversity. The resulting injuries of the accident were to cause Steve paralysis from the chest down.

## Steve McCormack... Could He Tell a Story

S TEVE hadn't been the best behaved young man in the world and had spent time in borstal. Due to the positioning of our beds, we would talk from opposite sides of the ward way into the hours, and how therapeutic! I would wake also from time to time in the night and find a nurse sitting by Steve just having the quietest of chats so as not to disturb others. We keep in touch now twenty-eight years after our most unexpected meeting and twenty-seven years after plonking myself with Lisa on his doorstep back in Ilfracombe that one year later. Steve and Julie moved back to the West Midlands from Ilfracombe in 1986 to be once again nearer to family and friends. There was always going to be the possibility for a requirement of help and assistance for Steve and as a precaution, if and when should said help or assistance ever be required, more dependable help be it someone in family or friend was in comparison, now on the doorstep as opposed to being miles away.

Although only ever being a very occasional 'tripper' to the West Midlands as a visitor to Steve and Julie, I have been to Molineux on two occasions watching West Ham play against their beloved Wolves. The first being an FA Cup 4th round 3-1 hammers victory in January 2004 and the second again being in January but the following year of 2005, finishing in what was the first season of name change from division one to the Championship in a Hammers 2-4 defeat. (Steve is a disabled season ticket holder and at both these encounters, I would get an in 'on the day' cost subsidised ticket as his helper.)

Steve still meets up with some of his old 'past' Wolves muckers before a match for a few pints and I became more and more knowledgeable of the roles they played as "Wolves Boys" twenty and thirty years prior. It was always a good excuse to use a visit of West Ham to the West Midlands but this was not in any way a regular custom due to football league divisional differences between the two clubs. A meet up with Steve and wife Julie was always looked forward to, but now it had all changed.

## Adopted Siblings Philip and Sarah/Population 400/The Blues Brothers

**I** WASN'T NOW just visiting Steve and Julie but was now visiting adopted children brother and sister siblings Philip and Sarah also. Philip, aged six, and Sarah, aged three at the time of adoption, had become legally adopted by Steve and Julie in 1995, after which Steve described it as "eighteen months of an intrusive and difficult adoption process". The family live in a small area known as Stanton Upon Hine Heath which Steve would describe as being a small tightknit community country place existence in Shropshire. The population he estimates at tops is approximately four hundred people: it has a pub appropriately called the Stanton Arms and he describes the area as very much a farming community with a church and village hall. Steve informed me that he did two years on the parish council and before retiring from voluntary duties, had campaigned successfully in having access and use of disabled toilets installed within the local village hall. This now family of four live in a bungalow with two acres of field; on my last visit which was the weekend of said 2-4 Hammers defeat in January 2005, they possessed two horses (Julie and Sarah both ride), and as a matter of course, a Staffordshire Bull Terrier (a breed of dog they are never without) in the name of Minnie The Moocher—Minnie, so named after the jazz song written in 1931 by Cabell (Cab) Calloway and so performed by him (then 73 years of age) as Curtis in one of Steve's favourite films 'The Blues Brothers' released in 1980.

It was this January weekend of 2005 that was to throw up one surprise that in no way had I envisaged. After the match and a couple of pints we returned to their bungalow home. The time was getting past 9pm and having had a bite to eat I was being polite and yet miffed that we had not left for the pub. Steve and Julie carried on as normal, the time having gone 9pm and we hadn't left for the pub and they're carrying on as normal—and this to me is so not normal behaviour. I'm being polite yet getting more and more miffed and we're still sitting in the bungalow. This isn't right, I'm thinking—what's this all about? Knowing their liking for an ale and along with their lack of get ready movement, I was puzzled even more, if not doing me in when then, out of the blue, there is a knock on a window. I asked Steve, "Who's that?" and Steve shrugged his shoulders in a 'I don't know, haven't got a clue' movement.

## Mr and Mrs Hospital Pal Paul and Nurse Heather Bladen

**T**WO PEOPLE enter the room in the shape of a man and a woman. Without any introduction to me other that a hello, they sit down and we talk. Steve and Julie carry on as normal offering a cup of tea or whatever; there's no mention of pub or going out and me, I'm being Mr Polite and beginning to think, "So, it's a night in then?" After I don't know how long but I doubt much more than five minutes, something was said and it was all change and the "set-up" all fell into place. I hadn't been introduced because I was expected to have recognised these surprise visitors! Now realising who they were, I jumped to my feet moving quickly across the room to greet them, now knowing exactly who they were and with a firm shaking of hands between the man and myself, I turned, faced the woman and with a mixture of embracement and emotional hugs, I whispered quietly into her ear: *Thank you, Thank you, Thank you*, as I repeated those meaningful, heartfelt feeling 'Thank you' words to this woman. For the few seconds this was taking place, my thoughts were instantaneously reminded again of my appreciation and gratitude towards the matron, sisters, staff nurses and nurses who had helped me and many through what was a most difficult and experiencing "in hospital" time twenty-five years previously—and this woman, by my words and actions, would have known this. I mention these members of hospital staff as obvious feelings of their efforts were more paramount in my mind when embracing this woman. Naturally and of course, no one forgets the incredible dedicated work and knowledge of the Consultants, Registrars, Doctors and Surgeons, but at this particular moment, it was the aftercare I had received that was foremost in my mind, and what I had been reminded of. Sometime back, a time in distance that I have no idea before this memorable moment, Steve had told me that when he had just started working in a hospital, he recalls as being the year of 2000 that without warning he had heard a voice behind him say, "It's you, it's you, isn't it?" And that before he could do anything a woman was beside him kneeling down beside his wheelchair, and it was Heather. The nurse Heather who had helped care for us with other nurses back in 1980 and who had later married our hospital in-patient friend Paul Bladen. Heather and Paul, after marrying, had moved away from Middlesex and Heather now worked at The Robert Jones and Agnes Hunt Orthopaedic Hospital, based in Oswestry, Shropshire, and this was the hospital of Steve and Heather's reunion and again coming together. So, twenty years after their first meeting and last seeing of each other in1980 at The Royal National Orphopaedic hospital in Stanmore, Steve and Heather, through a big coincidence, were to meet up again; but now they were, technically anyway, hospital colleagues. Heather was a nurse or Staff nurse then and Steve had just recently at that time started working in the Midland Centre for Spinal Injuries. In his time there since, he has continually worked in the spinal unit as a peer counsellor and is now a fully trained psychotherapist. He has also however been known to visit prisons on the basis of helping long-term internees prepare and adapt to life on the 'outside' on completion of sentence. Steve, now seeing Heather from time to time within the hospital, and with Heather now working as a theatre sister, had informed her and therefore Paul of the forthcoming Wolves West Ham match and of my travelling to the West Midlands as a match cum visit. Steve had seized this opportunity and with wife Julie as his confidante had arranged for this wonderful meet-up to happen and, yes, we did now go to the pub! Not the local Stanley Arms, however, but to The Fox in a place called Wem, six or so miles North West of the family home in Stanton Upon Hine Heath.

## Stuart and The Fox/Bungalow Charismatic Features/Smoke Visit/Camden Town Market NW1

S TUART WAS THE GAFFER and a Hammers fan at that. The Fox was chosen of course for my benefit; the pub was not very well supported that night customer-wise, which made for easier conversation. Stuart talked about his liking of Nathan's pie and mash along the Barking road and a hundred yards or so from the Boleyn pub on the corner of Green Street. After a few beers and with settled relaxation sinking in, a rousing chorus of 'Bubbles' was sung and Stuart appeared from around the other bar into the bar where we were; he stood behind the counter and added his vocal chords which, to be quite honest, was not already short in volume.

There are many charismatic features about Steve and Julie's bungalow home; they have a red telephone call box in the front garden and an old-fashioned jukebox jury-type jukebox in one of the rooms along with a pool table. Steve had acquired the pool table when a landlord he knew vacated his pub. Whenever I visit, a bed is always there for me. Steve and Julie in return have travelled down to London when "The Wolves" (Steve and Julie's expression) are playing the Hammers, or when just visiting, they stay either in The Express by Holiday Inn, Greenwich SE10 or The Travel Lodge, Poplar E14. They thoroughly enjoy coming down to "The Smoke" as they call London and I chauffeur drive their specially converted Volvo car for Steve's disability, giving them commentary and my knowledge when showing them the monopoly-board sights along with other major touristy parts of interest. Sunday has always been home-time day but not before the customary visit to the multi-racial and cosmopolitan market of Camden Town, a nice finish off and easy travel for the M1 and their journey home.


## Immediate Family

## Mum


**M**UM HAD BEEN EVACUATED as a ten-year-old in September 1939 to Deacon Street, Swindon, and returned as a fourteen-year-old to her parents' family East End home and pub The Hearts of Oak, not much more than a stone's throw from the north side of Blackwall Tunnel. Mum informs me children of the age of fourteen and above were not evacuated during the war but having been evacuated and then reaching the age of fourteen, children were returned home. Parents were not forced to have their children evacuated but the government strongly encouraged child evacuation to what was deemed safer areas from German bombing. Main cities such as London, Birmingham and Coventry were to be obvious targets as of course many other cities were also. For this reason less populated areas were favoured for evacuees, therefore out "in the country" village and towns were favoured. Children if at all possible would be sent to homes of family members such as grandparents, aunts or uncles; another consideration for happiness and trust would be family friends who, it was possible, the children would already be familiar with. However, if that option was not available, "host homes" would be a common alternative.

A public house on mum's side of the family was to be a "way of life". In 1881 her grandfather George Henry Arthur Sturges had been born in The British Flag public house 103 Calvert Road, Battersea SW11. In 1899 he was to marry a Minnie Dora Moult, two or so years his junior. Minnie Victoria Rose, my mum's mum and my Nan, was to be born in 1900 and along with younger brother Francis (known as Sam) was, just like their father, to be born in The British Flag also. My ancestry in pub life I can see goes back further than my Great Grandfather, but how far back before these given facts I do not know. My Nan was to grow up within The British Flag pub business and home but also worked as a civil servant. Nan was to marry in 1920 to Harold

Martin, a bus and tram driver who worked out of Chiswick and lived in Battersea, but now, after marriage, was to join his new family in the pub and home based in Calvert road.

My mum, Joan Edna Martin, just as her grandfather, mum and two brothers before her (Basil 1924 and Derek 1925), was to be born in The British Flag on 10th February 1929 and a consistent span of twenty-nine years was to be the separation birth times of who would have been my Great Grandfather, Nan and mum. Within a month of mum being born her grandmother had died at the age of either 46 or 47. Talking to mum after so many years, she admits it's hard for her to remember all the information she was fed as she got older, but one certainty that mum is totally aware of, is that soon after her never to be known Nan's passing, Sam, younger brother to her mother in a pre-prepared will, was to take over the running of The British Flag public house family business. My future Nan and granddad Martin then in the same year of 1929, took mum as a few months old baby girl and her two very young but older brothers Basil and Derek to East London. The now Martin side of the family were to take on a new public house business and home known as The Hearts of Oak, situated in St Leonard's Road, Poplar E14. It is possible a divided financial agreement may have given rise to the affordability of this new venture? Mum's granddad was soon to vacate The British Flag after his 48-49 years after Sam taking 'control' but continued to remain and live in the Battersea area. In June 1930 Harold was to be born and was the third of the three brothers that now completed mum's early family beginning in life. Harold, just like his two brothers and my mum his sister, was also to be born in a public house, but this time it was to be the new to the family Hearts of Oak. Nan and Granddad vacated The Hearts of Oak in 1958 as it was to be demolished along with much of its surroundings. The last day of opening as a pub and business was to be the 13th February but Nan and granddad were to remain in the living quarters until their departure shortly after. The 13th was also the day mum was to vacate The East End Maternity Home; dad had collected mum and by bus took baby me as a thirteen-day-old with them to The Hearts of Oak in what was as mentioned to be its final day of trade. The pub was very busy and after a short while I was taken upstairs out of the way of the mayhem; I can, however, imagine dad staying downstairs to down a pint or three?

*The British Flag that mums side of the
family were to live and run as a business
prior to 1881 and post 1929. In this
Picture Edie and Bill Taylor appear to be
Landlords but what year I haven't
The faintest*

*Bottom: The Hearts of Oak 1929-1958*

St Leonard's Road on the corner of Drew Street, 1956. J. Halls and Son, haulage contractors, are on the right, and in the distance is the Hearts of Oak pub. All of this and much more was swept away to build the northern approach to the Blackwall Tunnel, which was opened in 1962.

*A sign post pointing in the direction of the Blackwall Tunnel is seen placed above the people preparing to cross the side road; a lone gentleman walks past towards nan and granddad Martins Truman House The Hearts of Oak.*

## Dad

**D**URING THE SECOND WORLD WAR Dad (George Colin Johnson) was to be a member of the Home Guard. Born in November 1925 he had been prevented from being "called up" on medical grounds. In 1945 when working as an apprentice fitter, turner, engineer and gaining experience of all and whatever, dad as a sideline also worked as a barman in the Eagle pub on the corner of East London's Cotton Street and East India Dock road; as bang opposite as you can get as possible is Roberts, a shop that was to remain in name existence throughout the war years and for more than sixty years later, it was also the shop where as a young child, mum was to receive her first roller skates and stabilized pedal bike. The Eagle pub, mum informs me, was bombed on the 6th march 1945 by a German V2 rocket and the same day as my granddad Martin's birthday. My Nan on most afternoons would visit Mary, landlady of the Eagle, and this was such a day. Fortune for Nan was smiling as she had departed from her regular visit an hour or so before the devastation that followed, and it is true to say that all in the pub including Mary, and just like millions around the world along with others at this time during, the World War Two six-year period, having their lives terminated prematurely and not necessarily in the nicest of manners. Bill was Mary's husband and was away from the pub at the time, my dad to be had been asked to cover Bill's shift but had been prevented from doing so due to a family intervention. The V2 rocket was a devastating weapon and the upgraded, more powerful, sinister version of the pilot-less flying bomb V1 'doodlebug' that had been in conjunction, terrorising London and England's South East for much of the war. A flying bomb that was targeted from German occupied launch sites in Belgium, France and possibly Holland and that on fuel exhaustion, would drop instantly to ground. The fear of this bomb was the drone sounding of the engine, and for the people below the not knowing when it was going to cut out but due to past experience, knowing it was possible and probably likely to do so at any time. On this occasion some length of Cotton Street on the side of the pub was destroyed, but miraculously, on the other side of Cotton Street and in East India Dock road, the buildings including Roberts had remained; this, my assumption tells me, was probably due to the angle the weapon had landed.

At the time of this 'Wartime normality' in East London, Granddad was serving at the bar in the Hearts of Oak where Nan had now returned and mum, as a sixteen-year-old was upstairs preparing dinner. Mum tells me that many windows of the pub from the shock of the V2 bomb were shattered through, and she tells me of going downstairs and picking up and holding Peggy, the family dog, thus preventing her from walking over the smashed glass. Dad was later, after the Eagle pub bombing, asked to work at the Hearts of Oak. Dad's Johnson side of the family were to be bombed out of home twice and eventually settled in Portree Street E14, and after the war was to work in the South and East London Docks alike as a ship repairer. Dad was brother to Joyce, my granddad Colin had married Florence (Flo) and at this time, that was to be the family contingent. Oban Street was where mum seems to think was where the Johnsons had been bombed on both occasions and it was Oban Street that in time was to be where Joyce (Joycey) later marrying Fred Scanlan were to live with children Andrew, Lesley and Christine. The Johnsons and Scanlans were the most typical of East London families of the time and money was never at a premium. I remember sitting on the floor as a child with other seated members of the Johnson and Scanlan families in Portree Street, very close to the small open but mesh-protected coal fire helping to assemble individual attachments that if placed together, would make hand-held mirrors to be sold just to make those few extra coppers.

It was normal and quite acceptable for us children from older, now bigger family members to be given 'hand me downs' of the clothes once worn. Nanny John, as Flo was known to us kids and at times other family members also, organised a family loan club where money was given each Sunday over the year as preparation for buying presents for Christmas. Fred worked at the gasworks while Joycey worked in an office. Minnie, my nan's sister, was also but later after Granddad Colin's passing to live in the house in Portree Street and before retiring had held work with the fire brigade. Visiting the family in this Canning Town area of East London was all but mandatory on a Sunday afternoon; conversation often went to the West Ham day before Saturday match and how 'we had lost again' or 'West Ham done well yesterday'. It was during these conversations in the small living room around the fire and the adjacent scullery that the term 'Our Bobby' (Moore) was to be instilled in my memory. 'Our Bob' or 'Bobby' was always a topical player in these conversations of the mid-to-late sixties and to family members is a term picked up by me from this period that I would sometimes use if and when referring to Bobby Moore to them.

Over the years it is natural to have additions to and departures of family members. The Martin, Johnson and Scanlans of course are no different or exception as families, tragedy, upset and joys have happened and have all played their part as they do. Andrew and Lesley are two such parts of the family who have kept and continue to keep the West Ham tradition going. Now having families of their own, they attend Upton Park's Boleyn Stadium with family members as season ticket holders with 'Bubbles' still being Number One in their charts at get-togethers. Lesley makes a point though that it 'gets to her' these days, when at the ground the Hammers faithfully sing 'They' reach the sky as opposed to the correct wording of 'Nearly'.

## Brother Terry/Sister Elaine

**M**Y SISTER ELAINE (Laine or Lainey as she was more commonly if not affectionately known) had her own room, being a girl. Laine is eight years older than me and I would follow her around as sometimes a three/four or whatever year old I was brother would. Laine would often take me to a park or wherever; that wherever would include places like Farver Square, meaning Trafalgar Square, which is where I would enjoy feeding the pigeons. My pronunciation as a toddler, egg and nannal, was another expression I had for egg and bacon. Brother Terry and me shared a bedroom and we used to kick eight bells out of each other (or more so me out of him) as friendly fighting brothers do. I was always the main aggressor because, being ten years younger than Terry, I never thought that I could hurt him and that his "yelps" were part of his play act.

*An Elaine Sister Sandwich, Terry to the left and me to the right...July 2007*

# WEST HAM UNITED FOOTBALL PROGRAMMES

## HOME ISSUES

ALL PROGRAMMES MARKED WITH * WERE ATTENDED

AND MARKED WITH X IN TOP LEFT CORNER OF PROGRAMME

IF REQUIRED MATCH TICKETS WILL BE ENCLOSED WITHIN THE PROGRAMME

THERE ARE DUPLICATE ISSUES AMONGST THE COLLECTION

| Date | Opponents | Competition |
|------|-----------|-------------|
| **SEASON 59/60** | | |
| 24.10.59 | BLACKPOOL | LEAGUE DIV ONE |
| | | |
| **SEASON 60/61** | | |
| 22.08.60 | ASTON VILLA | LEAGUE DIV ONE |
| 27.08.60 | BOLTON | LEAGUE DIV ONE |
| 05.09.60 | MAN UNITED | LEAGUE DIV ONE |
| 19.11.60 | NOTTS FOREST | LEAGUE DIV ONE |
| 21.01.61 | CHELSEA | LEAGUE DIV ONE |
| | | |
| **SEASON 61/62** | | |
| 19.08.61 | MAN UNITED | LEAGUE DIV ONE |
| 28.08.61 | TOTTENHAM | LEAGUE DIV ONE |
| 02.09.61 | NOTTS FOREST | LEAGUE DIV ONE |
| 11.09.61 | PLYMOUTH | L/CUP 1ST ROUND |
| 16.09.61 | CHELSEA | LEAGUE DIV ONE |
| 18.09.61 | BLACKPOOL | LEAGUE DIV ONE |
| 30.09.61 | LEICESTER | LEAGUE DIV ONE |
| 09.10.61 | ASTON VILLA | L/CUP 2nd ROUND |
| 14.10.61 | BURNLEY | LEAGUE DIV ONE |
| 28.10.61 | SHEFFIELD WED | LEAGUE DIV ONE |
| 30.10.61 | MALMO (SWE) | FRIENDLY |
| 25.11.61 | EVERTON | LEAGUE DIV ONE |
| 09.12.61 | BOLTON | LEAGUE DIV ONE |
| 20.01.62 | ASTON VILLA | LEAGUE DIV ONE |
| 24.02.62 | IPSWICH TOWN | LEAGUE DIV ONE |
| 24.03.62 | MAN CITY | LEAGUE DIV ONE |
| 20.04.62 | CARDIFF CITY | LEAGUE DIV ONE |

SEASON 62/63

| | | |
|---|---|---|
| 02.03.63 | ARSENAL | LEAGUE DIV ONE |
| 02.04.63 | SHEFFIELD WED | LEAGUE DIV ONE |
| 04.05.63 | BLACKBURN | LEAGUE DIV ONE |

SEASON 63/64

| | | |
|---|---|---|
| 07.09.63 | SHEFFIELD UTD | LEAGUE DIV ONE |
| 25.11.63 | SWINDON | L/CUP 4th RD REPLAY |
| 30.11.63 | FULHAM | LEAGUE DIV ONE |
| 04.01.64 | CHARLTON | FA CUP 3rd ROUND |
| 18.01.64 | LIVERPOOL | LEAGUE DIV ONE |
| 29.01.64 | LEYTON ORIENT | FA CUP 4th ROUND |
| 08.02.64 | TOTTENHAM | LEAGUE DIV ONE |
| 22.02.64 | SHEFFIELD WED | LEAGUE DIV ONE |
| 29.02.64 | BURNLEY | FA CUP 6th ROUND |
| 07.03.64 | MAN UTD | LEAGUE DIV ONE |
| 21.03.64 | ARSENAL | LEAGUE DIV ONE |
| 23.03.64 | LEICESTER | L/CUP S/F (2nd LEG) |
| 27.03.64 | STOKE CITY | LEAGUE DIV ONE |
| 04.04.64 | BOLTON | LEAGUE DIV ONE |
| 17.04.64 | BIRMINGHAM | LEAGUE DIV ONE |
| 27.04.64 | ALL STARS 11 | JOHN LYALL TESTIMONIAL |

SEASON 64/65

| | | |
|---|---|---|
| 24.08.64 | MAN UTD | LEAGUE DIV ONE |
| 28.08.64 | NOTTS FOREST | LEAGUE DIV ONE |
| 07.09.64 | WOLVES | LEAGUE DIV ONE |
| 12.09.64 | TOTTENHAM | LEAGUE DIV ONE |
| 26.09.64 | SHEFFIELD UTD | LEAGUE DIV ONE |
| 07.10.64 | A.R.A LA GANTOISE (BELGIUM) | ECWC PRE-ROUND (2nd LEG) |
| 10.10.64 | ASTON VILLA | LEAGUE DIV ONE |
| 24.10.64 | SHEFFIELD WED | LEAGUE DIV ONE |
| 07.11.64 | BLACKBURN | LEAGUE DIV ONE |
| 21.11.64 | LEEDS | LEAGUE DIV ONE |

| | | |
|---|---|---|
| 24.14.64 | SPARTAK PRAHA | |
| | SOKOLOVO | ECWC 1st ROUND |
| | (CZECH) | (1st LEG) |
| 05.12.64 | LEICESTER | LEAGUE DIV ONE |
| 12.12.64 | FULHAM | LEAGUE DIV ONE |
| 28.12.64 | BIRMINGHAM | LEAGUE DIV ONE |
| 02.01.65 | STOKE CITY | LEAGUE DIV ONE |
| 09.01.65 | BIRMINGHAM | FA CUP 3rd ROUND |
| 23.01.65 | BURNLEY | LEAGUE DIV ONE |
| 13.02.65 | EVERTON | LEAGUE DIV ONE |
| 27.02.65 | LIVERPOOL | LEAGUE DIV ONE |
| 13.03.65 | SUNDERLAND | LEAGUE DIV ONE |
| 23.03.65 | LAUSANNE | |
| | SPORTS (SWISS) | ECWC Q/F (2nd LEG) |
| | | |
| 07.04.65 | REAL ZARAGOZA | |
| | CLUB | |
| | DEPORTIVA (SPAIN) | ECWC S/F (1st LEG) |
| 12.04.65 | CHELSEA | LEAGUE DIV ONE |
| 16.04.65 | WBA | LEAGUE DIV ONE |
| 23.04.65 | BLACKPOOL | LEAGUE DIV ONE |
| | | |
| SEASON 65/66 | | |
| 23.08.65 | SUNDERLAND | LEAGUE DIV ONE |
| 28.08.65 | LEEDS | LEAGUE DIV ONE |
| 06.09.65 | LIVERPOOL | LEAGUE DIV ONE |
| 11.09.65 | LEICESTER | LEAGUE DIV ONE |
| 25.09.65 | BLACKPOOL | LEAGUE DIV ONE |
| 27.11.65 | EVERTON | LEAGUE DIV ONE |
| 11.12.65 | NEWCASTLE | LEAGUE DIV ONE |
| 01.01.66 | NOTTS FOREST | LEAGUE DIV ONE |
| 12.02.66 | BLACKBURN | FA CUP 4th ROUND |
| 02.04.66 | BURNLEY | LEAGUE DIV ONE |
| 16.04.66 | ARSENAL | LEAGUE DIV ONE |
| | | |
| SEASON 66/67 | | |
| 20.08.66 | CHELSEA | LEAGUE DIV ONE |
| 29.08.66 | ARSENAL | LEAGUE DIV ONE |

| 14.09.66 | TOTTENHAM | L/CUP 2nd ROUND |
| 26.10.66 | NOTTS FOREST | LEAGUE DIV ONE |
| 19.11.66 | NEWCASTLE | LEAGUE DIV ONE |
| 03.12.66 | WBA | LEAGUE DIV ONE |
| 27.12.66 | BLACKPOOL | LEAGUE DIV ONE |
| 31.12.66 | LEICESTER | LEAGUE DIV ONE |
| 14.01.67 | STOKE CITY | LEAGUE DIV ONE |
| 21.01.67 | SHEFFIELD WED | LEAGUE DIV ONE |
| 28.01.67 | SWINDON | FA CUP 3rd ROUND |
| 08.02.67 | WBA | L/CUP S/F (2nd LEG) |
| 25.03.67 | BURNLEY | LEAGUE DIV ONE |
| 06.05.67 | MAN UTD | LEAGUE DIV ONE |
| 09.05.67 | TOTTENHAM | LEAGUE DIV ONE |

SEASON 67/68

| 19.08.67 | SHEFFIELD WED | LEAGUE DIV ONE |
| 21.08.67 | BURNLEY | LEAGUE DIV ONE |
| 02.09.67 | MAN UTD | LEAGUE DIV ONE |
| 16.09.67 | WOLVES | LEAGUE DIV ONE |
| 30.09.67 | LEEDS | LEAGUE DIV ONE |
| 07.10.67 | STOKE CITY | LEAGUE DIV ONE |
| 11.10.67 | BOLTON | L/CUP 3rd ROUND |
| 02.12.67 | SHEFFIELD UTD | LEAGUE DIV ONE |
| 26.12.67 | LEICESTER | LEAGUE DIV ONE |
| 03.02.68 | FULHAM | LEAGUE DIV ONE* |
| 23.03.68 | CHELSEA | LEAGUE DIV ONE |
| 29.03.68 | ARSENAL | LEAGUE DIV ONE |
| 06.04.68 | NEWCASTLE | LEAGUE DIV ONE* |
| 12.04.68 | NOTTS FOREST | LEAGUE DIV ONE* |
| 20.04.68 | LIVERPOOL | LEAGUE DIV ONE |
| 24.04.68 | SUNDERLAND | LEAGUE DIV ONE |
| 11.05.68 | EVERTON | LEAGUE DIV ONE |

SEASON 68/69

| 17.08.68 | NOTTS FOREST | LEAGUE DIV ONE |
| 26.08.68 | BURNLEY | LEAGUE DIV ONE |
| 31.08.68 | WBA | LEAGUE DIV ONE* |
| 25.09.68 | COVENTRY | LEAGUE DIV ONE |

| | | |
|---|---|---|
| 05.10.68 | SOUTHAMPTON | LEAGUE DIV ONE |
| 19.10.68 | SUNDERLAND | LEAGUE DIV ONE |
| 02.11.68 | QPR | LEAGUE DIV ONE* |
| 16.11.68 | LEICESTER | LEAGUE DIV ONE |
| 30.11.68 | MAN CITY | LEAGUE DIV ONE* |
| 28.12.68 | ARSENAL | LEAGUE DIV ONE POSTPONED |
| 04.01.69 | BRISTOL CITY | FA CUP 3rd ROUND* |
| 18.01.69 | WOLVES | LEAGUE DIV ONE POSTPONED |
| 22.02.69 | LIVERPOOL | LEAGUE DIV ONE* |
| 01.03.69 | NEWCASTLE | LEAGUE DIV ONE* |
| 14.03.69 | COVENTRY | LEAGUE DIV ONE |
| 21.03.69 | IPSWICH TOWN | LEAGUE DIV ONE* |
| 24.03.69 | WOLVES | LEAGUE DIV ONE |
| 29.03.69 | MAN UTD | LEAGUE DIV ONE |
| 08.04.69 | STOKE CITY | LEAGUE DIV ONE |
| 12.04.69 | CHELSEA | LEAGUE DIV ONE |
| 14.04.69 | SOUTHAMPTON (RESERVES) | COMBINATION CUP FINAL |
| 21.04.69 | ARSENAL | LEAGUE DIV ONE* |

SEASON 69/70

| | | |
|---|---|---|
| 09.08.69 | NEWCASTLE | LEAGUE DIV ONE* |
| 11.08.69 | CHELSEA | LEAGUE DIV ONE* |
| 23.08.69 | WBA | LEAGUE DIV ONE |
| 25.08.69 | ARSENAL | LEAGUE DIV ONE* |
| 03.09.69 | HALIFAX | L/CUP 2nd ROUND |
| 06.09.69 | TOTTENHAM | LEAGUE DIV ONE* |
| 20.09.69 | SHEFFIELD WED | LEAGUE DIV ONE* |
| 04.10.69 | BURNLEY | LEAGUE DIV ONE* |
| 06.10.69 | STOKE CITY | LEAGUE DIV ONE* |
| 25.10.69 | SUNDERLAND | LEAGUE DIV ONE* |
| 08.11.69 | CRYSTAL PAL | LEAGUE DIV ONE* |
| 22.11.69 | DERBY COUNTY | LEAGUE DIV ONE* |
| 06.12.69 | MAN CITY | LEAGUE DIV ONE* |
| 13.12.69 | EVERTON | LEAGUE DIV ONE* |
| 27.12.69 | NOTTS FOREST | LEAGUE DIV ONE* |
| 17.01.70 | MAN UTD | LEAGUE DIV ONE* |

| 07.02.70 | COVENTRY | LEAGUE DIV ONE* |
| 28.02.70 | SOUTHAMPTON | LEAGUE DIV ONE* |
| 14.03.70 | IPSWICH TOWN | LEAGUE DIV ONE* |
| 28.03.70 | LIVERPOOL | LEAGUE DIV ONE |
| 31.03.70 | WOLVES | LEAGUE DIV ONE* |
| 02.04.70 | LEEDS | LEAGUE DIV ONE* |

SEASON 70/71

| 17.08.70 | ARSENAL | LEAGUE DIV ONE* |
| 22.08.70 | CHELSEA | LEAGUE DIV ONE* |
| 31.08.70 | SOUTHAMPTON | LEAGUE DIV ONE* |
| 05.09.70 | EVERTON | LEAGUE DIV ONE* |
| 09.09.70 | HULL CITY | L/CUP 2nd ROUND |
| 19.09.70 | NEWCASTLE | LEAGUE DIV ONE* |
| 03.10.70 | BURNLEY | LEAGUE DIV ONE |
| 17.10.70 | TOTTENHAM | LEAGUE DIV ONE |
| 31.10.70 | BLACKPOOL | LEAGUE DIV ONE* |
| 14.11.70 | WOLVES | LEAGUE DIV ONE* |
| 16.11.70 | CELTIC | BOBBY MOORE TESTIMONIAL* |
| 28.11.70 | COVENTRY | LEAGUE DIV ONE* |
| 12.12.70 | LIVERPOOL | LEAGUE DIV ONE* |
| 26.12.70 | NOTTS FOREST | LEAGUE DIV ONE POSTPONED |
| 16.01.71 | LEEDS | LEAGUE DIV ONE* |
| 06.02.71 | DERBY COUNTY | LEAGUE DIV ONE* |
| 20.02.71 | MAN CITY | LEAGUE DIV ONE* |
| 24.02.71 | NOTTS FOREST | LEAGUE DIV ONE* |
| 06.03.71 | CRYSTAL PAL | LEAGUE DIV ONE* |
| 20.03.71 | IPSWICH TOWN | LEAGUE DIV ONE |
| 03.04.71 | MAN UTD | LEAGUE DIV ONE |
| 09.04.71 | WBA | LEAGUE DIV ONE* |
| 17.04.71 | STOKE CITY | LEAGUE DIV ONE |
| 01.05.71 | HUDDERSFIELD | LEAGUE DIV ONE* |

SEASON 71/72

| 14.08.71 | WBA | LEAGUE DIV ONE* |
| 23.08.71 | IPSWICH TOWN | LEAGUE DIV ONE* |
| 28.08.71 | EVERTON | LEAGUE DIV ONE* |

| | | |
|---|---|---|
| 30.08.71 | COVENTRY | LEAGUE DIV ONE* |
| 08.09.71 | CARDIFF CITY | L/CUP 2nd ROUND* |
| 11.09.71 | CHELSEA | LEAGUE DIV ONE* |
| 25.09.71 | STOKE CITY | LEAGUE DIV ONE |
| 06.10.71 | LEEDS | L/CUP 3rd ROUND |
| 09.10.71 | LEICESTER | LEAGUE DIV ONE* |
| 23.10.71 | WOLVES | LEAGUE DIV ONE |
| 27.10.71 | LIVERPOOL | L/CUP 4th ROUND |
| 06.11.71 | SHEFFIELD UTD | LEAGUE DIV ONE* |
| 17.11.71 | SHEFFIELD UTD | L/CUP 5thROUND* |
| 20.11.71 | MAN CITY | LEAGUE DIV ONE |
| 23.11.71 | EUROPEAN X1 | GEOFF HURST TESTIMONIAL* |
| 04.12.71 | ARSENAL | LEAGUE DIV ONE |
| 15.12.71 | STOKE CITY | L/CUP S/F (2nd LEG) |
| 18.12.71 | NEWCASTLE | LEAGUE DIV ONE* |
| 01.01.72 | MAN UTD | LEAGUE DIV ONE* |
| 15.01.72 | LUTON TOWN | FA CUP 3rd ROUND |
| 22.01.72 | DERBY COUNTY | LEAGUE DIV ONE |
| 14.02.72 | HEREFORD | FA CUP 4th ROUND |
| | | REPLAY (LOCK OUT) |
| 19.02.72 | CRYSTAL PAL | LEAGUE DIV ONE* |
| 04.03.72 | HUDDERSFIELD | LEAGUE DIV ONE* |
| 18.03.72 | NOTTS FOREST | LEAGUE DIV ONE |
| 31.03.72 | LEEDS | LEAGUE DIV ONE* |
| 01.04.72 | TOTTENHAM | LEAGUE DIV ONE* |
| 15.04.72 | LIVERPOOL | LEAGUE DIV ONE* |
| 01.05.72 | SOUTHAMPTON | LEAGUE DIV ONE |

SEASON 72/73

| | | |
|---|---|---|
| 14.08.72 | COVENTRY | LEAGUE DIV ONE* |
| 19.08.72 | LEICESTER | LEAGUE DIV ONE* |
| 02.09.72 | MAN UTD | LEAGUE DIV ONE* |
| 06.09.72 | BRISTOL CITY | L/CUP 2nd ROUND* |
| 16.09.72 | NORWICH | LEAGUE DIV ONE* |
| 30.09.72 | BIRMINGHAM | LEAGUE DIV ONE |
| 14.10.72 | SHEFFIELD UTD | LEAGUE DIV ONE* |
| 28.10.72 | CRYSTAL PAL | LEAGUE DIV ONE |

| 04.11.72 | WOLVES | LEAGUE DIV ONE |
| 18.11.72 | DERBY COUNTY | LEAGUE DIV ONE |
| 02.12.72 | NEWCASTLE | LEAGUE DIV ONE* |
| 16.12.72 | STOKE CITY | LEAGUE DIV ONE* |
| 26.12.72 | TOTTENHAM | LEAGUE DIV ONE* |
| 06.01.73 | LIVERPOOL | LEAGUE DIV ONE* |
| 27.01.73 | CHELSEA | LEAGUE DIV ONE* |
| 17.02.73 | WBA | LEAGUE DIV ONE* |
| 02.03.73 | IPSWICH TOWN | LEAGUE DIV ONE* |
| 17.03.73 | MAN CITY | LEAGUE DIV ONE |
| 31.03.73 | EVERTON | LEAGUE DIV ONE* |
| 04.04.73 | ISRAEL NAT'L X1 | PAUL HEFFER TESTIMONIAL* |
| 14.04.73 | LEEDS | LEAGUE DIV ONE* |
| 20.04.73 | SOUTHAMPTON | LEAGUE DIV ONE* |
| 28.04.73 | ARSENAL | LEAGUE DIV ONE* |

SEASON 73/74

| 25.08.73 | NEWCASTLE | LEAGUE DIV ONE* |
| 27.08.73 | IPSWICH TOWN | LEAGUE DIV ONE* |
| 08.09.73 | TOTTENHAM | LEAGUE DIV ONE* |
| 10.09.73 | QPR | LEAGUE DIV ONE* |
| 22.09.73 | LEICESTER | LEAGUE DIV ONE* |
| 06.10.73 | BURNLEY | LEAGUE DIV ONE |
| 08.10.73 | LIVERPOOL | L/CUP 2nd ROUND* |
| 27.10.73 | DERBY COUNTY | LEAGUE DIV ONE |
| 10.11.73 | SHEFFIELD UTD | LEAGUE DIV ONE |
| 24.11.73 | ARSENAL | LEAGUE DIV ONE |
| 08.12.73 | MAN CITY | LEAGUE DIV ONE* |
| 22.12.73 | STOKE CITY | LEAGUE DIV ONE |
| 01.01.74 | NORWICH | LEAGUE DIV ONE* |
| 05.01.74 | HEREFORD | FA CUP 3rd ROUND* |
| 12.01.74 | MAN UTD | LEAGUE DIV ONE* |
| 02.02.74 | BIRMINGHAM | LEAGUE DIV ONE |
| 16.02.74 | EVERTON | LEAGUE DIV ONE* |
| 02.03.74 | CHELSEA | LEAGUE DIV ONE |
| 16.03.74 | COVENTRY | LEAGUE DIV ONE* |
| 30.03.74 | LEEDS | LEAGUE DIV ONE |
| 12.04.74 | SOUTHAMPTON | LEAGUE DIV ONE* |

| | | |
|---|---|---|
| 13.04.74 | WOLVES | LEAGUE DIV ONE* |
| 27.04.74 | LIVERPOOL | LEAGUE DIV ONE* |

SEASON 74/75

| | | |
|---|---|---|
| 19.08.74 | LUTON TOWN | LEAGUE DIV ONE* |
| 24.08.74 | EVERTON | LEAGUE DIV ONE |
| 07.09.74 | SHEFFIELD UTD | LEAGUE DIV ONE* |
| 18.09.74 | TRANMERE | L/CUP 2nd RD REPLAY* |
| 21.09.74 | LEICESTER | LEAGUE DIV ONE* |
| 25.09.74 | BIRMINGHAM | LEAGUE DIV ONE* |
| 05.10.74 | DERBY COUNTY | LEAGUE DIV ONE* |
| 19.10.74 | IPSWICH TOWN | LEAGUE DIC ONE* |
| 02.11.74 | MIDDLESBROUGH | LEAGUE DIV ONE* |
| 16.11.74 | WOLVES | LEAGUE DIV ONE* |
| 07.12.74 | LEEDS | LEAGUE DIV ONE* |
| 14.12.74 | MAN CITY | LEAGUE DIV ONE* |
| 26.12.74 | TOTTENHAM | LEAGUE DIV ONE* |
| 18.01.75 | QPR | LEAGUE DIV ONE* |
| 25.01.75 | SWINDON | FA CUP 4th ROUND* |
| 01.02.75 | CARLISLE | LEAGUE DIV ONE* |
| 15.02.75 | QPR | FA CUP 5th ROUND* |
| 19.02.75 | LIVERPOOL | LEAGUE DIV ONE* |
| 28.02.75 | NEWCASTLE | LEAGUE DIV ONE* |
| 15.03.75 | BURNLEY | LEAGUE DIV ONE* |
| 28.03.75 | STOKE CITY | LEAGUE DIV ONE* |
| 29.03.75 | CHELSEA | LEAGUE DIV ONE* |
| 18.04.75 | COVENTRY | LEAGUE DIV ONE* |
| 21.04.75 | IPSWICH TOWN | FA YOUTH |
| | | YOUTH X1 CUP FINAL 1stLEG* |
| 28.04.75 | ARSENAL | LEAGUE DIV ONE* |
| 05.05.75 | 4 W.HAM TEAMS | WALLY St PIER TESTIMONIAL* |
| | | 1964 FA CUP WINNERS |
| | | V |
| | | 1975 FA CUP WINNERS |
| | | 1963 FA YOUTH C/W |
| | | V |
| | | 1975 FA YOUTH C/F |

SEASON 75/76

| | | |
|---|---|---|
| 23.08.75 | BURNLEY | LEAGUE DIV ONE* |
| 25.08.75 | TOTTENHAM | LEAGUE DIV ONE* |
| 06.09.75 | MAN CITY | LEAGUE DIV ONE* |
| 09.09.75 | BRISTOL CITY | L/CUP 2nd ROUND* |
| 20.09.75 | SHEFFIELD UTD | LEAGUE DIV ONE* |
| 01.10.75 | REIPAS LAHDEN | |
| | (FINLAND) | ECWC 1st RD 2nd LEG* |
| 04.10.75 | EVERTON | LEAGUE DIV ONE* |
| 08.10.75 | DARLINGTON | L/CUP 3rd ROUND* |
| 11.10.75 | NEWCASTLE | LEAGUE DIV ONE* |
| 25.10.75 | MAN UTD | LEAGUE DIV ONE* |
| 05.11.75 | ARARAT EREVAN | |
| | (U.S.S.R) | ECWC 2nd RD 2nd LEG* |
| 08.11.75 | COVENTRY | LEAGUE DIV ONE* |
| 22.11.75 | MIDDLES'BORO | LEAGUE DIV ONE* |
| 24.11.75 | TOTTENHAM | L/CUP 4th ROUND* |
| 29.11.75 | ARSENAL | LEAGUE DIV ONE* |
| 10.12.75 | A.C. FIORENTINO | |
| | (ITALY) | ANGLO-ITALIAN |
| | | CUP WINNERS CUP |
| | | FINAL 2nd LEG* |
| 20.12.75 | STOKE CITY | LEAGUE DIV ONE* |
| 27.12.75 | IPSWICH TOWN | LEAGUE DIV ONE* |
| 03.01.76 | LIVERPOOL | FA CUP 3rd ROUND* |
| 10.01.76 | LEICESTER | LEAGUE DIV ONE* |
| 24.01.76 | QPR | LEAGUE DIV ONE* |
| 31.01.76 | LIVERPOOL | LEAGUE DIV ONE* |
| 21.02.76 | DERBY COUNTY | LEAGUE DIV ONE* |
| 23.02.76 | LEEDS | LEAGUE DIV ONE* |
| 06.03.76 | BIRMINGHAM | LEAGUE DIV ONE* |
| 17.03.76 | F.C DEN HAAG | ECWC Q/F (2nd LEG)* |
| 27.03.76 | NORWICH | LEAGUE DIV ONE* |
| 03.04.76 | WOLVES | LEAGUE DIV ONE* |
| 14.04.76 | EINTRACHT | FRANKFURT |
| | (WEST GERMANY) | ECWC S/F (2nd LEG)* |
| 17.04.76 | ASTON VILLA | LEAGUE DIV ONE* |

SEASON 76/77

| | | |
|---|---|---|
| 23.08.76 | QPR | LEAGUE DIV ONE* |
| 28.08.76 | LEICESTER | LEAGUE DIV ONE* |
| 01.09.76 | BARNSLEY | L/CUP 2nd ROUND* |
| 11.09.76 | ARSENAL | LEAGUE DIV ONE* |
| 25.09.76 | SUNDERLAND | LEAGUE DIV ONE* |
| 02.10.76 | BRISTOL CITY | |
| | (RESERVES) | COMBINATION LEAGUE* |
| 06.10.76 | LEEDS | LEAGUE DIV ONE* |
| 16.10.76 | IPSWICH TOWN | LEAGUE DIV ONE* |
| 27.10.76 | QPR | LEAGUE DIV ONE* |
| 02.11.76 | FULHAM | FRANK LAMPARD TESTIMONIAL* |
| 06.11.76 | TOTTENHAM | LEAGUE DIV ONE* |
| 20.11.76 | NEWCASTLE | LEAGUE DIV ONE* |
| 04.12.76 | MIDDLESBROUGH | LEAGUE DIV ONE* |
| 18.12.76 | LIVERPOOL | LEAGUE DIV ONE* |
| 29.12.76 | COVENTRY | LEAGUE DIV ONE* (POSTPONED) |
| 03.01.77 | WBA | LEAGUE DIV ONE* |
| 08.01.77 | BOLTON | FA CUP 3rd ROUND* |
| 22.01.77 | ASTON VILLA | LEAGUE DIV ONE* |
| 12.02.77 | STOKE CITY | LEAGUE DIV ONE* |
| 26.02.77 | BRISTOL CITY | LEAGUE DIV ONE* |
| 12.03.77 | MAN CITY | LEAGUE DIV ONE* |
| 02.04.77 | EVERTON | LEAGUE DIV ONE* |
| 08.04.77 | BIRMINGHAM | LEAGUE DIV ONE* |
| 11.04.77 | NORWICH | LEAGUE DIV ONE* |
| 04.05.77 | COVENTRY | LEAGUE DIV ONE* |
| 07.05.77 | DERBY COUNTY | LEAGUE DIV ONE* |
| 16.05.77 | MAN UTD | LEAGUE DIV ONE* |

SEASON 77/78

| | | |
|---|---|---|
| 20.08.77 | NORWICH | LEAGUE DIV ONE* |
| 27.08.77 | MAN CITY | LEAGUE DIV ONE* |
| 10.09.77 | QPR | LEAGUE DIV ONE* |
| 24.09.77 | EVERTON | LEAGUE DIV ONE* |
| 03.10.77 | MIDDLESBROUGH | LEAGUE DIV ONE* |
| 08.10.77 | NOTTS FOREST | LEAGUE DIV ONE* |

| | | |
|---|---|---|
| 22.10.77 | ASTON VILLA | LEAGUE DIV ONE* |
| 31.10.77 | ENGLAND X1 | TREVOR BROOKING TESTIMONIAL* |
| 12.11.77 | WBA | LEAGUE DIV ONE* |
| 26.11.77 | LEEDS | LEAGUE DIV ONE* |
| 10.12.77 | MAN UTD | LEAGUE DIV ONE* |
| 26.12.77 | BIRMINGHAM | LEAGUE DIV ONE* |
| 31.12.77 | LEICESTER | LEAGUE DIV ONE* |
| 07.01.78 | WATFORD | FA CUP 3rd ROUND* |
| 21.01.78 | NEWCASTLE | LEAGUE DIV ONE* |
| 28.01.78 | QPR | FA CUP 4th ROUND* |
| 11.02.78 | BRISTOL CITY | LEAGUE DIV ONE* |
| 25.02.78 | ARSENAL | LEAGUE DIV ONE* |
| 11.03.78 | WOLVES | LEAGUE DIV ONE* |
| 24.03.78 | IPSWICH TOWN | LEAGUE DIV ONE* |
| 25.03.78 | CHELSEA | LEAGUE DIV ONE* |
| 01.04.78 | COVENTRY | LEAGUE DIV ONE* |
| 15.04.78 | DERBY COUNTY | LEAGUE DIV ONE* |
| 29.04.78 | LIVERPOOL | LEAGUE DIV ONE* |
| 02.05.78 | BOBBY MOORE'S X1 | VICTOR RAILTON MEMORIAL MATCH* |

SEASON 78/79

| | | |
|---|---|---|
| 19.08.78 | NOTTS COUNTY | LEAGUE DIV TWO* |
| 30.08.78 | SWINDON | L/CUP 2nd ROUND* |
| 02.09.78 | FULHAM | LEAGUE DIV TWO* |
| 16.09.78 | BRISTOL ROVERS | LEAGUE DIV TWO* |
| 23.09.78 | SHEFFIELD UTD | LEAGUE DIV TWO* |
| 07.10.78 | MILLWALL | LEAGUE DIV TWO* |
| 21.10.78 | STOKE CITY | LEAGUE DIV TWO* |
| 04.11.78 | PRESTON N E | LEAGUE DIV TWO* |
| 18.11.78 | CRYSTAL PAL | LEAGUE DIV TWO* |
| 02.12.78 | CAMBRIDGE UTD | LEAGUE DIV TWO* |
| 04.12.78 | TOTTENHAM | BILLY BONDS TESTIMONIAL* |
| 16.12.78 | CHARLTON | LEAGUE DIV TWO* |
| 26.12.78 | ORIENT | LEAGUE DIV TWO* |
| 30.12.78 | BLACKBURN | LEAGUE DIV TWO* |

| 10.02.79 | SUNDERLAND | LEAGUE DIV TWO* |
| 24.02.79 | OLDHAM | LEAGUE DIV TWO* |
| 10.03.79 | BRIGHTON | LEAGUE DIV TWO* |
| 24.03.79 | NEWCASTLE | LEAGUE DIV TWO* |
| 31.03.79 | LEICESTER | LEAGUE DIV TWO* |
| 09.04.79 | LUTON TOWN | LEAGUE DIV TWO* |
| 16.04.79 | CARDIFF | LEAGUE DIV TWO* |
| 24/04.79 | BURNLEY | LEAGUE DIV TWO* |
| 28.04.79 | WREXHAM | LEAGUE DIV TWO* |

SEASON 79/80

| 20.08.79 | CHELSEA | LEAGUE DIV TWO* |
| 25.08.79 | OLDHAM | LEAGUE DIV TWO* |
| 28.08.79 | BARNSLEY | L/CUP 2$^{nd}$ ROUND* |
| 15.09.79 | SUNDERLAND | LEAGUE DIV TWO* |
| 25.09.79 | SOUTHEND | L/CUP 3$^{rd}$ ROUND* |
| 29.09.79 | BURNLEY | LEAGUE DIV TWO* |
| 06.10.79 | NEWCASTLE | LEAGUE DIV TWO* |
| 08.10.79 | SOUTHEND | L/CUP 3$^{rd}$ ROUND (2$^{nd}$ REPLAY)* |
| 02.10.79 | LUTON TOWN | LEAGUE DIV TWO* |
| 03.11.79 | WREXHAM | LEAGUE DIV TWO* |
| 05.11.79 | SUNDERLAND | L/CUP 4$^{th}$ RD REPLAY* |
| 17/11.79 | SWANSEA | LEAGUE DIV TWO* |
| 24.11.79 | CARDIFF | LEAGUE DIV TWO* |
| 04.12.79 | NOTTS FOREST | L/CUP 5$^{th}$ ROUND* |
| 08.12.79 | BRISTOL ROVERS | LEAGUE DIV TWO* |
| 21.12.79 | CAMBRIDGE UTD | LEAGUE DIV TWO* |
| 08.01.80 | WBA | FA CUP 3$^{RD}$ REPLAY* |
| 12.01.80 | WATFORD | LEAGUE DIV TWO* |
| 19.01.80 | PRESTON N E | LEAGUE DIV TWO* |
| 09.02.80 | QPR | LEAGUE DIV TWO* |
| 16.02.80 | SWANSEA | FA CUP 5$^{th}$ ROUND* |
| 23.02.80 | LEICESTER | LEAGUE DIV TWO* |
| 08.03.80 | ASTON VILLA | FA CUP 6$^{th}$ ROUND* |
| 11.03.80 | NOTTS COUNTY | LEAGUE DIV TWO* |
| 22.03.80 | FULHAM | LEAGUE DIV TWO* |
| 05.04.80 | ORIENT | LEAGUE DIV TWO* |

| 22.04.80 | BIRMINGHAM | LEAGUE DIV TWO |
| 26.04.80 | SHREWSBURY | LEAGUE DIV TWO |
| 05.05.80 | CHARLTON | LEAGUE DIV TWO |

**SEASON 80/81**

| 16.08.80 | LUTON TOWN | LEAGUE DIV TWO |
| 30.08.80 | NOTTS COUNTY | LEAGUE DIV TWO |
| 02.09.80 | BURNLEY | L/CUP 2nd RD 2nd LEG |
| 13.09.80 | SHREWSBURY | LEAGUE DIV TWO* |
| 20.09.80 | WATFORD | LEAGUE DIV TWO* |
| 01.10.80 | CASTILLA C de F. (SPAIN) | ECWC 1st RD 2nd LEG |
| 07.10.80 | CARDIFF | LEAGUE DIV TWO* |
| 11.10.80 | BLACKBURN | LEAGUE DIV TWO* |
| 22.10.80 | POLITEHNICA TIMISOARA (ROMANIA) | ECWC 2nd RD 1st LEG* |
| 25.10.80 | BOLTON | LEAGUE DIV TWO* |
| 28.10.80 | BARNSLEY | L/CUP 4th ROUND* |
| 08.11.80 | GRIMSBY TOWN | LEAGUE DIV TWO* |
| 11.11.80 | BRISTOL CITY | LEAGUE DIV TWO* |
| 22.11.80 | SWANSEA | LEAGUE DIV TWO* |
| 02.12.80 | TOTTENHAM | L/CUP 5th ROUND* |
| 06.12.80 | SHEFFIELD WED | LEAGUE DIV TWO* |
| 20.12.80 | DERBY COUNTY | LEAGUE DIV TWO* |
| 27.12.80 | ORIENT | LEAGUE DIV TWO* |
| 03.01.81 | WREXHAM | FA CUP 3rd ROUND* |
| 31.01.81 | PRESTON N E | LEAGUE DIV TWO* |
| 10.02.81 | COVENTRY | L/CUP S/F (2nd LEG)* |
| 14/02.81 | CHELSEA | LEAGUE DIV TWO (LOCKED OUT) |
| 21.02.81 | CAMBRIDGE UTD | LEAGUE DIV TWO* |
| 04.03.81 | DINAMO TBLISI (U.S.S.R) | ECWC Q/F 1st LEG* |
| 07.03.81 | NEWCASTLE | LEAGUE DIV TWO* |
| 18.03.81 | DINAMO TBLISI (U.S.S.R) | (SPECIAL CONTINENTAL EDITION) |

| 21.03.81 | OLDHAM | LEAGUE DIV TWO* |
| 04.04.81 | BRISTOL ROVERS | LEAGUE DIV TWO* |
| 13.04.81 | SOUTHAMPTON | BOBBY FERGUSON* |
| | | TESTIMONIAL |
| 21.04.81 | QPR | LEAGUE DIV TWO* |
| 23.04.81 | TOTTENHAM | FA YOUTH CUP FINAL |
| | | (1st LEG)* |
| 02.05.81 | WREXHAM | LEAGUE DIV TWO* |

SEASON 81/82

| 29/08/81 | BRIGHTON | LEAGUE DIV ONE* |
| 12/09/81 | STOKE CITY | LEAGUE DIV ONE* |
| 22/09/81 | SOUTHAMPTON | LEAGUE DIV ONE* |
| 26/09/81 | LIVERPOOL | LEAGUE DIV ONE* |
| 10/10/81 | EVERTON | LEAGUE DIV ONE* |
| 27/10/81 | DERBY COUNTY | L/CUP 2nd ROUND* |
| 31/10/81 | MIDDLESBROUGH | LEAGUE DIV ONE* |
| 10/11/81 | WBA | L/CUP 3rd ROUND* |
| 21/11/81 | COVENTRY | LEAGUE DIV ONE* |
| 01/12/81 | WBA | L/CUP 3rd ROUND |
| | | 2nd REPLAY* |
| 05/12081 | ARSENAL | LEAGUE DIV ONE* |
| 19/12/81 | WOLVES | LEAGUE DIV ONE (POSTPONED) |
| 28/10/81 | IPSWICH TOWN | LEAGUE DIV ONE (POSTPONED) |
| 02/01/82 | EVERTON | FA CUP 3rd ROUND* |
| 09/01/82 | TOTTENHAM | LEAGUE DIV ONE (POSTPONED) |
| 30/01/82 | WBA | LEAGUE DIV ONE* |
| 02/02/82 | MAN CITY | LEAGUE DIV ONE* |
| 13/02/82 | BIRMINGHAM | LEAGUE DIV ONE* |
| 02/03/82 | IPSWICH TOWN | LEAGUE DIV ONE* |
| 06/03/82 | ASTON VILLA | LEAGUE DIV ONE* |
| 13/03/82 | NOTTS COUNTY | LEAGUE DIV ONE* |
| 27/03/82 | NOTTS FOREST | LEAGUE DIV ONE* |
| 06/04/82 | WOLVES | LEAGUE DIV ONE* |
| 10/04/82 | SWANSEA | LEAGUE DIV ONE* |
| 24/04/82 | LEEDS | LEAGUE DIV ONE* |
| 04/05/82 | SUNDERLAND | LEAGUE DIV ONE* |

| | | |
|---|---|---|
| 08/05/82 | MAN UTD | LEAGUE DIV ONE* |
| 10/05/82 | TOTTENHAM | LEAGUE DIV ONE* |

SEASON 82/83

| | | |
|---|---|---|
| 28/08/82 | WBA | LEAGUE DIV ONE* |
| 07/09/82 | IPSWICH TOWN | LEAGUE DIV ONE* |
| 11/09/82 | BIRMINGHAM | LEAGUE DIV ONE* |
| 25/09/82 | MAN CITY | LEAGUE DIV ONE* |
| 09/10/82 | LIVERPOOL | LEAGUE DIV ONE* |
| 26/10/82 | STOKE CITY | MILK CUP 2$^{nd}$ ROUND 2$^{nd}$ LEG* |
| 30/10/82 | MAN UTD | LEAGUE DIV ONE* |
| 13/11/82 | NORWICH | LEAGUE DIV ONE* |
| 23/11/82 | LINCOLN CITY | MILK CUP 3$^{rd}$ ROUND REPLAY* |
| 27/11/82 | EVERTON | LEAGUE DIV ONE* |
| 11/12/82 | COVENTRY | LEAGUE DIV ONE* |
| 21/12/82 | NOTTS COUNTY | MILK CUP 4$^{th}$ ROUND REPLAY* |
| 27/12/82 | SWANSEA | LEAGUE DIV ONE* |
| 01/01/83 | TOTTENHAM | LEAGUE DIV ONE* |
| 04/01/83 | LUTON TOWN | LEAGUE DIV ONE* |
| 22/01/83 | WBA | LEAGUE DIV ONE* |
| 19/02/83 | DUNDEE UTD | FRIENDLY* |
| 26/02/83 | SOUTHAMPTON | LEAGUE DIV ONE |
| 05/03/83 | BRIGHTON | LEAGUE DIV ONE* |
| 19/03/83 | STOKE CITY | LEAGUE DIV ONE |
| 02/04/83 | WATFORD | LEAGUE DIV ONE |
| 09/04/83 | SUNDERLAND | LEAGUE DIV ONE* |
| 23/04/83 | ASTON VILLA | LEAGUE DIV ONE* |
| 07/05/83 | NOTTS COUNTY | LEAGUE DIV ONE* |
| 10/05/83 | ARSENAL | LEAGUE DIV ONE* |

SEASON 83/84

| | | |
|---|---|---|
| 27/08/83 | BIRMINGHAM | CANON LGE DIV ONE* |
| 06/09/83 | LEICESTER | CANON LGE DIV ONE* |
| 10/09/83 | COVENTRY | CANON LGE DIV ONE |
| 24/09/83 | NOTTS COUNTY | CANON LGE DIV ONE |
| 15/10/83 | LIVERPOOL | CANON LGE DIV ONE* |
| 22/10/83 | NORWICH | CANON LGE DIV ONE* |
| 25/10/83 | BURY | MILK CUP 2$^{nd}$ ROUND 2$^{nd}$ LEG* |

| | | |
|---|---|---|
| 05/11/83 | IPSWICH TOWN | CANON LGE DIV ONE* |
| 08/11/83 | BRIGHTON | MILK CUP 3<sup>rd</sup> ROUND* |
| 27/11/83 | MAN UTD | CANON LGE DIV ONE* |
| 30/11/83 | EVERTON | MILK CUP 4<sup>th</sup> ROUND* |
| 10/12/83 | ARSENAL | CANON LGE DIV ONE* |
| 26/12/83 | SOUTHAMPTON | CANON LGE DIV ONE* |
| 31/12/83 | TOTTENHAM | CANON LGE DIV ONE* |
| 07/01/84 | WIGAN | FA CUP 3<sup>rd</sup> ROUND* |
| 21/01/84 | WBA | CANON LGE DIV ONE* |
| 31/01/84 | CRYSTAL PAL | FA CUP 4<sup>th</sup> ROUND REPLAY* |
| 04/02/84 | STOKE CITY | CANON LGE DIV ONE* |
| 21/02/84 | WATFORD | CANON LGE DIV ONE* |
| 10/03/84 | WOLVES | CANON LGE DIV ONE* |
| 31/03/84 | QPR | CANON LGE DIV ONE* |
| 14/04/84 | SUNDERLAND | CANON LGE DIV ONE* |
| 17/04/84 | LUTON TOWN | CANON LGE DIV ONE* |
| 05/05/84 | ASTON VILLA | CANON LGE DIV ONE* |
| 12/05/84 | NOTTS FOREST | CANON LGE DIV ONE* |
| 14/05/84 | EVERTON | CANON LGE DIV ONE* |
| 18/05/84 | TOTTENHAM | PAT HOLLAND TESTIMONIAL* |

SEASON 84/85

| | | |
|---|---|---|
| 25/08/84 | IPSWICH TOWN | CANON LGE DIV ONE |
| 04/09/84 | COVENTRY | CANON LGE DIV ONE |
| 08/09/84 | WATFORD | CANON LGE DIV ONE |
| 22/09/84 | NOTTS FOREST | CANON LGE DIV ONE |
| 06/10/84 | LEICESTER | CANON LGE DIV ONE* |
| 27/10/84 | ARSENAL | CANON LGE DIV ONE* |
| 06/11/84 | MAN CITY | MILK CUP 3<sup>rd</sup> ROUND REPLAY* |
| 10/11/84 | EVERTON | CANON LGE DIV ONE* |
| 17/11/84 | SUNDERLAND | CANON LGE DIV ONE* |
| 01/12/84 | WBA | CANON LGE DIV ONE* |
| 15/12/84 | SHEFFIELD WED | CANON LGE DIV ONE* |
| 22/12/84 | SOUTHAMPTON | CANON LGE DIV ONE* |
| 01/01/85 | QPR | CANON LGE DIV ONE* |
| 05/01/85 | PORT VALE | FA CUP 3<sup>rd</sup> ROUND* |
| 02/02/85 | NEWCASTLE | CANON LGE DIV ONE* |

| 04/02/85 | NORWICH | FA CUP 4th ROUND* |
| 23/02/85 | ASTON VILLA | CANON LGE DIV ONE* |
| 06/03/85 | WIMBLEDON | FA CUP 5th ROUND REPLAY* |
| 15/03/85 | MAN UTD | CANON LGE DIV ONE* |
| 06/04/85 | TOTTENHAM | CANON LGE DIV ONE* |
| 13/04/85 | CHELSEA | CANON LGE DIV ONE* |
| 27/04/85 | LUTON TOWN | CANON LGE DIV ONE* |
| 06/05/85 | NORWICH | CANON LGE DIV ONE* |
| 14/05/85 | STOKE CITY | CANON LGE DIV ONE* |
| 20/05/85 | LIVERPOOL | CANON LGE DIV ONE* |

SEASON 85/86

| 20/08/85 | QPR | CANON LGE DIV ONE* |
| 24/08/85 | LUTON TOWN | CANON LGE DIV ONE* |
| 31/08/85 | LIVERPOOL | CANON LGE DIV ONE* |
| 14/09/85 | LEICESTER | CANON LGE DIV ONE* |
| 24/09/85 | SWANSEA | MILK CUP 2nd ROUND 2nd LEG |
| 28/09/85 | NOTTS FOREST | CANON LGE DIV ONE |
| 12/10/85 | ARSENAL | CANON LGE DIV ONE* |
| 19/10/85 | ASTON VILLA | CANON LGE DIV ONE* |
| 02/11/85 | EVERTON | CANON LGE DIV ONE* |
| 16/11/85 | WATFORD | CANON LGE DIV ONE* |
| 30/11/85 | WBA | CANON LGE DIV ONE* |
| 14/12/85 | BIRMINGHAM | CANON LGE DIV ONE* |
| 28/12/85 | SOUTHAMPTON | CANON LGE DIV ONE POSTPONED |
| 01/01/86 | CHELSEA | CANON LGE DIV ONE POSTPONED |
| 25/01/86 | IPSWICH TOWN | FA CUP 4th ROUND* |
| 02/02/86 | MAN UTD | CANON LGE DIV ONE* |
| 03/03/86 | MAN UTD | FA CUP 5th ROUND* |
| 22/03/86 | SHEFFIELD WED | CANON LGE DIV ONE* |
| 31/03/86 | TOTTENHAM | CANON LGE DIV ONE* |
| 08/04/86 | SOUTHAMPTON | CANON LGE DIV ONE* |
| 12/04/86 | OXFORD UTD | CANON LGE DIV ONE |
| 15/04/86 | CHELSEA | CANON LGE DIV ONE |
|  |  | LOCK OUT/GET IN* |
| 21/04/86 | NEWCASTLE | CANON LGE DIV ONE* |
| 26/04/86 | COVENTRY | CANON LGE DIV ONE* |

| | | |
|---|---|---|
| 28/04/86 | MAN CITY | CANON LGE DIV ONE* |
| 30/04/86 | IPSWICH TOWN | CANON LGE DIV ONE* |
| 12/05/86 | TOTTENHAM | GERHARDT AMPOFO TESTIMONIAL* |

**SEASON 86/87**

| | | |
|---|---|---|
| 23/08/86 | COVENTRY | LEAGUE DIV ONE* |
| 02/09/86 | NOTTS FOREST | LEAGUE DIV ONE* |
| 06/06/86 | LIVERPOOL | LEAGUE DIV ONE* |
| 20/09/86 | LUTON TOWN | LEAGUE DIV ONE* |
| 07/10/86 | PRESTON N E | LITTLEWOODS CUP 2nd ROUND* |
| 11/10/86 | CHELSEA | LEAGUE DIV ONE* |
| 25/10/86 | CHARLTON | LEAGUE DIV ONE* |
| 02/11/86 | EVERTON | LEAGUE DIV ONE* |
| 18/11/86 | OXFORD UTD | LITTLEWOODS CUP 4th ROUND* |
| 22/11/86 | ASTON VILLA | LEAGUE DIV ONE* |
| 25/11/86 | CHELSEA | FULL MEMBERS CUP 3rd ROUND |
| 06/12/86 | SOUTHAMPTON | LEAGUE DIV ONE* |
| 20/12/86 | QPR | LEAGUE DIV ONE* |
| 27/12/86 | WIMBLEDON | LEAGUE DIV ONE* |
| 01/01/87 | LEICESTER | LEAGUE DIV ONE* |
| 27/01/87 | TOTTENHAM | LITTLEWOODS CUP Q/F* |
| 31/01/87 | ORIENT | FA CUP 3rd ROUND REPLAY* |
| 07/02/87 | OXFORD UTD | LEAGUE DIV ONE* |
| 09/02/87 | SHEFFIELD UTD | FA CUP 4th ROUND* |
| 25/02/87 | SHEFFIELD WED | FA CUP 5th ROUND REPLAY* |
| 14/03/87 | NORWICH | LEAGUE DIV ONE* |
| 24/03/87 | SHEFFIELD WED | LEAGUE DIV ONE* |
| 28/03/87 | WATFORD | LEAGUE DIV ONE* |
| 08/04/87 | ARSENAL | LEAGUE DIV ONE* |
| 14/04/87 | MAN UTD | LEAGUE DIV ONE* |
| 20/04/87 | TOTTENHAM | LEAGUE DIV ONE* |
| 02/05/87 | NEWCASTLE | LEAGUE DIV ONE* |
| 09/05/87 | MAN CITY | LEAGUE DIV ONE* |

**SEASON 87/88**

| | | |
|---|---|---|
| 15/08/87 | QPR | BARCLAYS DIV ONE* |
| 29/08/87 | NORWICH | BARCLAYS DIV ONE* |

| | | |
|---|---|---|
| 05/09/87 | LIVERPOOL | BARCLAYS DIV ONE* |
| 19/09/87 | TOTTENHAM | BARCLAYS DIV ONE |
| 03/10/87 | DERBY COUNTY | BARCLAYS DIV ONE |
| 06/10/87 | BARNSLEY | LITTLEWOODS CUP 2nd ROUND 2nd LEG |
| 10/10/87 | CHARLTON | BARCLAYS DIV ONE* |
| 25/10/87 | MAN UTD | BARCLAYS DIV ONE* |
| 07/11/87 | SHEFFIELD WED | BARCLAYS DIV ONE* |
| 10/11/87 | MILLWALL | SIMOD CUP 1st ROUND |
| 21/11/87 | NOTTS FOREST | BARCLAYS DIV ONE* |
| 05/12/87 | SOUTHAMPTON | BARCLAYS DIV ONE* |
| 19/12/87 | NEWCASTLE | BARCLAYS DIV ONE* |
| 26/12/87 | WIMBLEDON | BARCLAYS DIV ONE* |
| 13/02/88 | PORTSMOUTH | BARCLAYS DIV ONE* |
| 05/03/88 | OXFORD UTD | BARCLAYS DIV ONE* |
| 12/04/88 | ARSENAL | BARCLAYS DIV ONE* |
| 23/04/88 | COVENTRY | BARCLAYS DIV ONE* |
| 02/05/88 | CHELSEA | BARCLAYS DIV ONE* |

SEASON 88/89

| | | |
|---|---|---|
| 03/09/88 | CHARLTON | BARCLAYS DIV ONE* |
| 29/10/88 | LIVERPOOL | BARCLAYS DIV ONE* |
| 12/11/88 | NOTTS FOREST | BARCLAYS DIV ONE* |
| 26/11/88 | EVERTON | BARCLAYS DIV ONE* |
| 10/12/88 | SHEFFIELD WED | BARCLAYS DIV ONE* |
| 17/12/88 | TOTTENHAM | BARCLAYS DIV ONE* |
| 02/01/89 | WIMBLEDON | BARCLAYE DIV ONE* |
| 18/01/89 | ASTON VILLA | LITTLEWOODS Q/F* |
| 21/01/89 | MAN UTD | BARCLAYS DIV ONE* |
| 12/02/89 | LUTON TOWN | LITTLEWOODS CUP Q/F 1st LEG* |
| 18/03/89 | NORWICH | FA CUP 6th ROUND* |
| 27/03/89 | NORWICH | BARCLAYS DIV ONE* |
| 06/05/89 | LUTON TOWN | BARCLAYS DIV ONE* |

SEASON 89/90

| | | |
|---|---|---|
| 22/08/89 | BRADFORD CITY | BARCLAYS DIV TWO* |
| 26/08/89 | PLYMOUTH | BARCLAYS DIV TWO* |

| 09/09/89 | SWINDON | BARCLAYS DIV TWO* |
|---|---|---|
| 23/09/89 | WATFORD | BARCLAYS DIV TWO* |
| 30/09/89 | WBA | BARCLAYS DIV TWO* |
| 28/10/89 | OXFORD UTD | BARCLAYS DIV TWO* |
| 11/11/89 | NEWCASTLE | BARCLAYS DIV TWO* |
| 18/11/89 | MIDDLESBROUGH | BARCLAYS DIV TWO* |
| 02/12/89 | STOKE CITY | BARCLAYS DIV TWO* |
| 20/01/90 | HULL CITY | BARCLAYS DIV TWO* |
| 31/01/90 | DERBY COUNTY | LITTLEWOODS CUP 5th ROUND 2nd REPLAY* |
| 24/02/90 | BLACKBURN | BARCLAYS DIV TWO* |
| 28/02/90 | OLDHAM | LITTLEWOODS CUP S/F 2nd LEG* |
| 10/03/90 | PORTSMOUTH | BARCLAYS DIV TWO* |
| 31/03/90 | PORT VALE | BARCLAYS DIV TWO* |
| 02/05/90 | LEICESTER | BARCLAYS DIV TWO* |

SEASON 90/91

| 29/08/90 | PORTSMOUTH | BARCLAYS DIV TWO LOCKED OUT |
|---|---|---|
| 01/09/90 | WATFORD | BARCLAYS DIV TWO* |
| 15/09/90 | WOLVES | BARCLAYS DIV TWO* |
| 19/09/90 | IPSWICH TOWN | BARCLAYS DIV TWO* |
| 06/10/90 | HULL CITY | BARCLAYS DIV TWO* |
| 24/10/90 | BLACKBURN | BARCLAYS DIV TWO* |
| 27/10/90 | CHARLTON | BARCLAYS DIV TWO* |
| 12/11/90 | TOTTENHAM | BILLY BONDS TESTIMONIAL* |
| 17/11/90 | BRIGHTON | BARCLAYS DIV TWO* |
| 01/12/90 | WBA | BARCLAYS DIV TWO* |
| 15/12/90 | MIDDLESBROUGH | BARCLAYS DIV TWO* |
| 26/12/90 | OLDHAM | BARCLAYS DIV TWO* |
| 19/01/91 | LEICESTER | BARCLAYS DIV TWO* |
| 16/02/91 | CREWE | FA CUP 5th ROUND* |
| 24/02/91 | MILLWALL | BARCLAYS DIV TWO |
| 16/03/91 | SHEFFIELD WED | BARCLAYS DIV TWO* |
| 20/04/91 | SWINDON | BARCLAYS DIV TWO* |
| 08/05/91 | BRISTOL ROVERS | BARCLAYS DIV TWO* |

| | | |
|---|---|---|
| 11/05/91 | NOTTS COUNTY | BARCLAYS DIV TWO* |

SEASON 91/92

| | | |
|---|---|---|
| 17/08/91 | LUTON TOWN | BARCLAYS DIV ONE* |
| 31/08/91 | NOTTS COUNTY | BARCLAYS DIV ONE* |
| 07/09/91 | CHELSEA | BARCLAYS DIV ONE* |
| 21/09/91 | MAN CITY | BARCLAYS DIV ONE* |
| 05/10/91 | COVENTRY | BARCLAYS DIV ONE* |
| 26/10/91 | TOTTENHAM | BARCLAYS DIV ONE* |
| 11/01/92 | WIMBLEDON | BARCLAYS DIV ONE* |
| 01/02/92 | OLDHAM | BARCLAYS DIV ONE* |
| 29/02/92 | EVERTON | BARCLAYS DIV ONE* |
| 20/04/92 | CRYSTAL PAL | BARCLAYS DIV ONE* |

SEASON 92/93

| | | |
|---|---|---|
| 05/09/92 | WATFORD | BARCLAYS DIV ONE* |
| 07/11/92 | NOTTS COUNTY | BARCLAYS DIV ONE* |
| 21/11/92 | OXFORD UTD | BARCLAYS DIV ONE* |
| 16/01/93 | PORTSMOUTH | BARCLAYS DIV ONE* |
| 20/03/93 | TRANMERE | BARCLAYS DIV ONE* |
| 08/05/93 | CAMBRIDGE | BARCLAYS DIV ONE* |

SEASON 93/94

| | | |
|---|---|---|
| 14/08/93 | WIMBLEDON | CARLING PREMIER* |
| 28/08/93 | QPR | CARLING PREMIER* |
| 16/10/93 | ASTON VILLA | CARLING PREMIER* |
| 20/11/93 | OLDHAM | CARLING PREMIER* |
| 03/01/94 | SHEFFIELD UTD | CARLING PREMIER* |
| 08/01/94 | WATFORD | FA CUP 3rd ROUND* |
| 24/01/94 | NORWICH | CARLING PREMIER* |
| 26/02/94 | MAN UTD | CARLING PREMIER* |
| 07/03/94 | FA PREMIER LGE | BOBBY MOORE MEMORIAL MATCH* |
| 19/03/94 | NEWCASTLE | CARLING PREMIER* |
| 09/04/94 | EVERTON | CARLING PREMIER* |
| 07/05/94 | SOUTHAMPTON | CARLING PREMIER* |

SEASON 94/95

| 20/08/94 | LEEDS | CARLING PREMIER* |
|---|---|---|
| 05/10/94 | WALSALL | COCA COLA CUP 2<sup>nd</sup> ROUND 2<sup>nd</sup> LEG* |

| 20/08/94 | LEEDS | CARLING PREMIER* |
|---|---|---|
| 05/10/94 | WALSALL | COCA COLA CUP |
| | | 2nd ROUND 2nd LEG* |
| 08/10/94 | CRYSTAL PAL | CARLING PREMIER* |
| 26/10/94 | CHELSEA | COCA COLA CUP |
| | | 3rd ROUND* |
| 05/11/94 | LEICESTER | CARLING PREMIER* |
| 26/11/94 | COVENTRY | CARLING PREMIER* |
| 17/10/94 | MAN CITY | CARLING PREMIER* |
| 31/12/94 | NOTTS FOREST | CARLING PREMIER* |
| 14/01/95 | TOTTENHAM | CARLING PREMIER* |
| 25/02/95 | CHELSEA | CARLING PREMIER* |
| 30/04/95 | BLACKBURN | CARLING PREMIER* |
| 03/05/95 | QPR | CARLING PREMIER* |
| 14/05/95 | MAN UTD | CARLING PREMIER* |

SEASON 95/96

| 19/08/95 | LEEDS | CARLING PREMIER* |
|---|---|---|
| 11/09/95 | CHELSEA | CARLING PREMIER* |
| 04/10/95 | BRISTOL ROVERS | COCA COLA CUP |
| | | 2nd ROUND 2nd LEG* |
| 04/11/95 | ASTON VILLA | CARLING PREMIER* |
| 22/11/95 | LIVERPOOL | CARLING PREMIER* |
| 06/01/96 | SOUTHEND UTD | FA CUP 3rd ROUND* |
| 22/01/96 | MAN UTD | CARLING PREMIER* |
| 07/02/96 | GRIMSBY TOWN | FA CUP 4th ROUND* |
| 21/02/96 | NEWCASTLE | CARLING PREMIER* |
| 09/03/96 | MIDDLESBROUGH | CARLING PREMIER* |
| 13/04/96 | BOLTON | CARLING PREMIER* |
| 05/05/96 | SHEFFIELD WED | CARLING PREMIER* |

95/96 FA CUP MATCHES SPONSORED BY LITTLEWOODS

SEASON 96/97

| 24/08/96 | SOUTHAMPTON | CARLING PREMIER* |
|---|---|---|
| 25/09/96 | BARNET | COCA COLA CUP |
| | | 2nd ROUND 2nd LEG* |

| 29/09/96 | LIVERPOOL | CARLING PREMIER* |
|---|---|---|
| 26/10/96 | BLACKBURN | CARLING PREMIER* |
| 23/11/96 | DERBY COUNTY | CARLING PREMIER* |
| 27/11/96 | STOCKPORT | COCA COLA CUP 4th ROUND* |
| 08/10/96 | MAN UTD | CARLING PREMIER* |
| 01/01/97 | NOTTS FOREST | CARLING PREMIER* |
| 20/01/97 | LEEDS | CARLING PREMIER* |
| 29/01/97 | ARSENAL | CARLING PREMIER* |
| 24/02/97 | TOTTENHAM | CARLING PREMIER* |
| 19/04/97 | EVERTON | CARLING PREMIER* |
| 03/05/97 | SHEFFIELD WED | CARLING PREMIER* |

SEASON 97/98

| 02/08/97 | QPR | STEVE POTTS    TESTIMONIAL* |
|---|---|---|
| 30/08/97 | WIMBLEDON | CARLING PREMIER* |
| 20/09/97 | NEWCASTLE | CARLING PREMIER* |
| 27/09/97 | LIVERPOOL | CARLING PREMIER* |
| 29/09/97 | HUDDERSFIELD | COCA COLA CUP 2nd ROUND 2nd LEG* |
| 15/10/97 | ASTON VILLA | COCA COLA CUP    3rd ROUND* |
| 18/10/97 | BOLTON | CARLING PREMIER* |
| 03/11/97 | CRYSTAL PAL | CARLING PREMIER* |
| 19/11/97 | WALSALL | COCA COLA CUP 4th ROUND* |
| 29/11/97 | ASTON VILLA | CARLING PREMIER* |
| 03/01/98 (Programme dated 97) | EMLEY | FA CUP 3rd ROUND* |
| 06/01/98 | ARSENAL | COCA COLA CUP 5th ROUND* |
| 10/01/98 | BARNSLEY | CARLING PREMIER* |
| 14/02/98 | BLACKBURN | FA CUP 5th ROUND* |
| 02/03/98 | ARSENAL | CARLING PREMIER* |
| 11/03/98 | MAN UTD | CARLING PREMIER* |
| 17/03/98 | ARSENAL | FA CUP 6th ROUND REPLAY* |
| 30/03/98 | LEEDS | CARLING PREMIER* |
| 18/04/98 | BLACKBURN | CARLING PREMIER* |

| | | |
|---|---|---|
| 25/04/98 | SOUTHAMPTON | CARLING PREMIER* |
| 10/05/98 | LEICESTER | CARLING PREMIER* |

97/98 FA CUP MATCHES SPONSORED BY LITTLEWOODS

SEASON 98/99

| | | |
|---|---|---|
| 22/08/98 | MAN UTD | CARLING PREMIER* |
| 09/09/98 | WIMBLEDON | CARLING PREMIER* |
| 22/09/98 | NORTHAMPTON | WORTHINGTON CUP 2nd ROUND 2nd LEG* |
| 28/09/98 | SOUTHAMPTON | CARLING PREMIER* |
| 17/10/98 | ASTON VILLA | CARLING PREMIER* |
| 14/11/98 | LEICESTER | CARLING PREMIER* |
| 28/11/98 | TOTTENHAM | CARLING PREMIER* |
| 28/12/98 | COVENTRY | CARLING PREMIER* |
| 16/01/99 | SHEFFIELD WED | CARLING PREMIER* |
| 06/02/99 | ARSENAL | CARLING PREMIER* |
| 13/02/99 | NOTTS FOREST | CARLING PREMIER* |
| 20/03/99 | NEWCASTLE | CARLING PREMIER* |
| 05/03/99 | CHARLTON | CARLING PREMIER* |
| 17/04/99 | DERBY COUNTY | CARLING PREMIER* |
| 01/05/99 | LEEDS | CARLING PREMIER* |
| 18/05/99 | SHEFFIELD WED | FA PREMIER ACADEMY U-19 PLAY-OFF FINAL* |

SEASON 99/2000

| | | |
|---|---|---|
| 21/08/99 | LEICESTER | CARLING PREMIER* |
| 11/09/99 | WATFORD | CARLING PREMIER* |
| 03/10/99 | ARSENAL | CARLING PREMIER* |
| 21/11/99 | SHEFFIELD WED | CARLING PREMIER* |
| 15/12/99 | ASTON VILLA | WORTHINGTON CUP Q/F* |
| 18/12/99 | MAN UTD | CARLING PREMIER* |
| 11/01/00 | ASTON VILLA | WORTHINGTON CUP Q/F REPLAY* |
| 15/01/00 | ASTON VILLA | CARLING PREMIER* |
| 26/02/00 | EVERTON | CARLING PREMIER* |

| 29/04/00 | MIDDLESBROUGH | CARLING PREMIER* |
| 14/05/00 | LEEDS | CARLING PREMIER* |

SEASON 00/01

| 26.08.00 | MAN UTD | CARLING PREMIER* |
| 17.09.00 | LIVERPOOL | CARLING PREMIER* |
| 21.10.00 | ARSENAL | CARLING PREMIER* |
| 28.10.00 | NEWCASTLE | CARLING PREMIER* |
| 11.11.00 | MAN CITY | CARLING PREMIER* |
| 02.12.00 | MIDDLESBROUGH | CARLING PREMIER* |
| 09.12.00 | ASTON VILLA | CARLING PREMIER* |
| 13.01.01 | SUNDERLAND | CARLING PREMIER* |
| 31.01.01 | TOTTENHAM | CARLING PREMIER* |
| 01.03.01 | CHELSEA | CARLING PREMIER* |
| 11.03.01 | TOTTENHAM | FA CUP 6th ROUND* |
| 14.04.01 | DERBY COUNTY | CARLING PREMIER* |
| 21.04.01 | LEEDS | CARLING PREMIER* |
| 05.05.01 | SOUTHAMPTON | CARLING PREMIER* |

00/01 FA CUP MATCHES SPONSORED BY AXA

SEASON 01/02

| 25.08.01 | LEEDS | BARCLAYS PREMIER* |
| 23.09.01 | NEWCASTLE | BARCLAYS PREMIER* |
| 24.10.01 | CHELSEA | BARCLAYS PREMIER* |
| 03.11.01 | FULHAM | BARCLAYS PREMIER* |
| 15.12.01 | ARSENAL | BARCLAYS PREMIER* |
| 26.12.01 | DERBY COUNTY | BARCLAYS PREMIER* |
| 12.01.02 | LEICESTER | BARCLAYS PREMIER* |
| 06.02.02 | CHELSEA | FA CUP 4th ROUND REPLAY* |
| 23.02.02 | MIDDLESBROUGH | BARCLAYS PREMIER* |
| 16.03.02 | MAN UTD | BARCLAYS PREMIER* |
| 06.04.02 | CHARLTON | BARCLAYS PREMIER* |

01/02 FA CUP MATCHES SPONSORED BY AXA

SEASON 02/03

| 24.08.02 | ARSENAL | BARCLAYS PREMIIER* |

| | | |
|---|---|---|
| 31.08.02 | CHARLTON | BARCLAYS PREMIER* |
| 21.09.02 | MAN CITY | BARCLAYS PREMIER* |
| 27.10.02 | EVERTON | BARCLAYS PREMIER* |
| 17/11/02 | MAN UTD | BARCLAYS PREMIER* |
| 02.12.02 | SOUTHAMPTON | BARCLAYS PREMIER* |
| 26.12.02 | FULHAM | BARCLAYS PREMIER* |
| 04.01.03 | NOTTS FOREST | FA CUP 3rd ROUND* |
| 29.01.03 | BLACKBURN | BARCLAYS PREMIER* |
| 01.03.03 | TOTTENHAM | BARCLAYS PREMIER* |
| 12.04.03 | ASTON VILLA | BARCLAYS PREMIER* |
| 21.04.03 | MIDDLESBROUGH | BARCLAYS PREMIER* |
| 03.05.03 | CHELSEA | BARCLAYS PREMIER* |

SEASON 03/04

| | | |
|---|---|---|
| 16.08.03 | SHEFFIELD UTD | NATIONWIDE DIV 1* |
| 26.08.03 | BRADFORD CITY | NATIONWIDE DIV 1* |
| 28.09.03 | MILLWALL | NATIONWIDE DIV 1* |
| 15.10.03 | NORWICH | NATIONWIDE DIV 1* |
| 18.10.03 | BURNLEY | NATIONWIDE DIV 1* |
| 22.10.03 | NOTTS FOREST | NATIONWIDE DIV 1* |
| 29.11.03 | WIGAN | NATIONWIDE DIV 1* |
| 09.12.03 | STOKE CITY | NATIONWIDE DIV 1* |
| 13.12.03 | SUNDERLAND | NATIONWIDE DIV 1* |
| 26.12.03 | IPSWICH TOWN | NATIONWIDE DIV 1* |
| 10.01.04 | PRESTON N E | NATIONWIDE DIV 1* |
| 31.01.04 | ROTHERHAM | NATIONWIDE DIV 1* |
| 28.02.04 | CARDIFF | NATIONWIDE DIV 1* |
| 09.03.04 | WIMBLEDON | NATIONWIDE DIV 1* |
| 17/03/04 | CREWE | NATIONWIDE DIV 1* |
| 01.05.04 | WATFORD | NATIONWIDE DIV 1* |
| 18.05.04 | IPSWICH TOWN | DIV 1 PLAY-OFF SEMI-FINAL 2nd LEG* |

ALL CHAMPIONSHIP MATCHES (04/05) SPONSORED BY COCA COLA

SEASON 04/05

| | | |
|---|---|---|
| 10.08.04 | READING | CHAMPIONSHIP* |
| 14.09.04 | ROTHERHAM | CHAMPIONSHIP* |

| 18.09.04 | IPSWICH TOWN | CHAMPIONSHIP* |
|---|---|---|
| 28.08.04 | BURNLEY | CHAMPIONSHIP* |
| 02.10.04 | WOLVES | CHAMPIONSHIP* |
| 19.10.04 | STOKE CITY | CHAMPIONSHIP* |
| 23.10.04 | GILLINGHAM | CHAMPIONSHIP* |
| 27.11.04 | WATFORD | CHAMPIONSHIP* |
| 03.01.05 | SHEFFIELD UTD | CHAMPIONSHIP* |
| 23.01.05 | DERBY COUNTY | CHAMPIONSHIP* |
| 06.02.05 | CARDIFF | CHAMPIONSHIP* |
| 05.03.05 | PRESTON N E | CHAMPIONSHIP* |
| 15.03.05 | CREWE | CHAMPIONSHIP* |
| 09.04.05 | COVENTRY | CHAMPIONSHIP* |
| 16.04.05 | MILLWALL | CHAMPIONSHIP* |
| 29.04.05 | SUNDERLAND | CHAMPIONSHIP* |
| 14.05.05 | IPSWICH | CHAMPIONSHIP PLAY-OFF SEMI-FINAL 2nd LEG * |

SEASON 05/06

| 06.08.05 | CA OSASUNA (SPAIN) | OUT PERFORMANCE DISPLAY CUP* |
|---|---|---|
| 13.08.05 | BLACKBURN | BARCLAYS PREMIER* |
| 27.08.05 | BOLTON | BARCLAYS PREMIER* |
| 12.09.05 | ASTON VILLA | BARCLAYS PREMIER* |
| 24.09.05 | ARSENAL | BARCLAYS PREMIER* |
| 23.10.05 | MIDDLESBROUGH | BARCLAYS PREMIER* |
| 05.11.05 | WBA | BARCLAYS PREMIER* |
| 27.11.05 | MAN UTD | BARCLAYS PREMIER* |
| 17.12.05 | NEWCASTLE | BARCLAYS PREMIER* |
| 28.12.05 | WIGAN | BARCLAYS PREMIER* |
| 02.01.06 | CHELSEA | BARCLAYS PREMIER* |
| 23.01.06 | FULHAM | BARCLAYS PREMIER* |
| 28.01.06 | BLACKBURN | FA CUP 4th ROUND* |
| 04.02.06 | SUNDERLAND | BARCLAYS PREMIER* |
| 13.02.06 | BIRMINGHAM | BARCLAYS PREMIER* |
| 04.03.06 | EVERTON | BARCLAYS PREMIER* |
| 15.03.06 | BOLTON | FA CUP 5th ROUND REPLAY* |

| | | |
|---|---|---|
| 18.03.06 | PORTSMOUTH | BARCLAYS PREMIER* |
| 02.04.06 | CHARLTON | BARCLAYS PREMIER* |
| 15.04.06 | MAN CITY | BARCLAYS PREMIER* |
| 26.04.06 | LIVERPOOL | BARCLAYS PREMIER* |
| 07.05.06 | TOTTENHAM | BARCLAYS PREMIER* |
| | | |
| 12.08.06 | OLYMPIAKOS CFP (GREECE) | PRE SEASON FRIENDLY* |
| 19.08.06 | CHARLTON | BARCLAYS PREMIER* |
| 10.09.06 | ASTON VILLA | BARVLAYS PREMIER* |
| 14.09.06 (ITALY) | PALERMO UEFA CUP | 1st ROUND 1st LEG* |
| 17.09.06 | NEWCASTLE | BARCLAYS PREMIER* |
| 01.10.06 | READING | BARCLAYS PREMIER* |
| 29.10.06 | BLACKBURN | BARCLAYS PREMIER* |
| 05.11.06 | ARSENAL | BARCLAYS PREMIER* |
| 25.11.06 | SHEFFIELD UTD | BARCLAYS PREMIER* |
| 06.12.06 | WIGAN | BARCLAYS PREMIER* |
| 17.12.06 | MAN UTD | BARCLAYS PREMIER* |
| 26.12.06 | PORTSMOUTH | BARCLAYS PREMIER* |
| 30.12.06 | MAN CITY | BARCLAYS PREMIER* |
| 06.01.07 | BRIGHTON | FA CUP 3rd ROUND* |
| 13.01.07 | FULHAM | BARCLAYS PREMIER* |
| 27.01.07 | WATFORD | FA CUP 4th ROUND* |
| 30.01.07 | LIVERPOOL | BARCLAYS PREMIER* |
| 10.02.07 | WATFORD | BARCLAYS PREMIER* |
| 04.03.07 | TOTTENHAM | BARCLAYS PREMIER* |
| 31.03.07 | MIDDLESBROUGH | BARCLAYS PREMIER* |
| 18.04.07 | CHELSEA | BARCLAYS PREMIER* |
| 21.04.07 | EVERTON | BARCLAYS PREMIER* |
| 05.05.07 | BOLTON | BARCLAYS PREMIER* |

06/07 FA CUP MATCHES SPONSORED BY E.ON

| | | |
|---|---|---|
| 04.08.07 | AS ROMA (ITALY) | PRE SEASON FRIENDLY* |

SEASON 07/08

| | | |
|---|---|---|
| 11.08.07 | MAN CITY | BARCLAYS PREMIER* |
| 25.08.07 | WIGAN | BARCLAYS PREMIER* |
| 15.09.07 | MIDDLESBROUGH | BARCLAYS PREMIER* |
| 26.09.07 | PLYMOUTH | CARLING CUP   3rd ROUND* |
| 29.09.07 | ARSENAL | BARCLAYS PREMIER * |
| 21.10.07 | SUNDERLAND | BARCLAYS PREMIER * |
| 04.11.07 | BOLTON | BARCLAYS PREMIER * |
| 25.11.07 | TOTTENHAM | BARCLAYS PREMIER * |
| 12.12.07 | EVERTON | CARLING CUP Q/F* |
| 15.12.07 | EVERTON | BARCLAYS PREMIER* |
| 26.12.07 | READING | BARCLAYS PREMIER* |
| 19.12.07 | MAN UTD | BARCLAYS PREMIER* |
| 05.01.08 | MAN CITY | FA CUP 3rd ROUND* |
| 12.01.08 | FULHAM | BARCLAYS PREMIER* |
| 30.01.08 | LIVERPOOL | BARCLAYS PREMIER* |
| 09.02.08 | BIRMINGHAM | BARCLAYS PREMIER* |
| 01.03.08 | CHELSEA | BARCLAYS PREMIER* |
| 15.03.08 | BLACKBURN | BARCLAYS PREMIER* |
| 08.04.08 | PORTSMOUTH | BARCLAYS PREMIER* |
| 19.08.08 | DERBY COUNTY | BARCLAYS PREMIER* |
| 26.04.08 | NEWCASTLE | BARCLAYS PREMIER* |
| 11.05.08 | ASTON VILLA | BARCLAYS PREMIER* |

HOME GAMES ATTENDED BUT NO PROGRAMMES

| | | |
|---|---|---|
| 84/85 | BRISTOL CITY | MILK CUP |
| 87/88 | LUTON TOWN | BARCLAYS DIVISION ONE |
| | CHARLTON | FA CUP 3rd ROUND |
| | EVERTON | BARCLAYS DIVISION ONE |
| | WATFORD | "      "      " |
| 88/89 | ASTON VILLA | "      "      " |
| | ARSENAL | "      "      " |
| | NEWCASTLE | "      "      " |

# WESTHAM UNITED FOOTBALL PROGRAMMES

### AWAY ISSUES

ALL PROGRAMMES MARKED WITH * WERE ATTENDED
AND MARKED WITH X IN TOP LEFT CORNER OF PROGRAMME
IF REQUIRED MATCH TICKETS WILL BE ENCLOSED WITHIN THE PROGRAMME
THERE ARE DUPLICATE/TRIPLICATE ISSUES AMONGST THE COLLECTION

| Date | Opponents | Competition |
| --- | --- | --- |
| SEASON 52/53 | | |
| 06.04.53 | FULHAM | LEAGUE DIV TWO |
| SEASON 53/54 | | |
| 16.01.54 | FULHAM | LEAGUE DIV TWO |
| SEASON 54/55 | | |
| 11.04.55 | FULHAM | LEAGUE DIV TWO |
| SEASON 56/57 | | |
| 18.08.56 | FULHAM | LEAGUE DIV TWO |
| SEASON 57/58 | | |
| 12.10.57 | CHARLTON | LEAGUE DIV TWO |
| 01.02.58 | FULHAM | LEAGUE DIV TWO |
| SEASON 62/63 | | |
| 11.02.63 | FULHAM | FA CUP 3$^{rd}$ ROUND REPLAY |
| SEASON 63/64 | | |
| 25.01.64 | LEYTON ORIENT | FA CUP 4$^{th}$ ROUND |
| 14.03.64 | MAN UTD | FA CUP S/F (HILLSBOROUGH) |
| 02.05.64 | PRESTON N E | FA CUP FINAL (WEMBLEY) |
| SEASON 64/65 | | |
| 28.11.64 | CHELSEA | LEAGUE DIV ONE |

| | | |
|---|---|---|
| 16.01.65 | TOTTENHAM | LEAGUE DIV ONE |
| 19.04.65 | WBA | LEAGUE DIV ONE |
| 19.05.65 | TSV MUNCHEN | ECWC FINAL |
| | 1860 | (WEMBLEY) |

SEASON 65/66

| | | |
|---|---|---|
| 20.11.65 | ARSENAL | LEAGUE DIV ONE |

SEASON 66/67

| | | |
|---|---|---|
| 23.08.66 | ARSENAL | LEAGUE DIV ONE |
| 28.03.67 | ASTON VILLA | LEAGUE DIV ONE |

SEASON 67/68

| | | |
|---|---|---|
| 23.09.67 | FULHAM | LEAGUE DIV ONE |

MID SEASON

| | | |
|---|---|---|
| 29.07.68 | CRYSTAL PALACE | FRIENDLY |

SEASON 68/69

| | | |
|---|---|---|
| 21.09.68 | CHELSEA | LEAGUE DIV ONE |
| 26.10.68 | ARSENAL | LEAGUE DIV ONE |
| 11.01.69 | QPR | LEAGUE DIV ONE |
| 19.04.69 | TOTTENHAM | LEAGUE DIV ONE* |

SEASON 69/70

| | | |
|---|---|---|
| 20.08.69 | CHELSEA | LEAGUE DIV ONE* |
| 24.03.70 | CRYSTAL PALACE | LEAGUE DIV ONE* |

SEASON 70/71

| | | |
|---|---|---|
| 07.08.70 | ORIENT | FRIENDLY |
| 26.09.70 | HUDDERSFIELD TOWN | LEAGUE DIV ONE |
| 24.10.70 | CRYSTAL PALACE | LEAGUE DIV ONE* |
| 19.12.70 | CHELSEA | LEAGUE DIV ONE |
| 22.01.71 | CHARLTON | FRIENDLY* |
| 13.04.71 | BURNLEY | LEAGUE DIV ONE |
| 10.05.71 | ORIENT | DAVE HARPER |
| | | TESTIMONIAL |

SEASON 71/72

| | | |
|---|---|---|
| 26.01.72 | STOKE CITY | LGE CUP S/F REPLAY (HILLSBOROUGH) |
| 26.01.72 | STOKE CITY | LGE CUP S/F 2$^{nd}$ REPLAY (OLD TRAFFORD) |
| 26.02.72 | HUDDERSFIELD TOWN | FA CUP 5$^{th}$ ROUND |
| 04.05.72 | MILLWALL | HARRY CRIPPS TESTIMONIAL* |

SEASON 72/73

| | | |
|---|---|---|
| 29.08.72 | ARSENAL | LEAGUE DIV ONE |
| 09.09.72 | CHELSEA | LEAGUE DIV ONE* |
| 05.12.72 | CHARLTON | CHARLIE HALL TESTIMONIAL* |
| 24.03.73 | CRYSTAL PALACE | LEAGUE DIV ONE* |
| 09.04.73 | GILLINGHAM | BRIAN YEO TESTIMONIAL* |

SEASON 73/74

| | | |
|---|---|---|
| 01.09.73 | NORWICH CITY | LEAGUE DIV ONE* |
| 04.09.73 | QPR | LEAGUE DIV ONE* |
| 26.12.73 | CHELSE | LEAGUE DIV ONE* |
| 29.12.73 | TOTTENHAM | LEAGUE DIV ONE* |
| 06.04.74 | ARSENAL | LEAGUE DIV ONE* |

SEASON 74/75

| | | |
|---|---|---|
| 14.09.74 | TOTTENHAM | LEAGUE DIV ONE* |
| 08.10.74 | FULHAM | LGE CUP 3$^{rd}$ ROUND* |
| 12.10.74 | COVENTRY CITY | LEAGUE DIV ONE* |
| 15.10.74 | EVERTON | LEAGUE DIV ONE |
| 12.11.74 | CHARLTON | PETER REEVES TESTIMONIAL* |
| 30.11.74 | QPR | LEAGUE DIV ONE* |
| 03.12.74 | MILLWALL | BILLY NEIL TESTIMONIAL* |
| 21.12.74 | CHELSEA | LEAGUE DIV ONE* |

| | | |
|---|---|---|
| 28.12.74 | STOKE CITY | LEAGUE DIV ONE* |
| 04.01.75 | SOUTHAMPTON | FA CUP 3rd ROUND* |
| 11.01.75 | LEEDS UNITED | LEAGUE DIV ONE* |
| 28.01.75 | SWINDON TOWN | FA CUP |
| | | 4th ROUND REPLAY* |
| 22.02.75 | WOLVES | LEAGUE DIV ONE* |
| 08.03.75 | ARSENAL | FA CUP 6th ROUND* |
| 18.03.75 | BIRMINGHAM | LEAGUE DIV ONE |
| 22.03.75 | SHEFFIELD UNITED | LEAGUE DIV ONE* |
| 05.04.75 | IPSWICH TOWN | FA CUP S/F |
| | | (VILLA PARK)* |
| 09.04.75 | IPSWICH TOWN | FA CUP S/F REPLAY |
| | | (STAMFORD BRIDGE)* |
| 03.05.75 | FULHAM | FA CUP FINAL |
| | | (WEMBLEY)* |

SEASON 75/76

| | | |
|---|---|---|
| 09.08.75 | DERBY COUNTY | FA CHARITY SHIELD |
| | | (WEMBLEY)* |
| 19.08.75 | LIVERPOOL | LEAGUE DIV ONE |
| 30.08.75 | QPR | LEAGUE DIV ONE* |
| 27.10.75 | ORIENT | PETER ALLEN |
| | | TESTIMONIAL* |
| 12.11.75 | TOTTENHAM | LGE CUP 4th ROUND* |
| 07.02.76 | TOTTENHAM | LEAGUE DIV ONE* |
| 03.03.76 | F.C. DEN HAAG | ECWC 1st ROUND (1st LEG) |
| 20.03.76 | ARSENAL | LEAGUE DIV ONE* |
| 05.05.76 | R.S.C. ANDERLECHT | ECWC FINAL* |
| | BELGIUM | (HEYSEL STADIUM) |
| | | BRUSSELS |
| | R.S.C. ANDERLECHT | OFFICIAL SOUVENIR |
| | BELGIUM | PROGRAMME* |
| 06.04.76 | FULHAM | COMBINATION LGE |

SEASON 76/77

| | | |
|---|---|---|
| 04.09.76 | STOKE CITY | LEAGUE DIV ONE* |
| 18.09.76 | BRISTOL CITY | LEAGUE DIV ONE* |

| | | |
|---|---|---|
| 21.09.76 | CHARLTON | LGE CUP 3rd ROUND* |
| 30.10.76 | WBA | LEAGUE DIV ONE* |
| 23.11.76 | FULHAM | LES BARRETT TESTIMONIAL* |
| 27.12.76 | BIRMINGHAM | LEAGUE DIV ONE* |
| 01.01.77 | TOTTENHAM | LEAGUE DIV ONE* |
| 29.01.77 | ASTON VILLA | FA CUP 4th ROUND* |
| 05.02.77 | LEICESTER CITY | LEAGUE DIV ONE* |
| 19.02.77 | ARSENAL | LEAGUE DIV ONE* |
| 22.03.77 | IPSWICH TOWN | LEAGUE DIV ONE* |
| 04.04.77 | QPR | LEAGUE DIV ONE* |
| 09.04.77 | COVENTRY CITY | LEAGUE DIV ONE* |

SEASON 77/78

| | | |
|---|---|---|
| 24.08.77 | LEICESTER CITY | LEAGUE DIV ONE* |
| 17.09.77 | BRISTOL CITY | LEAGUE DIV ONE* |
| 01.10.77 | ARSENAL | LEAGUE DIV ONE* |
| 15.10.77 | WOLVES | LEAGUE DIV ONE* |
| 29.10.77 | IPSWICH TOWN | LEAGUE DIV ONE* |
| 05.11.77 | COVENTRY CITY | LEAGUE DIV ONE* |
| 03.12.77 | LIVERPOOL | LEAGUE DIV ONE* |
| 17.12.77 | WBA | LEAGUE DIV ONE* |
| 27.12.77 | CHELSEA | LEAGUE DIV ONE* |
| 02.01.78 | NORWICH CITY | LEAGUE DIV ONE* |
| 31.01.78 | QPR | FA CUP 4th ROUND REPLAY* |
| 04.02.78 | QPR | LEAGUE DIV ONE* |

SEASON 78/79

| | | |
|---|---|---|
| 26.08.78 | CRYSTAL PALACE | LEAGUE DIV TWO* |
| 28.10.78 | BRIGHTON | LEAGUE DIV TWO* |
| 21.11.78 | FULHAM | LEAGUE DIV TWO* |
| 25.11.78 | LEICESTER CITY | LEAGUE DIV TWO* |
| 23.12.78 | LUTON TOWN | LEAGUE DIV TWO* |
| 06.01.79 | NEWPORT COUNTY | FA CUP 3rd ROUND* |
| 17.02.79 | MILLWALL | LEAGUE DIV TWO* |
| 14.04.79 | ORIENT | LEAGUE DIV TWO* |
| 21.04.79 | CHARLTON | LEAGUE DIV TWO* |

SEASON 79/80

| | | |
|---|---|---|
| 01.09.79 | WATFORD | LEAGUE DIV TWO* |
| 04.09.79 | BARNSLEY | LGE CUP 2nd ROUND |
| | | 2nd LEG |
| 22.09.79 | QPR | LEAGUE DIV TWO* |
| 01.10.79 | SOUTHEND UNITED | LGE CUP 3rd ROUND |
| | | REPLAY* |
| 13.10.79 | LEICESTER CITY | LEAGUE DIV TWO* |
| 27.10.79 | NOTTS COUNTY | LEAGUE DIV TWO* |
| 31.10.79 | SUNDERLAND | LGE CUP 4th ROUND* |
| 10.11.79 | FULHAM | LEAGUE DIV TWO* |
| 14.11.79 | CHELSEA | LEAGUE DIV TWO* |
| 01.12.79 | CHARLTON | LEAGUE DIV TWO* |
| 12.12.79 | NOTTS FOREST | LGE CUP 5th ROUND |
| | | REPLAY* |
| 01.01.80 | ORIENT | LEAGUE DIV TWO* |
| 05.01.80 | WBA | FA CUP 3rd ROUND* |
| 26.01.80 | ORIENT | FA CUP 4th ROUND* |
| 19.02.80 | BURNLEY | LEAGUE DIV TWO* |
| 01.03.80 | LUTON TOWN | LEAGUE DIV TWO* |
| 14.03.80 | NEWCASTLE UNITED | LEAGUE DIV TWO* |
| 29.03.80 | SWANSEA CITY | LEAGUE DIV TWO* |
| 01.04.80 | CAMBRIDGE UNITED | LEAGUE DIV TWO* |
| 07.04.80 | BIRMINGHAM | LEAGUE DIV TWO* |
| 12.04.80 | EVERTON | FA CUP SEMI-FINAL |
| | | (VILLA PARK)* |
| 16.04.80 | EVERTON | FA CUP S/F REPLAY* |
| | | (ELLAND ROAD) |
| 10.05.80 | ARSENAL | FA CUP FINAL |
| | | WEMBLEY |

SEASON 80/81

| | | |
|---|---|---|
| 09.08.80 | LIVERPOOL | FA CHARITY SHIELD |
| | | (WEMBLEY)* |
| 23.09.80 | CHARLTON | LGE CUP 3rd ROUND* |
| 27.09.80 | CAMBRIDGE UNITED | LEAGUE DIV TWO* |
| 01.11.80 | BRISTOL ROVERS | LEAGUE DIV TWO* |

| 15.11.80 | LUTON TOWN | LEAGUE DIV TWO* |
| 26.12.80 | QPR | LEAGUE DIV TWO* |
| 06.01.81 | WREXHAM | FA CUP 3rd ROUND REPLAY* |
| 12.01.81 | WREXHAM | FA CUP 3rd ROUND 2nd REPLAY* |
| 27.01.81 | COVENTRY CITY | LGE CUP S/F 1st LEG* |
| 28.02.81 | WATFORD | LEAGUE DIV TWO* |
| 14.03.81 | LIVERPOOL | LEAGUE CUP FINAL (WEMBLEY)* |
| 01.04.81 | LIVERPOOL | LEAGUE CUP FINAL REPLAY* (VILLA PARK) |
| 18.04.81 | ORIENT | LEAGUE DIV TWO* |

SEASON 81/82

| 02.09.81 | TOTTENHAM | LEAGUE DIV ONE* |
| 19.09.81 | WBA | LEAGUE DIV ONE* |
| 03.10.81 | BIRMINGHAM | LEAGUE DIV ONE* |
| 17/10/81 | ASTON VILLA | LEAGUE DIV ONE* |
| 24.10.81 | NOTTS COUNTY | LEAGUE DIV ONE* |
| 07.11.81 | NOTTS FOREST | LEAGUE DIV ONE* |
| 16.01.82 | BRIGHTON | LEAGUE DIV ONE* |
| 23.01.82 | WATFORD | FA CUP 4th ROUND* |
| 21.08.82 | CHARLTON | PRE-SEASON FRIENDLY* |

SEASON 82/83

| 31.08.82 | LUTON TOWN | LEAGUE DIV ONE* |
| 02.10.82 | ARSENAL | LEAGUE DIV ONE* |
| 10.11.82 | LINCOLN CITY | MILK CUP 3rd ROUND* |
| 20.11.82 | TOTTENHAM | LEAGUE DIV ONE* |
| 29.12.82 | WATFORD | LEAGUE DIV ONE* |

SEASON 83/84

| 03.09.83 | TOTTENHAM | CANON LGE DIV ONE* |

| | | |
|---|---|---|
| 17.09.83 | WBA | CANON LGE DIV ONE* |
| 06.12.83 | EVERTON | MILK CUP 4<sup>th</sup> ROUND REPLAY* |
| 02.01.84 | NOTTS COUNTY | CANON LGE DIV ONE* |
| 28.01.84 | CRYSTAL PALACE | FA CUP 4<sup>th</sup> ROUND* |
| 07.02.84 | QPR | CANON LGE DIV ONE* |
| 18.02.84 | BIRMINGHAM | FA CUP 5<sup>th</sup> ROUND* |
| 28.04.84 | MAN UTD | CANON LGE DIV ONE* |
| 07.05.84 | ARSENAL | CANON LGE DIV ONE* |

SEASON 84/85

| | | |
|---|---|---|
| 16.02.85 | WIMBLEDON | FA CUP 5<sup>th</sup> ROUND* |
| 09.03.85 | MAN UTD | FA CUP 6<sup>th</sup> ROUND* |

SEASON 85/86

| | | |
|---|---|---|
| 12.03.86 | SHEFFIELD WED | FA CUP 6<sup>th</sup> ROUND* |

SEASON 86/87

| | | |
|---|---|---|
| 26.12.86 | TOTTENHAM | TODAY LGE DIV ONE* |
| 10.01.87 | ORIENT | FA CUP 3<sup>rd</sup> ROUND* |
| 02.02.87 | TOTTENHAM | LITTLEWOODS CUP Q/F REPLAY* |

SEASON 87/88

| | | |
|---|---|---|
| 17/10/87 | OXFORD UNITED | BARCLAYS DIV ONE* |
| 30.01.88 | QPR | FA CUP 4<sup>th</sup> ROUND* |

SEASON 90/91

| | | |
|---|---|---|
| 14/04.91 | NOTTS FOREST | FA CUP SEMI-FINAL* (VILLA PARK) |

CHARITY MATCH

| | | |
|---|---|---|
| 11.10.92 | KEITH PEACOCK'S | |
| | CHARLTON OLD BOYS | |
| | V | |
| | FRANK LAMPARD'S | PLAYED AT |
| | WEST HAM OLD BOYS | WELLING UTD FC* |

SEASON 94/95

| | | |
|---|---|---|
| 28.01.95 | QPR | LITTLEWOODS FA CUP 4th ROUND* |
| 06.05.95 | CRYSTAL PALACE | CARLING PREMIER* |

SEASON 95/96

| | | |
|---|---|---|
| 16.09.95 | ARSENAL | CARLING PREMIER* |
| 02.12.95 | BLACKBURN | CARLING PREMIER* |

SEASON 96/97

| | | |
|---|---|---|
| 04.01.97 | WREXHAM | LITTLEWOODS FA CUP 3rd ROUND* |
| 18.03.97 | WIMBLEDON | CARLING PREMIER* |

SEASON 97/98

| | | |
|---|---|---|
| 08.03.98 | ARSENAL | LITTLEWOODS FA CUP 6th ROUND* |
| 13.04.98 | SHEFFIELD WED | CARLING PREMIER* |

I had been to Blackpool as a singly for the weekend; the last and first time had been a two/three hour pit stop with Bob from 'behind the post' after an away match against Blackburn in season 95/96. I was due to go home on the Bank Holiday Monday morning and although not having a ticket chose to divert my journey home via Sheffield Wednesday. A nice scenic route over The Peak District and no problem getting in—there were plenty of available seats in the West Ham enclosure and immediately on entering, was being called down to and lucky enough to meet up with lads I knew: Joe (Greyhound Pub, Eltham H/St SE9) and Dave (Dartford)

| | | |
|---|---|---|
| 05.05.98 | CRYSTAL PALACE | CARLING PREMIER* |

SEASON 98/99

| | | |
|---|---|---|
| 30.01.99 | WIMBLEDON | CARLING PREMIER* |

PRE SEASON

| | | |
|---|---|---|
| 30.07.99 | CHARLTON | KEITH PEACOCK TESTIMONIAL* |

SEASON 99/00

| | | |
|---|---|---|
| 26.12.99 | WIMBLEDON | CARLING PREMIER* |

SEASON 00/01

| 28.01.01 | MAN UTD | AXA FA CUP |
| | | 4th ROUND* |

9000 allocation and anyone wanting to go by coach when booking match tickets were given the option of travel free of charge. Between 115 and 140 coaches were made available; taking up this offer with Bob 'from behind the post', coaches on the day began to leave Barking around 7am. Good day, excellent performance and a great 1-0 against the odds result, Paolo Di Canio 74th minute or was it 76th? Remaining minutes to the 90 plus 6 minutes added on time seemed an eternity.

SEASON 02/03

| 18.09.02 | CHARLTON | BARCLAY   RESERVE LGE* |
| 22.01.03 | CHARLTON | BARCLAY PREMIER* |

"BOYS OF '86" + GUESTS

| 07.09.03 | HEYBRIDGE SWIFTS X1 | FRIENDLY* |

SEASON 03/04

| 25.01.04 | WOLVES | FA CUP 4th ROUND* |
| 09.05.04 | WIGAN ATHLETIC | NATIONWIDE DIV 1* |
| 29.05.04 | CRYSTAL PALACE | NATIONWIDE |
| | | PLAY-OFF FINAL* |
| | | (MILLENNIUM STADIUM) |

SEASON 04/05

| 15.01.05 | WOLVES | CHAMPIONSHIP* |
| 08.05.05 | WATFORD | CHAMPIONSHIP* |
| 30.05.05 | PRESTON NE | CHAMPIONSHIP |
| | | PLAY-OFF FINAL* |
| | | (MILLENNIUM STADIUM) |

CHAMPIONSHIP MATCHES SPONSORED BY COCA COLA

SEASON 05/06

| 17.09.05 | FULHAM | BARCLAY PREMIER* |
| 31.12.05 | CHARLTON | BARCLAY PREMIER* |

| | | |
|---|---|---|
| 07.01.06 | NORWICH | FA CUP 3rd ROUND* |
| 18.02.06 | BOLTON WANDERERS | FA CUP 5th ROUND* |
| 23.04.06 | MIDDLESBROUGH | FA CUP SEMI FINAL* (VILLA PARK) |
| 13.05.06 | LIVERPOOL | FA CUP FINAL* (MILLENNIUM STADIUM) |

SEASON 06/07

| | | |
|---|---|---|
| 11.11.06 | MIDDLESBROUGH | BARCLAYS PREMIER* |
| 01.01.07 | READING | BARCLAYS PREMIER* |

PRE SEASON

| | | |
|---|---|---|
| 01.08.07 | WELLING UTD | FRIENDLY* |

SEASON 07/08

| | | |
|---|---|---|
| 01.09.07 | READING | BARCLAYS PREMIER* |

AWAY MATCHES ATTENDED WITH OFFICIAL PROGRAMMES ISSUED IN NEWSPAPER FORM

SEASON 72/73

| | | |
|---|---|---|
| 21.05.73 | DERBY COUNTY | LEAGUE DIV ONE* |

SEASON 75/76

| | | |
|---|---|---|
| 15.11.75 | DERBY COUNTY | LEAGUE DIV ONE* |
| 31.03.76 | EINTRACHT FRANKFURT | ECWC S/F 1st LEG* |

SEASON 76/77

| | | |
|---|---|---|
| 11.12.76 | DERBY COUNTY | POSTPONED |

SEASON 77/78

| | | |
|---|---|---|
| 19.11.77 | DERBY COUNTY | LEAGUE DIV ONE* |

SEASON 79/80

| | | |
|---|---|---|
| 08.09.79 | PRESTON N E | LEAGUR DIV TWO* |
| 15.12.79 | SHREWSBURY TOWN | LEAGUE DIV TWO* |

Don't remember much about this one at all, only that we lost 0-3 and although not funny at the time, so many fans were pushing at the gates to get out the ground with 20 minutes to go; they wanted to get out because West Ham (Come on You Irons) really were THAT BAD!

AWAY MATCHES ATTENDED, NO PROGRAMMES BUT MATCH TICKETS IN HAND

94/95

| | | |
|---|---|---|
| 07.01.95 | WYCOMBE WANDERERS | FA CUP 3rd ROUND |

97/98

| | | |
|---|---|---|
| 04.08.97 | CHARLTON ATHLETIC | SIMON WEBSTER |
| | | BENEFIT MATCH |

BOLEYN GROUND LIVE BEAM BACKS

| | |
|---|---|
| SEASON 02/03 | |
| 05.04.03 | SOUTHAMPTON* |
| SEASON 03/04 | |
| 21.03.04 | MILLWALL* |
| SEASON 04/05 | |
| 23.04.05 | BRIGHTON* |

NO PROGRAMMES ISSUED FOR BEAM BACKS BUT TICKETS IN HAND

## COMMENTS – WHAT PEOPLE HAVE SAID

"When you are playing you don't realise how passionate supporters are. Graham's words bring home the passion that is in a true West Ham supporter and it's nice to be able to read thoughts, experiences and stories from the terraces. As players we do not always realise what goes through the minds of supporters. It is a well known fact that West Ham supporters are amongst the most passionate, loyal, knowledgeable and understanding fans"
**Alan Devonshire and Tony Gale (West Ham United)**

"The words written in this book are how many of us West Ham Fans would love to be able to put in writing. Not only is it a very interesting and enjoyable read, it also invokes so many of my own personal memories. Like Graham I have many fond memories and stories of my time following the 'Irons, and this book is a must for any true West Ham Fan."
**Len Herbert (Secretary of the Boys of '86)**

"This book has been written straight from the heart of an obviously devoted Hammers Fan. There were sections that just forced a trip back down memory lane. **Brilliant"**
**Paul W**

"Loved the book and I can only imagine the pictures before me, and how it must have been in those days… **COYI"**
**'Iron' Bert (Belgium)**

"'Any Old Iron' was an excellent read; it made me feel like I was there. I visited England with my parents when I was a child and I haven't had the privilege of watching the Mighty Hammers at Upton Park or any English stadium yet. Reading your book came pretty close to capturing that feeling and for that I Thank You."
**Enrique Mejia (Italy)**

"I honestly thought it was great. From start to finish the author has got the correct balance between football and the social side to his life. Obviously the book is primarily about his passion for, and association with West Ham United but the author allows the reader to learn something about the man who has given so much of his time following his beloved Hammers. The writer's views come over very well, from his admiration and respect for past players of a previous era, and the joy of witnessing them on so many occasions, to how he now feels about the modern game"
**Darren Conner (Crayford)**

"A Great Book Graham, makes us **proud to be West Ham Fans**"
**Andy Whu Tillman (Sweden)**

"A Great read from a real fan and true to life. **Brilliant**"
**Steve Waite (Camberley)**

"I really enjoyed this book. It is written by a consummate Hammers Fan, whose love for his team comes across clearly. It is a refreshing change to read a book about football that has absolutely nothing to do with the well documented blight of our game, the violence. This book is a social document of the author's experience growing up in and around East London. You do not need to originate from the setting to capture the flavour of the time, and the central theme of his pursuit of his team ties it together nicely. There is a comprehensive history of West Ham's fortunes over this time and some good incisive comments about not only the club but the game in general. **Try It**"
**Wolfmanmac**

"A very enjoyable look into the trials and tribulations of a football fan who loves his club, where any fan of any club can also associate themselves with the Shenanigans that happen on away trips around the country."
**Robby**

"A real ripping yarn of amazing facts and data from yesteryear. Once you start reading "Any Old Iron" it's difficult to put the book down as you get enthralled into the author's passion for West Ham United. Full of fantastic memorabilia and places you can relate to from the past. If you like soccer, you'll love this book, regardless as to whether or not you are a West Ham supporter."
**Hissing Sid**

"Bought the book in Holland, got it hi-jacked by a Liverpool fan mate of mine, said it was one of the best books he ever read, I get it back Monday, only loaned it to him because he was laid up sick in bed... **COYI**"
**Dave Condron**

"Can't say I'm surprised by the 5* reviews on Amazon.co.uk and other reviews I've been informed of since. I only finished the book yesterday but they all fell into place. I thought the book "Charming" but more importantly **a most honest, humorous, detailed, informative and Factual read... Well Done**"
**Martyn Newbold (Belvedere)**

"A Must Have Read.........**WHUTWD, COYI, OLAS, 'AOI'**"
**Alison Verrent Taylor (Bexley)**

"The best West Ham United Book I have ever read"
**OLAS Editor Gary Firmager, West Ham's Number 1 Fanzine**

"A Very Interesting Book"
**Fossie**

"Can You Imagine...
Fever Pitch (Nick Hornby), mixed with The Secret Diary of Adrian Mole (Sue Townsend), with a flavour of Paddy Clarke Ha Ha Ha (Roddy Doyle), read to you with the genuine charm of Danny Baker, then you have this book. **ENJOY!!!**"
**Michael Voce**

"A real trip down memory lane, a very entertaining and informative read from a most knowledgeable author. There are a number of games Graham attended that I was at, it was like turning the clock back, even the defeats (and there were a few) brought a smile"
**Martin Davis (Stoke)**

"'Any Old Iron', one man's story of how in many ways West Ham United played a part in his life's journey, but it's not all doom and gloom, in fact it is very funny in places. Great attention to detail is shown in the many match reports and his story in general. **All in all, an enjoyable read**"
**Chris Deady (Erith)**

"Loved the book and a fantastic read from the heart of a West Ham Fan…
**Excellent… Excellent… Excellent"**
**Steve Jubb (Plumstead)**

"Went everywhere looking for this book in book shops and got swamped with the usual Man United, Liverpool rubbish. Finally found it on Amazon (on the missus's account of course) and loved every minute of it. The way the author describes everything makes you feel like you are there too. An excellent read and would definitely recommend it to all Hammers fans looking for a great read."
**Viviane Freegard**

"Picked up this book from the Door Hinge Micropub in Welling. I was an Eltham Hammer like Graham. I lived behind the Dutch House pub and never missed many home or away matches '75 to the '80's. This book had so many happy memories for me. It was written in a way a true fan of that era would tell it. A great read and as an inscription, I put this was my life."
**Keith Heyward**

Author Contact: AnyoldirongmJ@gmail.com